W9-BKA-222

Delusion and Reality

Delusion and Reality

GAMBITS, HOAXES, & DIPLOMATIC ONE–UPMANSHIP IN VIETNAM

János Radványi

Introduction by
GEORGE W. BALL

GATEWAY EDITIONS, LIMITED / *South Bend, Indiana*

Manufactured in the United States of America

Library of Congress Catalog Card Number: 78-57066

International Standard Book Number: 0-89526-693-8

To the memory of my father,
Géza Radványi

CONTENTS

PREFACE ix
ACKNOWLEDGMENTS xii
INTRODUCTION BY GEORGE W. BALL xiii

CHAPTER I
Stalin's Vietnam Policy 1
Dien Bien Phu: A Desperate Gamble 5
Hanoi's Decision to Liberate the South 10

CHAPTER II
The Washington Assignment 28
A Shift in Kremlin Policy 36
A New Phase of the Conflict 41

CHAPTER III
The Pyongyang Visit 53
The Meeting Between Foreign Minister Péter and Secretary Dean Rusk 61
Bleak Prospects 70

CHAPTER IV
The Bombing Pause Debate 76
International Complexities 82
The Chinese Factor 85
Final Arguments 91

CHAPTER V
Expansion of the Christmas Truce 97
The Decision 107

CHAPTER VI
The Harriman Mission 116
The Polish Initiative 124
The Humphrey–Kosygin Meeting 130
The Byroade Channel 132
The Resumption of the Bombing 137
The Budapest File 142

CHAPTER VII *The Two-front Battle* 147
Economic Aid for the DRV 157
The Shelepin Mission 160
The Tashkent Spirit 169
The Mongol Interlude 176

CHAPTER VIII *More Peace Feelers and Peace Hoax* 187
The Polish Episode—
the "Marigold Affair" 192
Moscow Channel 201
The Wilson–Kosygin Episode 204

CHAPTER IX *Péter's News Conference* 214
A Personal Decision 229

EPILOGUE 239
From the Tet Offensive to Paris
Peace Negotiations 241
Global Diplomacy and
the Vietnamese War 246
The Final Settlement 251

NOTES 269
BIBLIOGRAPHY 283
INDEX 289

PREFACE

This study combines personal recollection with historical insight. Some of the chapters follow a traditional scholarly approach in their meticulous scrutiny of all available sources and the careful checking out of the various possible interpretations. But the highlights of the introductory chapters and the major stories incorporate first-hand impressions as well as my own reflections on how the Soviet, the East European, the Chinese, and the Vietnamese Communists perceived the vital issues of the war and the question of the peace settlement. My direct involvement in Vietnamese affairs and my contact with high-level Communist and American officials provided me with the unique opportunity to appraise critically the process by which the decisions were reached and implemented.

In mid-1970 I started to expand an article I had originally published in *Life* magazine two years earlier. With a generous Rockefeller Foundation Grant and the support of my university I spent a summer at the Center for International Studies at Princeton and another summer at the Institute of Political Studies at Stanford University. I travelled extensively for interviews with many of the principal participants on the American side. Moreover, I had occasion to examine the diplomatic volumes of the "Pentagon Papers," released under the Freedom of Information Act. Then, back in my peaceful Mississippi home, I put on paper the kaleidoscopic exposés of the behind-the-scenes diplomatic initiatives, international horse-tradings, and bizarre occasions of make-believe diplomacy.

My major story starts on Christmas Day 1965 and lasts through January 1966. In these agonizing weeks, when I was firmly yet falsely convinced that mediation efforts could bring an end to the war, a number of interrelated developments occurred. The Hungarians and Poles presented themselves as honest brokers to initiate negotiations between Hanoi and Washington. The Soviet Union continued its two-front battle against the United States and China. While the Sino-Soviet conflict became more acute, the leaders in the Kremlin decided to move in militarily to Mongolia, deploying troops along the

Mogol-Chinese border. At the same time they sent Politburo member Shelepin to Hanoi to expand military aid to Ho Chi Minh, in the hope of bringing the North Vietnamese Communists over from the Chinese to the Soviet camp. Meanwhile, Mao Tse-tung adamantly opposed any negotiated settlement of the war. A pacifist mood swept through North Vietnam as a result of the long bombing pause; the Communist leadership stamped out dissension and continued its drive for the "liberation" of South Vietnam.

While writing about the Russian attitude throughout the war, I found, inadvertently, that several high officials in the Johnson, as well as the Nixon, administration were inclined to think that Moscow was "interested" in assisting Washington to extricate itself from the war. After the Soviet-supported North Vietnamese military campaign of 1972 and the general offensive of 1975, however, this assumption proved false. Moscow shed no crocodile tears that the long war in Vietnam had disrupted American society, had damaged the relations of the United States with a number of its allies, and had cast serious doubts on the reliability and endurance of American commitments all around the world.

But interestingly enough, no one—neither the Americans, the Russians, nor the Chinese—came out on top at the end of the war. No one, that is, save the North Vietnamese. All others lost out either diplomatically, militarily, or politically. For Russia, it was failure to establish hegemony in Southeast Asia. For China, it was failure to secure a return for their aid to North Vietnam. For America, it was a failure all around.

Neither I nor, for that matter, can any of the participants involved in those months of false expectations and diplomatic dead ends presume to possess the final word on the events presented in this book; the task of drawing conclusions must rest with my readers and, beyond this, with history. Meanwhile, I believe that my study can provide a new light on Russian, East European, and Chinese roles in the Vietnam War and on the broader questions of crisis diplomacy that arose during the conflict. Moreover, I am hopeful that my detailed operational analysis of Communist decision-making will contribute not only to an understanding of problems involved in making foreign policy but also to the anticipation and, we must all hope, the avoidance of future East-West conflicts.

ACKNOWLEDGMENTS

I owe a major debt of gratitude to many people for their cooperation and assistance. I am particularly thankful for the continued support and academic professionalism of J. Chester McKee, vice-president for research at Mississippi State University. To Gordon A. Craig and John W. Lewis I am especially grateful, for it was their early and continued enthusiasm that encouraged me to undertake this project.

Among the many friends and colleagues who have read all or parts of the manuscript and who have given me the most valuable advice and criticism, I am especially appreciative to George W. Ball, William P. Bundy, Glover Moore, Charles B. MacDonald, and Dean Rusk; also to Jacob D. Beam, John A. Gronouski, W. Averell Harriman, Herbert B. Jacoby, Stephan Kertesz, Leslie Tihany, and William Westmoreland for their highly professional comments. Needless to say I alone bear responsibility for the facts and views presented.

In preparing the manuscript I was crucially dependent upon the unfailing assistance and good judgment of Carol Norton. I am further indebted to Gertrude P. Holland for her excellent editorial advice. I benefited from the assistance in research and library matters provided by Anna Hoseman and Denise Ford. Mrs. Carol Sprayberry deserves many thanks for careful typing of the manuscript. Hoover Institution Press at Stanford kindly gave permission to reprint portions of my book, *Hungary and the Superpowers.* I am deeply grateful also to the staff of Gateway Editions, Ltd., for the patience and understanding assistance in seeing the book through publication.

Finally to my wife, who gave me support and perspective when things looked darkest, I am most thankful. Her enthusiasm for the book helped me overcome the difficulties of writing diplomatic history as it unfolded.

INTRODUCTION
George W. Ball

During the agonizing years of 1965 and 1966, President Johnson and his closest advisors were eager to find a way out of the Vietnam morass. At the same time, the President was not prepared to make concessions that would, in any significant way, compromise the objective for which the United States had fought the war—the maintenance of a South Vietnam free of North Vietnam domination. The administration's peace initiatives were limited by the pervasive worry that withdrawal might destroy America's credibility and authority, and by an obsessive concern that the faintest sign of weakness or irresolution might trigger the disintegration of the jerry-built government in Saigon, which, like an eighteenth-century heroine, seemed always on the verge of collapse. President Johnson in particular was strongly influenced by personal pride—"I will not be the first American President to lose a war"—and by a brooding fear of vicious attack from the American right-wing—which he described to me as "the real lurking monster." He was, in my observation, substantially less concerned at the mounting opposition on the campuses, which he wrote off as a product of left-wing agitation. Nor was he much influenced by the views of America's allies, who, because they had not helped in the fight, lacked the credentials to cavil.

At the same time, the President was troubled in mind and spirit by America's deepening involvement, which seemed to require an endless deployment of men and materiel—while the goal of victory proved a recurrent mirage. He felt responsible for the mounting casualties; and, as a famous graduate of the Senate, he was naturally preoccupied by the fear of losing Congressional support for what was clearly becoming an increasingly unpopular war. No matter how great our military effort, we seemed unable to bring the struggle to an acceptable conclusion, while the barometric needle continued to oscillate cyclically from hope to disappointment to hope.

As the months wore on, the dour face of reality increasingly intruded into White House counsels. Secretary McNamara, who had direct responsibility for the military conduct of the war, became outspokenly eager for negotiation, hoping to achieve through diplomatic means what we were persistently denied on the battlefield. Dean Rusk took a more stoic view of the ups and downs of fortune; reading the situation against his Korean War experiences, he remained convinced that, if only we stuck at it long enough, we would win.

The diplomatic equation was a complex one with many unknowns and variables. To pursue successful diplomacy, a nation must accurately predict how its antagonist is likely to respond to signals, secret or overt, passed directly or through intermediaries. An essential ingredient is the depth and reliability of intelligence, which, in our case, was sometimes—consciously or, as a result of bureaucratic reflex, subconsciously—distorted in the theater of war. Caution also warned us that the other side would try to feed us misleading information or create deceptive impressions.

Even more critical than raw information was its interpretation. That depended on understanding the adversary's assessment of its own situation, its staying power, and, finally, its long-term plans, ambitions, and apprehensions. The interpretative task was greatly complicated by the profound differences of philosophy and culture that separated the two sides; conditions we would reject as intolerable were endurable hardships to the North Vietnamese. Besides, we were new to the struggle and in a hurry; Hanoi had been fighting for a quarter of a century. For us it was a regional entanglement and, despite the apocalyptic terms in which the President tended to describe it, it still had only marginal strategic implications; for them it was an obsessive central objective. So we operated under vastly different conceptions of acceptable solutions and time spans.

What complicated the problem even more was the nature of the supporting cast on Hanoi's side. The political rivalry between the major powers on whose help North Vietnam depended—the Soviets and the Chinese—was difficult to factor into our calculations. In addition, there were minor players, such as the Eastern European states—including Hungary, which was

Professor Radványi's point of vantage—each with its own tactical motivations and cultural conditioning. Each state, and even its individual leaders, possessed ambitions that might relate not so much to the central game on the board as to a subsidiary competition within the Warsaw Pact group. How, for example, could an Eastern European state use the Vietnam situation to improve its own position in relation to Moscow—or to Peking? How were its moves or reactions affected by its rivalry with the other Warsaw Pact nations? How could the White House know when and whether to trust an encouraging statement from one of the minor states—or even from a superpower? Was a small power acting out its own fantasies or pursuing a central strategy prescribed by a major power that, in turn, might or might not correspond to the views or intentions of Hanoi?

I find Professor Radványi's book particularly fascinating, since he provides definite answers to questions that were the subject of intense speculation at the upper reaches of the Johnson Administration. He shows us how Moscow and its client states fostered misleading reports to encourage bombing pauses that would enable North Vietnam to speed up its infiltration and the resupply of its forces in the South. He describes the elaborate interplay between Moscow and the other Warsaw Pact governments and the manner in which Moscow ordered—or, at least, sought to control—every move. He discloses how ambitious members of satellite bureaucracies tried to improve their own prestige by starting the foxes we doggedly pursued—skeptically but with wistful hope. He sets at rest the contentions still mindlessly repeated that we might have achieved a negotiating breakthrough had we handled more sympathetically the U Thant-Stevenson exchange, the Fanfani proposals, the British initiative, the Polish intervention, and so on. Finally, he discloses the outrageous fabrications of Foreign Minister Péter of Hungary, which intrigued even a dubious Dean Rusk and bemused the President. In contrast to that perfidy, Professor Radványi's own integrity and courage stand out dramatically; when, as Charge d'Affaires of the Hungarian Embassy in Washington, he learned that Péter's proposal was a cruel fiction, he resigned in disgust and requested asylum in America.

The poignant message that emerges from this book is how futile was the hope of President Johnson and his advisors that by diplomacy reinforced with bombs we could ever persuade Hanoi to abandon its fanatical ambitions to dominate the South. Yet, against all hard evidence, that hope lingered on—encouraged by false signals from Moscow and its client states—while a beleaguered administration studied fluctuating reports from the theater of combat that tended toward an optimistic bias. With our resources so overwhelming, not only in quantitative but qualitative terms, we should—at some point —be able to force Hanoi to the bitter conclusion that the struggle was not worth the cost—or so it appeared to certain of the President's top advisors addicted to the bloodless logic of a mechanistic age. Unfortunately the argument left no room for the intangibles that finally made the difference—spirit, ideological commitment, and the brutal discipline imposed by a relentless leadership; since those factors could not be quantified, they did not count.

We had the bombs and the big battalions and sooner or later we must win. Thus the bait we used to entice Hanoi to the negotiating table was little more than a rejuggling of words so as to make our own objectives seem more palatable without materially changing our basic position.

An embattled White House thus regarded it as an article of faith that the iron law of number would sooner or later force the North Vietnamese to recognize the bankruptcy of their ambition; and, when the hard-bitten leaders in Hanoi finally reached that conclusion, they would, with Communist deviousness, presumably communicate with us in enigmatic form through indirect or unlikely channels. So we must be at all times alert to detect the faintest wisp of smoke.

Meanwhile, as I felt at the time and, it seems to me, as Professor Radványi has now demonstrated, we tended to confuse negotiating initiatives with a restless search for channels of communication when, in fact, we had nothing to communicate. Though the President sent highly visible emissaries all over the world in the hope of finding a negotiating opening, that was more to show our desire for peace than any realistic approach to a diplomatic solution. Channels were always available were we prepared to say anything to which the other side might be ready to respond.

What Professor Radványi ultimately makes clear, of course, is how ill-starred was the whole American effort in Vietnam. If that was a lesson he and his administration could not face, President Johnson still prepared the way for America to accept reality. By freezing troop commitments and withdrawing from the presidential race, he gave his successor the chance to extricate us quickly on terms at least as good as were finally achieved almost four years later.

But that was not to be, for Nixon still clung to the same vain hope that Hanoi could be made to cry: "Enough." Thus it was not until April 20, 1972, that Kissinger told Brezhnev that the United States would no longer insist on North Vietnamese troops being withdrawn north of the DMZ, but would be willing to conclude a peace under which an estimated 100,000 could remain in the South. A month later, he sweetened the American position by suggesting to the Russians that the return of all American prisoners was not a condition precedent to the end of the bombing of North Vietnam—although Nixon had publicly stated just the opposite one week earlier. Moreover, Kissinger indicated that the United States was prepared to back a tri-partite electoral commission in South Vietnam which would include elements from the Viet Cong, together with that ever convenient fiction, the neutralists—although the United States had hitherto resolutely rejected a tri-partite commission because of Saigon's concern that it could evolve into a coalition government.

What happened thereafter everyone knows. The arrangements our nation concluded precipitated the capitulation of the South, as it was clear they must inevitably do; and the tragic sequel to the North Vietnamese victory is still unfolding in the inside pages of American newspapers.

Professor Radványi's book illuminates a foggy chapter of American history when leaders were tempted to misread diplomatic signals in their desire to find a political way out of a military disaster. If offers careful documentation of the hazards and complexities that accompany any dealing with the Communist powers.

I first knew János Radványi in 1965 or 1966, when, as Charge d'Affaires of the Hungarian Embassy (ambassadors were not then maintained in either country), he would call on me in my capacity as Under Secretary of State. Even at our first meetings, he impressed me as not in the mold of Iron Curtain diplomats. Open and straightforward, and with a relaxed manner, he displayed a sense of humor and gaiety rarely found in an envoy from behind the Iron Curtain. I remember particularly one long lunch at his Embassy when he recounted some hilarious diplomatic experiences. Unlike the other Warsaw Pact diplomats, he did not repeat formulae learned by rote but reacted as a warm and sympathetic individual.

Later, after I had left the government, he came to see me in New York. As I had already learned from the newspapers, he had recently defected. Briefly, he and his wife had been provided with protection in a safe house, but he was now on his own, with neither a job nor the professional credentials that could provide the *laissez-passez* to a new occupation. Clearly he needed help.

I mobilized a few friends—McGeorge Bundy, chairman of the Ford Foundation, Robert Roosa, who had served as Under Secretary of the Treasury during my years in Washington, and several others. With the valiant help of Dean Carl Spaeth at Stanford University, arrangements were made for Mr. Radványi and his wife to move to the West Coast, where, through brilliance and assiduous effort, he earned a doctorate in history. Today he is a highly regarded professor at Mississippi State University.

The chapters that follow are a lucid and beautifully written account of events in Saigon, Moscow, Peking, and Budapest that add enlightening detail to the heart-breaking Vietnam tragedy.

G. W. B.
May 1978

Delusion and Reality

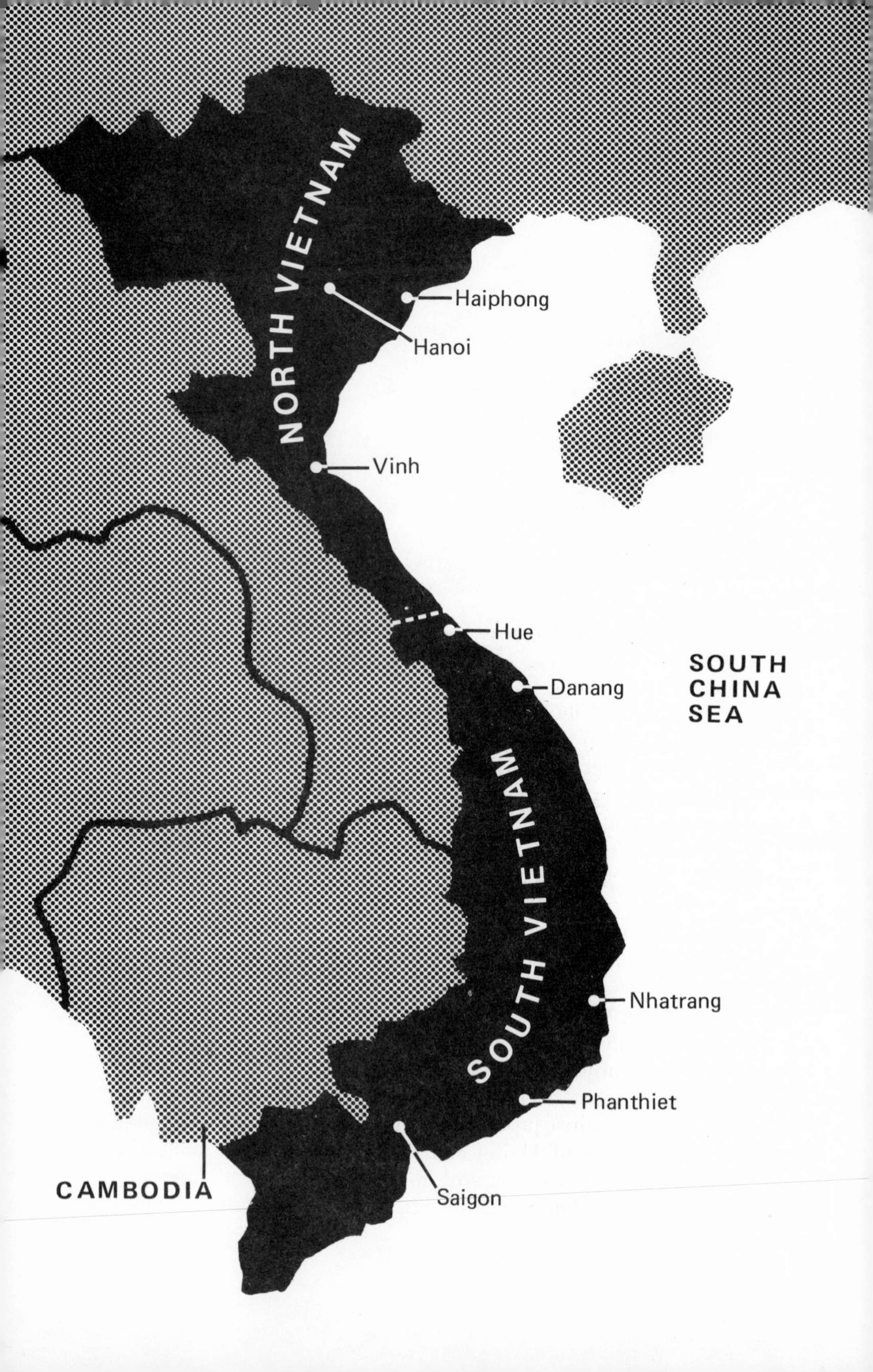
NORTH VIETNAM
Haiphong
Hanoi
Vinh
Hue
Danang
SOUTH CHINA SEA
SOUTH VIETNAM
Nhatrang
Phanthiet
Saigon
CAMBODIA

CHAPTER I

Stalin's Vietnam Policy

Spring 1945 was a time of swiftly unfolding events in Southeast Asia, especially in Vietnam. The Japanese, who up to that time had been willing to tolerate a Vichy French administration in Indochina, discovered preparations for a pro-de Gaulle uprising. In March, the Kempetai (the Japanese secret police) arrested all persons suspected of being leaders of the plot, interned all French troops and civil servants, and quickly put together a somewhat shaky but acceptable pro-Japanese Vietnamese regime headed by Emperor Bao Dai.

In the meantime the Vietnam Lap Dong Minh Hoi (Vietnamese Independence League) under Ho Chi Minh, better known as the Viet Minh resistance forces, established a liberated zone along the Chinese border. From this base, equipped with American light machine guns and captured Japanese war materials, they infiltrated the Red River Delta and moved close to Hanoi. In August, 1945, Ho issued a general appeal for an armed uprising against Japanese forces. His call to arms and his subsequent capture of Hanoi coincided with the dropping of atomic bombs on Hiroshima and Nagasaki and Japan's unconditional surrender. On September 2, Ho stood on the balcony of Hanoi's opera house and proclaimed the establishment of the Democratic Republic of Vietnam and himself the president of the new Republic. The burst of enthusiasm that swept through the crowd of half a million Vietnamese who listened to Ho's declaration, however, was not echoed in Moscow. The Communist press barely mentioned this first Communist-led, anti-colonial revolution in Asia. The Kremlin issued no congratulatory telegram, and Stalin made no move to extend recognition to the new Democratic Republic.[1]

Nor did the news of the Vietnam revolution create any sensation elsewhere in Eastern Europe, where in any case the majority of the people would have had difficulty even locating Indochina on a map. At that time (1945-47) I was a student at the Academy of Foreign Affairs in Budapest, where the post-war Hungarian coalition government trained its prospective diplomatic officers. In this school, in the course of discussions on current international problems, I did hear the Viet Minh and Ho Chi Minh mentioned, but only briefly: our Marxist teacher explained that it was the devastating Soviet drive in Manchuria in the last six days of World War II which made possible the uprising in Indochina leading to the establishment of the Democratic Republic of Vietnam (DRV). He neglected to mention that Ho Chi Minh launched his guerrilla war against the Japanese without Soviet assistance, and he failed to point out that the American victory over Japan might well have aided the Viet Minh cause.

Our classroom discussions also covered the Franco-Vietnamese negotiations of 1946, which failed to produce lasting French recognition of the Democratic Republic of Vietnam within the Indochina Federation and the French Union. We were outraged when we learned that French naval vessels bombarded Haiphong; this we interpreted as the signal for a return of French colonial power to Indochina. We also heard of the Viet Minh retaliation against the French in Hanoi, which was to touch off the eight-year-long Franco-Vietnamese War. Privately, I believed that Ho Chi Minh would have been willing to work out an accommodation with the French colonial administration had he not been double-crossed and forced to defend himself.

I was a Communist out of conviction, having joined the Hungarian Communist party in 1940. I was interned in and escaped from a Nazi labor camp during the war, and thereafter, under strict party discipline, had fought the Germans in the partisan underground until the war ended. Because I was a Communist, I was on Ho Chi Minh's side.

From 1947 until 1950, however, Vietnam was beyond my professional province. In the Foreign Ministry, where I began work as a desk officer in late 1947, I dealt with Soviet-Hungarian reparations and international economic problems. The next year I received my first foreign assignment, as an attaché in Turkey. By then the division of Europe had become a fact, rigid and irreversible. Hungary, together with the other East European countries, was firmly in the Soviet orbit; the rest of Europe was protected from further Stalinist encroachment by the American "containment policy." Stalin's attempt to revise the Montreux convention of 1936 concerning the straits and his claim to the provinces of Kars and Ardahan in eastern Anatolia strained relations between the Turkish and Soviet governments. I lived the not very pleasant life of an East European diplomat in Ankara, the Turkish capital, since our policy had to follow identically that of the Russians. I dealt mainly with trade questions and to a lesser extent concerned myself with international politics. That was the time when Stalin had put up his blockade around Berlin, and I expected that the Cold War would soon turn into a hot one. I recall the sense of relief I felt, after the blockade was lifted, when the Soviet ambassador to Turkey, A.V. Lavritshchev, told me that Berlin was not deemed worth a new world war.

It was in Ankara, too, that I learned of the "excommunication" of President J. Broz Tito from the Soviet camp. This action came as a shock to me, for I had been his liaison officer in December 1947 when he went to Budapest to sign a "Friendship and Assistance Treaty" with the Hungarians and considered him an outstanding figure in the international Communist movement; it was hard for me to imagine how Stalin could justify his charges that Tito was an "imperialist agent." It was painful and embarrassing, but of course necessary, for me to cut all ties with the Yugoslav friends in the Turkish capital, and

I was not unhappy when Stalin's military pressure and economic blockade backfired by uniting Yugoslavia behind Tito. This view, however, I kept to myself.

I was transferred from Ankara to home service in 1949, but stayed in Budapest only a few months before being sent again abroad, this time to Paris to head the political department of the Hungarian Legation there. By then Vietnam had become one of the central issues in the broadening Cold War. The Communist bloc intensified its anti-American propaganda by branding the conflict a "Washington-instigated dirty war" *(sale guerre)*. The World Council of Peace, one of Stalin's front organizations, launched a vigorous "stop the French aggression" offensive. The new ruler of China, Mao Tse-tung, was even more active with regard to Vietnam. He not only began to supply arms, ammunition, and military advisers to the Viet Minh but also extended diplomatic recognition to the Democratic Republic of Vietnam. Stalin had no other choice but to follow suit, and, ten days after Red China did so, on January 31 the Soviet Union granted economic aid and established diplomatic relations with the Democratic Republic of Vietnam.[2]

Not surprisingly, the French Communist party mobilized itself behind Ho Chi Minh's war effort. Together with the Confederation General du Travail, it organized protest demonstrations, strikes, and walk-outs, and party intelligence workers began sabotaging military hardware moving through French ports to Indochina.

Until formal relations between the Soviet Union and the Democratic Republic of Vietnam were established, Stalin used the French Communist party as a communication channel to the Vietnamese Communists. This I learned in the fall of 1950, when French Communist party Secretary General Maurice Thorez came to a dinner party at our legation. As one of Stalin's long-time close collaborators in the international Communist movement, Thorez at that time probably knew more than anyone else about the Russian leader's thinking on Vietnam. At one point during the party, I found myself in a conversation with Thorez, his wife Jeanette Vermeersch, and the Hungarian Minister Zoltán Szánto. The French party leader spoke freely of his party's go-between role and stated that Stalin had been absolutely right in his cautious approach toward entanglement in the Vietnamese affair, not only because of the remote geographic location of Vietnam but because of the weakness of Ho Chi Minh's guerrillas vis-à-vis the French expeditionary forces: Stalin simply did not want to take part in a venture that showed no substantial prospect of success. Moreover, according to Thorez, Stalin was somewhat distrustful of Ho and his group. He felt Ho had gone too far in his wartime collaboration with British intelligence and the Office of Strategic Services (better known as the OSS), and Ho had consistently displayed an unwillingness to seek Stalin's advice and consent prior to taking action. As an example, Thorez mentioned that when Ho Chi Minh dissolved the Indochinese Communist party in 1945 he (Thorez) had a hard time convincing Stalin that the liquidation was transitory, a mere tactic to gain political support from the Vietnamese nationalists.[3] Naturally the Vietnamese comrades had been bitter about Moscow's apparent indifference to their struggle, Thorez acknowledged, but the French party had been powerless to change Stalin's attitude until after Mao Tse-tung was victorious in China and the Korean War began. The Vietnam war then became a useful second front in the fight against the French colonialists and their American supporters.

I was somewhat surprised at what Thorez said. Minister Szánto, however, who had worked for the Comintern and had lived in Moscow and known Stalin rather well, was not. He told me after the party that Thorez's summation of Stalin's attitudes and policies on Vietnam was entirely accurate.

Dien Bien Phu: A Desperate Gamble

The spring of 1953 marked the beginning of a new era. On March 5 Stalin was dead; his feared police chief Lavrentii P.

Beria had been liquidated, and in the Kremlin Stalin's one-man rule had been replaced by collective dictatorship. Prime Minister Georgii Malenkov promised more food and consumer goods for the Russian people; the new party chief, Nikita S. Khrushchev, embarked on the destruction of the Stalin myth by exposing the terror and crimes of the late dictator. In foreign policy, change appeared to be the order of the day. Moscow's reconciliation with Tito, its signing of the Austrian State Treaty, and its willingness to end the war in Korea were viewed as milestones in this direction.

As far as Vietnam was concerned, both Moscow and Peking had to face the grim reality that the Viet Minh guerrilla forces were on the brink of collapse after their long fight against a stronger foe. It was evident that if Ho Chi Minh was to be rescued what was needed was either a negotiated political settlement or a massive Chinese military intervention in Vietnam. But the Chinese, after their losses in Korea, had turned to more pressing problems at home and had embraced a policy of peaceful coexistence abroad. At the same time, the post-Stalin leadership in the Soviet Union was preoccupied with internal problems and favored a lessening of international tensions. In addition, all three interested parties on the Communist side—Moscow, Peking, and Ho Chi Minh—were concerned about possible American intervention in Vietnam or a Korean-type "united action" by the Western powers. Accordingly, at the Big Four foreign ministers' meeting in Berlin in February 1954, Soviet Foreign Minister V. Molotov tendered his offices to arrange a cease-fire in Indochina. French Foreign Minister George Bidault gladly accepted the offer, and within three months an international conference convened in Geneva, with France, Vietnam, the Viet Minh, the United Kingdom, the United States, the USSR, and the Chinese People's Republic, as well as representatives of Cambodia and Laos, participating. In three months the parties had worked out a compromise solution of the eight-year-old Franco-Viet Minh war in Indochina, an accord which provided for the temporary division of Vietnam into two parts, North and South, with a common boundary along the 17th parallel and with a demilitarized zone on each side of the parallel. It was agreed that Vietnam would be reunited by national plebescite in two years. The French agreed to remove their troops from the North, now controlled entirely by Ho Chi Minh, within 300 days, and Ho promised to withdraw his Viet Minh units from the South. Finally, all parties consented to the creation of an International Control Commission, with representatives from Canada, India, and Poland, to supervise the movement of all armed forces and the release of prisoners of war and to oversee control of the frontiers, ports, and airfields. Separate agreements were reached on the cessation of hostilities in Cambodia and in Laos.[4]

Thus in 1954 the Indochina war ended on terms more agreeable to the Communists than the West knew. At the time I had little access to background information about the situation in Indochina and the motives that prompted Moscow, Peking, and the Viet Minh to go to Geneva. Five years later, in the spring of 1959, I visited Hanoi as a member of a Hungarian party and government delegation, at which time I had the opportunity to get some inside information on the decision. It was there that I learned the dramatic story of the fall of Dien Bien Phu, as retold by General Vo Nguyen Giap, which resulted in the ending of the war.

During that visit our delegation toured the recently opened Museum of the Revolution in Hanoi with General Giap as our guide. In one of the thirty halls of the modestly appointed museum, our attention was directed to a group photograph taken at the famous French Socialist party National Congress at Tours in 1920. Included in the group was a youthful Ho Chi Minh, who had spoken at the Congress on behalf of the oppressed colonial peoples of Asia and had voted with Communists Marcel Cachin and Paul Vaillant-Couturier against the Socialists. Another picture showed Ho in a British prison in Hong Kong in 1931. A third depicted Ho in the Kremlin with Soviet party leader N. S. Khrushchev in 1957, and another, taken in the same year, showed him in Peking with Mao Tse-tung. We also inspected a display of documents of the Indochinese Communist party and its successor, the Lao Dong party. Included in the display were documents relating to the Seventh Comintern Congress in 1935, where Ho represented the five-year-old United Vietnamese Communist party and endorsed the Comintern's anti-Fascist and anti-Japanese popular front policy. The museum preserved some of the papers and personal belongings Ho carried with him in the 1940s in the grottoes of Viet Bac, where the first units of the Viet Minh guerrilla army were organized. But if Ho's role was particularly dramatized throughout the museum, it was not entirely at the expense of his comrades; many of his close collaborators—Pham Van Dong, Le Duan, Giap, and others—were also much in evidence.

In the central hall of the Museum was a papier-maché model of the Dien Bien Phu battlefield. When we arrived at this display, General Giap stepped to a lectern on one side of the model, bade the Hungarians be seated on wooden benches facing him, and with the aid of a long bamboo pointer launched into a lecture like a university professor. The battle of Dien Bien Phu, he told us, was the last desperate exertion of the Viet Minh army. Its forces were on the verge of complete exhaustion. The supply of rice was running out. Apathy had spread among the populace to such an extent that it was difficult to draft new fighters. Years of jungle warfare had sent morale in the fighting units plunging to the depths.

On this note, the Supreme War Council met, remained in session for several days, and finally came to the decision that the impossible must be attempted: a surprise assault, a decisive battle. The mountain-girted valley of Dien Bien Phu was chosen as the scene of the battle on the assumption that General Navarre, the commander of the French expeditionary forces, would consider that well fortified stronghold an unlikely target of attack. This decision revealed that Giap and his colleagues knew something of the strategic thinking of the French military school. They gambled on the failure of the postwar French military leadership to draw a lesson from its defeat at that other "impregnable" fortress, the Maginot line, during World War II. The calculations proved correct.

The French did not foresee the move because it was doubtless impossible for them to imagine how units and material could be brought to the scene through the dense surrounding jungles in numbers and strength necessary to wage a battle. It was indeed a difficult undertaking, said Giap. First, a detailed reconnoitering of the terrain had to be effected in a relatively short time; second, the transportation of the forces had to be organized. The first objective was carried out by soldiers on bicycles and on foot who carried no load; to each soldier was assigned one coolie to carry ammunition and rice rations for both. The problem of transporting artillery batteries was solved with elephants and buffaloes. The general even gave the elephants military grades of rank.

When his forces reached the target area, Giap ordered a general rest of three days. During this period political officers circulated among the troops trying to raise morale. "The French are not gods" the men were told time and again. This agitation was sorely needed, Giap observed, because the soldiers were truly terrified.

The first phase of the battle was conducted in typical guerrilla warfare fashion. The Viet Minh attacked by night, each time blowing up one or two pillboxes reached via subterranean tunnels dug during the day. At first Giap even permitted the French resupply transport aircraft to come and go undisturbed, and the French command concluded the pillbox demolitions were just another series of partisan attacks. It was only later that the Viet Minh brought up artillery and kept the only runway on the Dien Bien Phu airfield under constant fire. At this juncture the French tried to resupply their base by parachute drops, but the parachuted packages were captured. Meanwhile, the Viet Minh batteries moved frequently so that by the time the French artillery registered their old positions they were concentrated elsewhere. Giap's forces increased their pressure systematically until they were attacking the base day and night from all sides. Cut off from the outside world, without supplies, the French military command recognized the hopelessness of its situation and surrendered.

What Giap had highlighted to us had not been incorporated in his book, *Dien Bien Phu,* neither was it reported in Western accounts following the battle. Only Soviet party leader Khrushchev revealed in his memoirs how desperate Ho Chi Minh's situation was before the battle.[5] It is equally important to remember that Giap in his book did not acknowledge the substantial Chinese aid, especially that of the heavy artillery pieces which were instrumental in breaking the French defense line; on the other hand, he did not blame the Russians for failing to support the Viet Minh in its life and death struggle.

We were deeply impressed by the general's presentation; everyone listened attentively, and the delegation members asked many questions. When Foreign Minister Endre Sik asked what would have happened had the Americans granted the military assistance the French were requesting, what would have happened if the Americans had intervened, the general answered with candor that one of the reasons the Viet Minh went to the Geneva Conference was that the Soviets and the Chinese, as well as the Ho Chi Minh leadership, assessed this possibility as a real danger. This remark reaffirmed what I had heard, upon assuming the direction of the Asian and African department of the Hungarian Foreign Ministry in 1958, about Moscow's concern over the possibility of American involvement.

Hanoi's Decision to Liberate the South

The Foreign Ministry had been reorganized a year earlier along geographical and political lines, much like most other foreign ministries in the socialist countries of Eastern Europe, after the Soviet model.* Six geographical and two international political departments were established within the ministry in 1957, and four more were added in 1961. The foreign minister, his five deputies (each responsible for different depart-

*From 1958 onward, the Soviet Foreign Ministry invited the East Europeans to Moscow each year to study procedural and structural matters. In 1960, Deputy Foreign Minister Frigyes Puja headed the Hungarian delegation. He took with him three political department heads, the head of the Ministerial Secretariat, the director of the personnel department, and the party secretary of the ministry. As one of the political department heads I was also a member of the delegation.

ments), and the party secretary constituted the operational directorate of the Ministry, which held daily meetings to transmit precise instructions from the party headquarters to the deputy foreign ministers. In addition, the minister delivered briefings on significant international political developments and discussed reports, proposals, travel of official Foreign Ministry delegations abroad, Ministry reorganization plans, etc., with his deputies. The deputy ministers then forwarded instructions to the department heads, and we in turn relayed these instructions through our deputies to the desk officers.

My department managed problems relating to Hungary's bilateral relations with Asian and African countries. Our first and foremost task was to write memorandums for leading government and party organs and to prepare proposals on questions affecting political matters. In addition, we conducted negotiations to establish diplomatic relations; we participated at international forums; assisted in the expansion of trade and cultural exchange; and dealt with special visa and consular cases, with V.I.P. visits, and occasionally with international propaganda matters. We paid constant attention to events in the four Asian socialist countries: the People's Republic of China, Korea, Mongolia, and the Democratic Republic of Vietnam. At Soviet bidding, we also made concerted efforts to develop good relations with India, Indonesia, Syria, Egypt, and Sudan. We paid less attention to Pakistan, Burma, Ceylon, Nepal, Iraq, Saudi Arabia, and Jordan. We had diplomatic relations with the leftist regime of Sékou Touré of Guinea at that time, and we also participated in preliminary talks to establish relations with the Japanese government, but we had no particular official interest in the Philippines, Malaysia, Thailand, Cambodia, South Vietnam, or South Africa.

Part of our continuing function was to provide our Asian embassies with political guidance. At the same time, we requested from them reports, analyses, and all available information on specified subjects of interest. The missions abroad gathered their information primarily from public sources (e.g., the press and official publications) and from meetings with government officials, politicians, newsmen, economists, and businessmen. The usefulness of material received from missions in the friendly socialist countries was limited for three reasons: first, diplomatic representatives in those countries invariably received their information from a controlled press or from official sources; second, their movements were strictly controlled in such major interest sectors as Peking, Hanoi, and Pyongyang (but not in Ulan Bator), and they were subject to rigorous travel restrictions; and third, it was not considered quite "cricket" to seek out non-official sources or have contact with dissenters.*

The missions in the Third World countries faced a more delicate situation than those in the socialist countries. Our diplomatic officers in Djakarta and New Delhi, for example, could observe political events closely, could travel freely, and had access to all kinds of information, with the result that our embassies there frequently reported the truth or at least the half-truth. Simultaneously, however, they felt constrained to interject a point of view into their reports to prove their loyalty to the party lest they be branded as "deviationists under a hostile influence."

All in all, our foreign missions played a relatively minor and many times misleading role in providing a picture of the outside world. But there were other sources of information that were taken more seriously. One, obviously, was the Soviet Foreign Ministry. Another, and for different reasons, was the Hungarian intelligence community, the military intelligence reports being especially thorough. We also read the Western press and received extensive reports from a foreign radio monitoring service. Finally, diplomats accredited to Budapest were sometimes a rich source of enlightenment, as were reports from Hungarians who made business trips abroad.

*As long as these general rules were observed our ambassadors and chargés in the Asian socialist countries escaped blame even when events proved their reports were distorted. On the other hand, undue objectivity and criticism of the party or government of a host socialist country might well result in the reporter's recall to Budapest. Both the Foreign Ministry and the party headquarters feared that the over-zealous diplomat might endanger good relations with the host country and create friction inside the Communist commonwealth. After 1962, however, when the Sino-Soviet rift became public and the Soviet Union changed its policy line in regard to China, the Hungarian ambassadors in Peking began sending reports about the "Mao Tse-tung clique" to Budapest.

Like all Asian countries, the Democratic Republic of Vietnam in 1958 maintained an embassy in Budapest. It was headed by Chargé d'Affaires ad interim Nguyen Duc Thieng and was located in one of the city's most elegant sections. Ambassador Nguyen Thanh Ha, the DRV representative in Prague, was also accredited to Budapest, although he usually appeared only on ceremonial occasions, such as Vietnamese or Hungarian holidays.

In public at least, the short-statured Vietnamese conducted themselves in a singularly unpretentious manner. The few diplomatic and administrative members of the embassy who mingled with diplomats of the socialist countries and occasionally were seen at the parties of the Indian embassy lived a mysteriously Spartan existence. Only the chief of the embassy was allowed to bring his wife with him, while the rest of the personnel saw their families only every three years when they returned to Hanoi for vacation. The reason for this, the Vietnamese explained to us with apparent pride, was that the diplomatic service was looked upon as a form of military service, to be filled by the select and seasoned few. In the course of their long guerrilla wars the Vietnamese had to become accustomed to living apart from their families for years at a time, and, furthermore, only those who had spent at least eight years in the jungle during the guerrilla war against the Japanese or the French could even qualify for the diplomatic service. They considered the practice of separation advantageous because it assured that the diplomat would not forget his homeland amid the comforts of Europe. (The Chinese diplomatic service operated under the same basic premise, but there the ambassadors were selected from participants in the Long March.)

Chargé Thieng's main activity was to obtain as much economic aid as possible for his country. He paid more visits to the industrial departments of the Hungarian Communist party and to the Ministries of Heavy and Light Industry than to the Foreign Ministry. His embassy was also active in propaganda. Press Secretary Cao Anh Kiet diligently traveled in the cities and provinces, searching out factories, agricultural cooperatives, and state farms, and giving lectures about war against the French and "the sinful machinations of American imperialism in Southeast Asia." He always stressed that his government looked upon the bifurcation of Vietnam as a merely temporary situation.

In private conversations with me, Chargé Thieng related details of the 1954 Geneva Conference and the developing South Vietnamese situation that were entirely new to me. He explained that the Viet Minh had always stood on firm ground in the South in terms of political influence. According to him, the Ho Chi Minh leadership had agreed to sign the 1954 Geneva agreement first and foremost because it felt certain that this influence could be preserved for years if necessary. He did not mention that the Chinese and the Russians pressed them at Geneva to sign the agreements. But he emphasized that additional cadres could be trained in North Vietnam and sent to the South, and in due time the situation in South Vietnam would become ripe for partisan action. In addition, Thieng—himself a Southerner—expected the imminent overthrow of "the American puppet," Diem. The South Vietnamese dictator had no popular support and was known to be extremely corrupt; indeed the chargé had information that he had secretly transferred American aid money to French and Swiss bank accounts in his own name.

My visit to North Vietnam in the spring of 1959 was not my first. I had been there late in 1958 on a routine inspection tour to report on the functioning of the Hungarian Embassy in Hanoi. Since the North Vietnamese capital was at that time not a significant post for Hungary, the activities of the embassy were actually directed by a chargé d' affaires.

In November 1958 the chargé in Hanoi had fallen seriously ill and had to be rushed back to Hungary; since then all embassy affairs had been in the hands of a young secretary named József Kertész, whose task was to supervise the delivery of Hungarian economic aid to Vietnam and to report back to Budapest Hanoi's never-ending requests for more aid. In performing this task he had enjoyed trouble-free relations with the Vietnamese Foreign Ministry. Like other socialist diplomats in Hanoi, he also maintained contact with the International Department of the Central Committee of the Vietnamese Worker's party and occasionally served as a party-to-party courier transmitting sealed messages from Budapest to Hanoi and back.

The diplomatic quarter in Hanoi was located in an area of the city formerly occupied by the French, an area that bore a marked physical resemblance to the famed French Quarter in New Orleans. Despite the pleasant surroundings, however, the everyday life in the foreign missions was not comfortable. Vietnamese security police armed with machine guns were posted at every embassy building, checking the credentials of all visitors who came and went, and subjecting all Vietnamese nationals to physical search. The Ministry of the Interior seldom allowed diplomats to travel in the countryside; the reason given was that South Vietnamese spies were operating in the villages and the surrounding jungle, and the safety of foreigners could not be guaranteed.

Hanoi itself was colorful and clean, and in 1958 the reconstruction after the ravages of war was complete. Children played peacefully on the backs of the huge turtles on Golden Turtle Islet in the middle of lotus-covered Little Lake. The historic one-footed Lotus Pagoda nearby and the adjoining flower market made the site a splendid attraction for tourists, Vietnamese soldiers on leave, and the wives of visiting Russian, Chinese, and East European advisers. The open-air food market was filled with fruit, vegetables, and fish of every description. The once flourishing commercial district, however, was almost deserted; most of its stores had been nationalized and there was a severe shortage of basic commodities. All over the city, the streets were safe day and night. After 1954 the police deported the city's underground elements, mainly thieves and prostitutes, to distant mines and closed some 400 opium dens and gambling houses.

The Hungarian diplomats made themselves familiar figures at the cocktail parties, receptions, and film showings hosted by the other diplomatic missions, and they were always present at social programs organized by the host Vietnamese. Kertész was especially active on the social scene, but despite all his best efforts he was able to obtain little privileged information. He told me resentfully that political matters in Hanoi were discussed only with the Russians or the Chinese and from time to time with the Poles, who were members of the International Control Commission for Indo-China. But he had learned from private sources that Chinese economic aid was beginning to supersede Russian aid and Chinese popularity was definitely growing. Back in Budapest, I reported this rather novel and, in my view, important observation, but nobody seemed to take it seriously.

During my spring 1959 visit to Vietnam, I went as the foreign policy expert in an official Hungarian party and government delegation headed by Prime Minister and Politburo member Ferenc Münnich. When our special plane, an Aeroflot TU 104 rented from the Soviet Union, touched down at the Hanoi airport on the afternoon of April 19, Prime Minister Pham Van Dong was on hand to greet the delegation, and after a short protocol ceremony we proceeded to the Presidential Palace, where President Ho Chi Minh awaited us.

During our week-long visit we were lodged in a palace that had been built for the French governor-general. The Vietnamese outdid themselves to make us welcome. French-trained chefs cooked our food; French wines and Napoleon cognacs graced every dinner, and at formal banquets we even drank Cordon Rouge champagne captured from French supply depots. One evening we were honored by a gala performance of the Vietnamese National Folk Ensemble in the garden of the palace. Our hosts also organized an unforgettable voyage in the Gulf of Tonkin. On that voyage we sailed through enchanting Along Bay (which with its three thousand tiny rocky islands is proudly referred to by the Vietnamese as the eighth wonder of the world) to a seaside resort on a smaller bay that had been a favorite recreation place of the French. This spot was now used as a military base, but in preparation for our one-day stay there the Vietnamese had tidied up a few of the buildings. We went swimming in the ocean—true, amidst great security precautions. The Vietnamese had completely closed off the little bay with fishing boats and barks and outside this cordon torpedo boats circled and throbbed relentlessly. What is more, beside each Hungarian bather swam three little Vietnamese security officers. It was a comic, grotesque experience but our host assured us earnestly that all the precautions were necessary because one must always anticipate South Vietnamese sabotage activity.

Back from that adventure and in less troubled water, so to speak, we visited a machine factory and the university in Hanoi, a fish processing plant in Haiphong, and an open-pit anthracite mine at Hon Gai. In the port of Haiphong we saw mainly Russian and Polish ocean-going vessels, but at one place alongside the docks, surprisingly, a Swedish ship was berthed. The port itself appeared rather desolate, and everywhere one could see blown-up pillboxes once used by the French, fire-gutted warehouses, and other traces of war.

In the course of our tour in the provinces we went to see the Thein Phon agricultural cooperative, which had been selected with special care from among the so-called model cooperatives and christened "Hungarian-Vietnamese Friendship Cooperative" in honor of our visit. It was a rice-growing operation; with its paddies under water and separated from one another by low dams, it was like stepping backward into another century. Some of the field workers were engaged in the endless task of lifting water over the dams by means of primitively designed foot-powered paddles. Women in black pajama-like *cu-nao* clothing stood knee-deep in the water, thinning out the rice plants, while men walked back and forth behind wooden plows pulled by buffaloes. Small boys darted about the paddies spearing fish with sharpened bamboo lances or more sedately transported their catch in baskets hanging from both ends of a bamboo pole thrown over their shoulders. A burning sun suffused the scene, and only woven bamboo hats afforded any of these people protection from its rays.

By way of wheeled transport, the cooperative boasted a grand total of two bicycles, one of which was the treasured property of the president of the cooperative, the other that of the secretary of the Lao Dong (Communist) party. The tour ended in a general meeting between field laborers and visitors at which the president of the cooperative gave an account of production results. When this report ended, General Giap, who had accompanied the delegation along with Deputy Foreign Minister Ung Van Khiem, rose to speak. First he explained to the local audience the approximate geographic location of Hungary. He then went on to explain how in Hungary, as in the DRV, the peasant workers had banded together in agricultural cooperatives—but in Hungary, he adjured, the peasants had progressed farther along this road. There, 85 to 90 percent of the land was already worked by cooperative farming, and "the achievements have been splendid." Then the general put a question to his countrymen: If in Hungary the peasants can achieve this result, can not Vietnamese peasants do the same? A young man in the audience jumped from his place as if jerked by wires and shouted, "We can do it, too!" Now here, I thought to myself, is a most interesting technique for promoting agricultural cooperatives. What is the reason behind it?

In the course of subsequent conversations with Giap and Khiem, we learned that the Vietnamese party leadership had encountered difficulties in its efforts to force the pace of agricultural collectivization. A lot of human sacrifice had been demanded in the process, and a lot of tension generated. Unfortunately, certain local leaders, seeing enemies of the people everywhere, had resorted to terrorist measures. Thousands of well-to-do peasants had to be resettled, and in numerous cases those who offered resistance were physically liquidated; landlords who were unable to flee to the South had been executed without exception. And what was even worse, said Giap, several thousand party members had been unjustly expelled from the party, jailed, and in some cases tortured and executed. It was the general's belief that the members of the Central Committee, intoxicated by the victory over the French, had thought it could do anything without limits, and failed to pay sufficient attention to the feelings of the people. They forgot that the war was won only because the party was able to mobilize the masses through patriotism.

Finally, he said, Ho Chi Minh had become alerted to these errors during the period of turbulence in the Communist camp that followed Khrushchev's denunciation of Stalin's crimes at the Communist party of the Soviet Union (CPSU) Twentieth Congress in 1956. Ho's grave concern was heightened especially after the Polish reform movement and the dissolution of cooperatives in Hungary during the anti-Communist uprising there. Thereafter the pace of agricultural reorganization in

Vietnam had slowed down. Meanwhile, of course, the crisis had created a drop in food production. There had been small protest riots among the peasants in Nghe An and elsewhere, and some intellectuals around the university and in literary circles had become restless. But, as Giap put it, the party leadership learned from the 1956 Hungarian lesson; and although it had no choice but to crush any rebellions without delay, it had taken steps to normalize its relations with tribal chiefs and Buddhist leaders, and a sincere effort was being made to honor centuries-old customs and national sentiments.

In the course of these remarkably frank disclosures, I noticed, however, that Giap failed to mention how, after the fiasco, party Secretary-General Truong Chinh, the man in charge of carrying out the collectivization, became a scapegoat and was replaced in his post by Politburo member Le Duan. Nor did he touch upon another aspect I considered important: in the wake of the Soviet Twentieth Party Congress, Khrushchev warned Ho Chi Minh that a forced collectivization campaign in the North could shatter Ho's political image in the South and make the unification of the country impossible.

The general ended our conversation at the cooperative on an optimistic note. He reminded us that in olden times, during the colonial period and before, the northern part of Vietnam always depended on rice transported from the south and that the French were convinced that plantations could be established no farther north than the 15th parallel. The North had now demonstrated that even rubber and coffee could be practicably produced above the 17th parallel—and what was even more important, northern rice production was now sufficient (at 303 kilograms per capita) to avoid the pre-harvest famine that for centuries had stalked the North annually.

Although what we saw in North Vietnam was impressive indeed—perhaps mainly because of the novel and sometimes exotic nature of the country—the most interesting moments in our visit came during talks we held with the leaders of the country. Usually we held our discussions in the early morning hours, before the sultry heat enveloped the city like a curtain of steam, or in the late afternoon, after the temperature dropped somewhat. President Ho Chi Minh received the Hungarian delegation in his modestly furnished private residence in company with his closest collaborators: Premier Pham Van Dong, Politburo member Le Duan, and Defense Minister General Giap. The residence stood in a corner of the Palace garden, well hidden by trees and shrubs and of course tightly sealed off from the rest of the park by security guards. Our Vietnamese friends told us this house had been used during French rule as servants' quarters.

I had heard many conflicting opinions about Ho Chi Minh, and like everyone in the delegation I was anxious to meet him. Back in 1952 in Paris, Pierre Courtade, the editor of the Communist newspaper *L'Humanité,* had told me that Ho was the Tito of the Far East—a staunch nationalist Communist and nothing more. Yugoslav trade union leader Svetozar Vukmanović Tempo, who had known Ho well from the time they were both active in the Comintern, agreed with this assessment; it was not merely by chance, I was told, that Ho Chi Minh received a hero's welcome when he visited Belgrade in 1947. Hungarian party chief Kádár held a contrary view. In public as well as in private, he said that Ho Chi Minh was an outstanding internationalist who had done much to spread communism in Indo-China. Prime Minister Münnich's view was that Ho was a lucky man to have survived Stalin's blood purges—lucky to have been in China and in the Vietnamese jungles while his former boss, Michael Borodin, and his other more accessible friends from the Far Eastern Bureau of the Comintern were liquidated one by one.

Vyacheslav M. Molotov, whom I had seen in Ulan Bator on my way to Hanoi, held a poor opinion of Ho Chi Minh and his deputy Pham Van Dong. According to him, both were stubborn men, interested only in Vietnam and not in the international movement. I heard other opinions, too—some that Ho was close to Moscow, others that his most intimate ties were with Peking.

Quite apart from the diverse opinions, an atmosphere of revolutionary romanticism surrounded Ho. His "Prison Diary"—a collection of melancholic poems written while he was imprisoned by Chiang Kai-shek's authorities as a suspected spy during World War II—had been published in Vietnamese,

French, English, and Russian; and effective propaganda had made him a national hero, a legend, a man capable of the most rigorous self-denial in the interest of serving the people. My own judgment, based on observation of his actions, was that behind the popular image was a shrewd, ruthlessly ambitious and highly intelligent Marxist colonial revolutionary whose life was dedicated to uniting Vietnam under his own sway. In 1959 this frail man with the iron resolve was one of the very few party leaders in the Communist camp who presided over a politburo and central committee that could claim an extraordinary record of cohesion and consensus. What is more, he was one of the few Communist chiefs who, like Yugoslavia's Tito, had come to power after a long and successful guerrilla war rather than as an appointee of Moscow or Peking. Indeed, during the struggle between the two Communist giants, Ho was to remain neutral and to profit thereby.

When he met with our delegation at his modest quarters on the Palace grounds, President Ho followed a formal greeting and exchange of customary courtesies with a general inquiry about the Hungarian situation and Hungarian affairs, then quickly focused upon the specific. He wanted to know what the Hungarian Communist party's final assessment of the 1956 "counter-revolution" was, and what lessons the Hungarian Politburo had drawn from that series of events. In particular, I thought, he seemed concerned about the current state of nationalism and national unity, the connection between the party and the masses.

These were delicate questions for Prime Minister Münnich, and his responses showed it. He essayed a rather trite reply to the effect that the Hungarian people, with the help of the Soviet Union, had not only scored a signal victory over a "counter-revolution" inspired by fascists and imperialists but were now enthusiastically engaged in the construction of a truly socialist society. It was the same kind of fare expounded daily in the Hungarian press for anyone who cared to read.[6] Ho acknowledged this statement with the polite observation that during and after the events of 1956 the Hungarian workers had enriched the treasury of the international workers' movement with valuable "experiences." In Vietnam, he said, these events had been studied carefully for the lessons they held.

At this point, Ho launched into a concise, candid review of the internal situation of the DRV, with special emphasis on the subject of religions. He had been able to normalize his relations with the Buddhists and Taoists, he stated, but not with the Catholics. This remained a problem, he said, despite the fact that about 60 percent of the Northern Catholics—more than half a million of them—had gone South. Those who remained in the North were obdurately uncooperative, and those who had gone to the South now formed a political base for Ngo Din Diem and weakened Ho's influence there. Catholicism was quite as dangerous as "American imperialism" and neo-colonialism, he averred; and, frankly, he had not yet developed a suitable means to fight it. How had the Hungarian party leadership handled this situation in view of the fact that over 50 percent of Hungary's population was Catholic?

The question came with startling abruptness and caught the Hungarians off guard, not only for what it revealed of Ho's knowledge of Hungary, but because it touched another sore spot. Politburo member Károly Kiss, the second man in the delegation, was the first to find his tongue. According to Hungarian experience, Kiss said, if both party and state are strong, the Catholic hierarchy willy-nilly must accept and respect this fact and dare not engage openly in oppositionist political activity. Hence the relationship between church and state becomes "normalized," and to one looking at it from the outside, at least, state-church relations appear to be good. If the state leadership shows weakness vis-à-vis the church, however, or if the internal political situation becomes unstable, then a collision between state and church is unavoidable.

Ho Chi Minh took note of this rather simplistic summation with a mildly mocking smile. He too had tried this method, he remarked quietly, but without much success, and for the time being he found he could do nothing better than keep the Catholics under tight surveillance and control.

To change the subject, Münnich now asked about the situation in the South. Here the bearded poet-statesman yielded the floor to a former Southern guerrilla leader, the sober-visaged

Le Duan. Le Duan, Ho explained, was the Politburo member in charge of South Vietnamese affairs and had recently returned from an extended tour of the South.

Le Duan quietly explained that the situation in the South was slowly but surely turning to the advantage of the North. Political workers and party cadres working there had instructions from Hanoi to "dissolve" among the peasants in the countryside and among the intellectuals in the cities, to find niches in the everyday life of the society, and indeed, where possible, to infiltrate the army and the government. In the agitprop (political agitation and progaganda) sphere, said Le Duan, party cadres working in the South seized every opportunity to expose the corruption of the Diem regime and to support popular grievances. These tactics had begun to bear fruit; the influence of the party was growing.

Naturally, there had been difficulties. Special attention had been devoted to maintaining good relations with the Buddhist clergy, a sometimes difficult task because many Buddhist leaders lacked confidence in the party workers and, perhaps more important, the party workers themselves often failed to understand this tactic and dogmatically refused to participate. Furthermore, Diem also had been actively organizing, and with the aid of the Catholic Church, the landlords, and certain others he had achieved a certain degree of stability. The Northerners whose fear of communism and naive receptivity to "hostile" propaganda had driven them south were of course a prime source of support for the Diem puppet government; in addition, the lies they spread about conditions in the North had done great harm to the DRV. And yet, in spite of these difficulties, Le Duan was confident that the Diem regime would soon collapse and that the final results would prove positive.

Le Duan also spoke at some length about how Diem and his cohorts pursued the policy of the strong hand, not only against the Communists and liberal-minded leftist elements, but against the Buddhists as well. Their internal security police had built up a network on the French model that covered all of South Vietnam, and from the Deuxième Bureau and perhaps through the Americans they had obtained the names of numerous Communist and progressive cadres. Their methods were brutal and effective. Fortunately, the Politburo member added with a thin smile, the Northerners too were conversant with French methods and thus not wholly bereft of defenses; but even so, their casualties had been enormous.

Le Duan spoke only briefly on the question of reunification of North and South Vietnam. As a matter of fact, he totally discounted the possibility of a reunification through elections as stipulated in the 1954 Geneva Agreements. All parties concerned had known full well that an election in 1956 would result in a Communist victory, and, therefore, he noted calmly, no one in Hanoi had been surprised when Diem and the Americans blocked the holding of an election that year. Clearly, such an election would never take place and reunification could be effected only through military means. The election issue still had great value for progaganda purposes, however, and Le Duan asked that it be stressed in the joint communiqué to be issued by the two parties at the conclusion of our visit. It was quickly agreed, therefore, that the communiqué would hold the American imperialists and the South Vietnamese authorities accountable for their violation of the Geneva Agreements and for the incorporation of South Vietnam as an autonomous state into the South East Asia Treaty Organization.

At this point the veteran Communist leader Pham Van Dong took over the conversation and discoursed at length on the worries caused by South Vietnamese guerrilla leaders residing in Hanoi. Day by day, he said, these comrades were increasing their pressure on members of the Politburo to endorse all-out military action in South Vietnam. Pham Van Dong acknowledged that emotionally this eagerness was understandable, but it would be folly to begin such an action before the North became strong enough to back it up and before the situation was ripe in the South. Then in a half-finished sentence he hinted that the Southern comrades should not be asked to wait too long.

On April 25 the Hungarian and Vietnamese delegations gathered for their final formal meeting. Prime Minister Münnich and his counter-part, Pham Van Dong, accepted without change the draft of a joint communiqué worked out in advance by propaganda experts on both sides. Then followed a tedious ceremony of signing the communiqué and a farewell reception given by the Vietnamese in an enormous military tent set up in the palm-girdled Palace garden. For this last occasion Ho Chi Minh appeared with his entire general staff. Also present were members of the diplomatic corps, a few Buddhist priests, and a fair representation of other special notables.

In one corner of the tent, clustered together and talking among themselves, were the South Vietnamese living in Hanoi. Apparently the Northern leadership regarded them rather like poor relations—to be tolerated but virtually ignored. At any rate, no one seemed to pay much attention to them. After Pham Van Dong and Münnich exchanged the customary toasts, the guests mingled in relaxed, chatting groups. Urged on by curiosity, I started a conversation with one of the South Vietnamese, Nguyen Huu Tho. It transpired that he was a lawyer, had attended a university in Paris, and spoke excellent French. He told me he had been living in Hanoi since 1954 but often went to South Vietnam on party business. Part of his family lived in Saigon and had spread the report that he was dead. He flatly stated that the situation in South Vietnam was ripe for revolutionary guerrilla activity. The peasants there were deeply embittered because the present landlords exploited them in the same way the landlords of a hundred years ago had exploited their forebearers; the intellectuals were alienated by the all-pervading corruption; the Buddhists chafed under Diem's Catholic rule. But still the guerrillas must stay their hand, he concluded with heavy sarcasm, because Hanoi contended the time was not right for action. He then asked whether Ho, Pham Van Dong, or Le Duan had disclosed any new plans to the Hungarians concerning the "liberation" of the South. I eluded the question.

On our way home we stayed for several days in Peking and had long meetings with the Chinese leaders, who were keen to hear about our experiences in Vietnam. While Foreign Minister Sik briefed his counterpart, Ch'en Yi, I was instructed to inform Wang Yu-t'ien, the director of the Soviet and East European departments in the Chinese Foreign Ministry. Both seemed particularly concerned about what we knew of the South Vietnamese situation. The Chinese foreign minister expected Ho Chi Minh to begin the unification process soon.

The subject of Vietnam came up again during our meeting with Mao Tse-tung. He spoke of Ho as an old friend with whom he had always enjoyed harmonious relations, blamed Stalin for all Ho's difficulties, and observed that Stalin had never understood Asian Communists. It was his own hope, he declared, that one day the Communists would come to power in France, making possible the solution of the Vietnam problem within the framework of a French Union under Maurice Thorez and Jacques Duclos. Meanwhile, Mao stated, China would continue to back the Vietnamese in their efforts to liberate their country.

We had a two-day stopover in Moscow on May 16–17, and Frol Kozlov, the first deputy prime minister, invited us to a luncheon in the Kremlin. Just before we started to eat, Khrushchev made an unannounced appearance. Clad in a Ukrainian rubashka (shirt) and apparently in high spirits, he sailed into an animated conversation with Premier Münnich that ranged over a broad field of foreign affairs. On the West Berlin question, he told us that Gromyko's reports from the ongoing Conference of Foreign Ministers in Geneva were not very encouraging; in any case, he remarked scathingly, he preferred to keep Germany divided. He then asked several questions about Mao Tse-tung and was pleased when Münnich told him the Hungarians had a low opinion of the latest Chinese innovation, the commune movement. Khrushchev confided that at one time the Soviet Union also had wanted to transform its kolkhozes (collective farms) into industrial complexes, but the experience did not work; he added that "Mao is not a man who learned from the mistakes of others."

The Soviet leader showed no interest whatsoever in Vietnam. Indeed, when Münnich enthusiastically tried to tell him about some of the highlights of our Hanoi visit, Khrushchev all but yawned in his face. I found this attitude rather strange inasmuch as the Fifteenth Plenum of the Central Committee of the Lao Dong party in May had for the first time called for an armed struggle against the "Diem clique" and the Americans. With Le Duan's briefing on the South Vietnamese situation and my lawyer friend's question about the liberation of the South still fresh in my memory, it seemed obvious to me that Ho Chi Minh and his Politburo had finally made the decision to start a war in the South. Yet Khrushchev, for reasons unknown to me, seemed totally unconcerned.

CHAPTER II

The Washington Assignment

The May 1959 resolution of the Fifteenth Plenum of the Central Committee of the Lao Dong party marked the beginning of the long-range revolutionary warfare against the anti-Communist South Vietnamese and their American supporters. As in the previous Franco-Viet Minh war, Hanoi's intervention took the form of the well-tested protracted guerrilla warfare. And as always Vo Nguyen Giap took charge of the overall direction of military operations. Otherwise the political and organizational work was handled by Le Duc Tho, a Politburo member and secretary of the Central Committee; and day-to-day operations were conducted by the Reunification Department of the Central Committee, headed by one of the ablest generals of the Vietnamese People's Army, Nguyen Van Vinh. Special border crossing units quietly transported ammunition, food, and medicine southward across the demilitarized zone and through the panhandle of Laos to supply the scattered Viet Cong bases. By early 1960, bases for training infiltrators had been set up on Son Tay, near Hanoi, in Nghe An Province and in Xuan Mai.[1]

At the Third Congress of the Lao Dong party in Hanoi in

September 1960, the Soviet Communist party delegate, N. A. Mukhitdinov (first secretary of the Uzbekistan Central Committee), was politely applauded after he underlined the overall importance of "peaceful coexistence" between capitalist and socialist societies and only secondarily denounced colonialism.[2] The Congress gave a tremendous reception, on the other hand, to the Chinese delegate, Li Fu-ch'un of the Chinese Communist party's Politburo, who forcefully propounded a "people's liberation war" against the "American imperialists and their Vietnamese lackeys." And when Ho Chi Minh rose to speak he brought down the house with a vehement attack against the Diem regime of South Vietnam and its American supporters, a vow to unify Vietnam, and, most significant of all, a proposal for the formation of a "united front" for the "liberation" of South Vietnam.[3]

In a matter of months Ho's united front grew into the National Front for the Liberation of South Vietnam (NLF); and in the same period the nucleus of the Liberation Army of South Vietnam appeared on the scene. The initial Viet Cong main force consisted of no more than 8 to 10 battalions with 5,500 men, plus some 30,000 poorly equipped and poorly trained regional and local guerrillas. But in three years this relatively small force was to grow into a respectable army of 30 battalions.[4] Meanwhile the membership of the NLF doubled and redoubled until by early 1962 it reached approximately 250,000 to 300,000. The Front was initially comprised of farmers from the Mekong river and town dwellers from Saigon, Danang, Hue, and elsewhere. Among the rank and file were Viet Minh Communists, socialists, liberals—even adherents of the religious Cao Dai and Hoa Hao sects. In 1960, thousands of hardcore ethnic Southeners who had gone north to regroup after 1954, were sent back south. They took command posts in the Viet Cong guerrilla units and layed the foundation of the People's Revolutionary party, the Southern branch of the Lao Dong party. Basically following the Viet Minh tactic of appealing to Vietnamese nationalism, the NLF guerrillas soon made significant political and military advances.[5]

Despite growing Communist pressure, Vietnam was not at this time Washington's chief preoccupation. The Kennedy administration had just survived the agonizing Bay of Pigs fiasco in Cuba and had recently faced a dangerous confrontation with the Russians in Berlin. With respect to Southeast Asia, a possible Communist takeover in Laos—and not the collapse of the Diem government of South Vietnam—was the main concern of policy-makers in the White House. Nevertheless, economic and military aid programs were expanded; the U.S. military advisory group was widened; training centers for South Vietnamese counter-insurgency forces were organized. By the end of 1963, 16,000 U.S. military personnel were stationed in South Vietnam. U.S. fliers and helicopter pilots were often engaged in combat missions. But U.S. ground forces were not sent to Vietnam. Meanwhile, American efforts to pressure President Diem into much needed political and administrative reforms fell through. Diem's so-called Strategic Hamlet program, a population relocation plan in the rural areas, ended in complete failure. Graft and corruption of key government officials reached unprecendented heights. Finally, the brutal suppression of the Buddhist movement added fuel to the fire which ultimately led to the overthrow of Ngo Dinh Diem in November 1963.

Yet neither the considerable increase in the size of the American military effort nor Diem's assassination and the subsequent military coup in South Vietnam stirred up much interest among Eastern Europeans. We Hungarians learned the details of the evolving situation in Vietnam from reports forwarded to the Foreign Ministry by our embassies in Moscow, Peking, and Hanoi as well as by our legations in Paris and Washington. Accounts coming from the two Western capitals contained interesting details, though little that one could not read in *Le Monde* and the *New York Times.* Reports from the Eastern capitals, based on information from the host countries' foreign ministries, were at first filled with inside information and quite intriguing. As time went on, however, they became increasingly trite, until one could have learned as much from the Chinese newspaper *Jen-min Jih-pao* or the Vietnamese *Nhan Dan.* This was particularly evident after the meeting of the twelve Communist bloc leaders, held in June 1960 in Bucharest, where Khrushchev had his famous confrontation with the Chinese, hastening the rupture between the two Communist giants. Thereafter the Chinese Foreign Ministry became increasingly secretive and the Vietnamese more rigid with Soviet bloc diplomats, with the result that the inside stories we received came almost exclusively from Moscow and were biased accordingly.

In the meantime my personal involvement in Vietnam came to a temporary halt. After my return from the DRV, I spent the latter half of 1959 dealing with African matters. In July we welcomed a government delegation from Guinea, headed by Deputy Premier and Defense Minister Keita N. Famara. Like the other Soviet bloc countries, we accorded sizable aid to the badly shaken economy of the leftist regime of President Sékou Touré. In August, I in turn visited Sékou Touré in Conakry and discussed further extension of our economic and political collaboration. From Guinea I proceeded to Accra where I spent a week of long, hard bargaining with Economic Minister Kojo Botsio and concluded the first trade agreement between Hungary and Ghana.

In April 1960, I was apointed protocol chief. In my new job I was in daily contact with all the diplomatic corps accredited to Budapest and had to see that the party and the government were properly represented at their receptions.[6] Another facet of my duties was to prepare and carry through visits from heads of state. Among my guests in 1960–61 were President Antonin Novotný of Czechoslovakia, Gheorghiu-Dej of Rumania, Sukarno of Indonesia, Kwame Nkrumah of Ghana, and Ernesto "Che" Guevara of Cuba. One of my special and frequent guests was N. S. Khrushchev, for whom we organized hunting parties. In 1961, I accompanied Premier Münnich on his good will tour of South East Asia, where we visited Prime Minister Jawaharlal Nehru in India, General Ne Win in Burma, and President Sukarno in Indonesia. The next year I escorted Deputy Premier Béla Biszku to the national day celebration of Walter Ulbricht's East Germany.

In spring 1962, I was relieved of my duties as protocol chief and appointed to head the Hungarian legation in Washington, D.C. As a routine procedure, Foreign Minister János Péter, who had selected me for the post, had first to report his choice to his superior, Dezső Nemes, the Politburo member responsible for Hungarian foreign affairs. He then discussed the appointment with the political and military intelligence agencies, since they had strong centers for intelligence operations (better known as residenturas) built in the legation in Washington. And finally, he also informed the Soviet ambassador to Hungary, Vladimir Ivanovits Ustinov, of the forthcoming assignment. When all these parties concurred, the proposal was sent to the Politburo for final approval, and there it was accepted without dispute.[7]

It was late March when I arrived in Washington, bringing with me vaguely formulated instructions from the Kádár government to discover a means of breaking the six-year impasse in Hungarian-U.S. relations and removing the "Hungarian Question" from the agenda of the United Nations General Assembly. It was a complex assignment. The United States government was determined to keep alive the debate on the question of the Russian invasion of Hungary in 1956 and did so in the General Assemby by sponsoring resolutions for restoration of freedom to the Hungarian people and by withholding its recognition of the Hungarian credentials until amnesty was granted to those political prisoners who had been incarcerated in the wake of the revolution. Neither Moscow nor Budapest could afford a political amnesty under what looked like American pressure. Nevertheless, the annually recurring debate was a perpetual source of irritation to the Soviet Union and an effective means to bar the Kádár government's international acceptance.

Under these circumstances, I had to proceed with extreme caution, selling the idea of amnesty to Budapest as the only option to break the deadlock, and at the same time convincing the Americans that to press for amnesty would reduce the chances of a positive result.

On October 20, after seven months of negotiations, I at last obtained a memorandum from the State Department, which stated that instead of amnesty the United States wanted the Hungarian government either to take convincing public steps to assure that the consequences of the events of 1956 would be erased or to issue an authoritative statement to that effect. In exchange, the State Department promised to end the debate on the "Hungarian Question" and expressed readiness to normalize bilateral relations. This was a good compromise, but I had been in the service long enough to know that a diplomatic step of such major importance had to be coordinated first with Moscow. Moreover, it was evident that the realization of the proposals contained in the memorandum hinged entirely on the outcome of a most dangerous confrontation of the two superpowers—the Cuban missile crisis, which had erupted in the meantime.

Naturally during the days of that crisis nobody cared about my memorandum. But once the humiliating fiasco of Khrushchev's attempt at nuclear blackmail was over, the Kremlin leadership sought an all-round relaxation of East-West tension. It was now ready to install a "hot-line" between Moscow and Washington as a special device to avoid future crises; it began seriously to consider a nuclear test ban treaty; and it was also willing to accept the American formula for Hungarian-U.S. rapprochement. Accordingly, Budapest announced a sweeping amnesty, and Washington dropped the "Question of Hungary" from the agenda of the United Nations.[8]

The resolution of the embarrassing "Question of Hungary" at the United Nations not only ended the seven-year-long isolation of the Kádár government but made possible a speedy normalization of its relations with the West. In addition it gave the Hungarian party leadership a sense of security to proceed with further relaxation of internal pressure. In this new mood the government eased travel regulations to and from Hungary; it even signed an agreement with the Vatican restoring the right of the Hungarian branch of the Church to form a hierarchy and to communicate freely with the Holy See.[9] These developments, together with the general amnesty, made the situation of the Hungarian people comparatively better than that of the peoples living in any other country in the Soviet bloc, with the possible exception of Poland.

Naturally this process of liberalization was welcomed in Washington and opened the way for diplomatic reconciliation between the two countries. It came at a time when the two superpowers had concluded a treaty to ban the testing of nuclear weapons in the earth's atmosphere, in space, and under water, and evidently this major international development also improved the chances for bilateral normalization of relations between Hungary and the United States. As Hungary's representative, I was present at the signing of the Nuclear Test Ban Treaty at the White House in the summer of 1963 and at that time detected among State Department officials a reinforced belief that the United States was ready to adopt a friendlier attitude toward the Kádár government and to treat his regime on equal footing with the other East European Communists.

The change in American attitude was confirmed early in October 1963 when President Kennedy authorized the sale of surplus wheat and other farm commodities to the draught-stricken Soviet Union and other East European countries, including Hungary. Characteristically, Budapest doubted whether the Americans would readily sell us wheat; I had to send cable after cable to convince the Communist party headquarters that the grain was available and that Soviet Ambassador Anatoliy Dobrynin had received the same assurances as I. When I finally received instructions to approach the State Department for a 30 million dollar wheat and corn purchase, the deal was concluded in record time. A transitory difficulty developed when Senator Karl Mundt introduced an amendment to the foreign aid appropriations bill which would have prohibited the Export-Import Bank or any other federal agency from guaranteeing the loans we needed to finance the deal. The clouds disappeared, however, when the administration persuaded Congress to permit Export-Import Bank credit guarantees to the Soviet bloc countries if President Kennedy felt this action to be in the national interest.[10] Despite the administration's efforts, at the end, party chief Kádár, still fearful that future grain deals with the United States would be hazardous, decided to make plans to achieve self-sufficiency in wheat production.

During the "peaceful coexistence" (as the Khrushchevian détente was named), I arranged for a high level Hungarian agricultural delegation to visit major experiment stations and farms in Iowa, Indiana, and Michigan and to meet Agriculture Secretary Orville Freeman and other leading experts in the field. On the cultural front, I entered into talks with Harrison

Brown, the foreign secretary of the National Academy of Sciences, who was responsible for the Soviet-American scientific exchange program and was concerned that the Americans had no similar program with other Eastern European countries. After preliminary negotiations in Washington, Professor Brown visited Budapest and reached an agreement with the Hungarian Academy of Sciences concerning the details of an exchange program. I also worked out an agreement with the Ford Foundation under which Hungarian intellectuals and scientists would receive travel and study grants. (Regrettably the Hungarian intelligence service subsequently used the Foundation program as a cover for their operations in the United States.)

There were, of course, some debit entries on the ledger of normalization. The future of Cardinal József Mindszenty, whose residence in political asylum at the American Legation in Budapest since 1956 had caused considerable friction between the two governments, remained unsolved, despite the fact that the interested parties—the Hungarian government, the Vatican, and the American government—had reached a tacit understanding that the Cardinal should accept a safe-conduct from Hungary to a post promised by the Vatican. Mindszenty refused to leave Hungary, and neither the Vatican nor the Americans were at that time willing to put pressure on him.[11]

In addition, we had to face the fact that because of U. S. Congressional opposition Hungary could not receive the "most favored nation" treatment for its export goods. We had difficulties also in obtaining access to advanced American technology. We were denied among other things the purchase of computer technology because it had strategic value to the Soviet bloc; then Budapest wanted to open consular offices in New York and Cleveland, but the State Department judged the proposal untimely. Concerned at the slow progress, I urged upon Ambassador Llewellyn E. Thompson the importance of maintaining forward momentum in peaceful settlements. I even went so far as to suggest that if it were not possible to agree promptly on some further step with the Soviets the Americans might consider some moves with smaller East European countries, such as Hungary. While I pressed the issue in Washington the Hungarian Foreign Ministry proposed starting formal talks through the American Legation in Budapest. Finally, once the 1964 presidential election was over and President Johnson was re-elected, things started moving. By late fall of that year the State Department announced itself ready to begin the long deferred talks between the two countries with preliminary discussions on cultural exchanges and an early consideration of pending financial matters. The Hungarian Foreign Ministry concurred, and on December 4, 1964, the formal bilateral negotiations started in Budapest.

On the same day Secretary of State Dean Rusk and Hungary's foreign minister, János Péter, had a half-hour conversation at the American United Nations Mission in New York. Péter and Rusk touched upon the major political trends in Europe, U. S. plans for the nuclear armed NATO fleet (the so-called Multilateral Force, or MLF), and a possible non-proliferation treaty. They briefly reviewed Hungarian-American trade relations, tourism, and cultural exchange, each assuring the other that an enlarged volume of trade and expanded cultural contacts would be desirable. The discussion was held in a friendly and businesslike atmosphere but produced no reverberating breakthroughs. This high level meeting and the formal negotiations in Budapest, however, signaled a genuine turn in the relationship between the two countries. Some optimists in the Hungarian Foreign Ministry were even predicting that Budapest and Washington would soon exchange ambassadors. But alas, the Kremlin's decision to support the "Liberation of South Vietnam" and the massive American intervention "to insure that aggression should not succeed" temporarily put an end to the Soviet-American détente and at the same time put an end to chances of improving our relations with the United States.

A Shift in Kremlin Policy

The sudden change in world politics resulting from the expansion of the war in Vietnam came as a surprise to the Hungarian diplomatic corps. To begin with, no one in the Foreign Ministry or at the Legation in Washington expected that the Americans, having witnessed the bitter experiences of the French, would get involved in a ground war in Vietnam. Nor did we believe that Brezhnev and his Politburo in the Kremlin would be interested in moving back to Vietnam, which had been abandoned by Khrushchev as a place where the Soviet Union should not waste money and energy. Personally I also thought that neither one of the superpowers would allow itself to become chained to the fortune of a small and relatively insignificant power in Southeast Asia—and that possibility existed in Vietnam. But I was wrong—things had gone too far for the superpowers to stay on the sidelines.

Possibly my miscalculation was due to the fact that during the Khrushchev years and even at the time of the Tonkin Gulf incident in August 1964 Hungarian party and government officials showed little interest in events in Southeast Asia. The news of the clash between a U. S. naval vessel and North Vietnamese torpedo boats caused hardly a ripple in Budapest, although it should have been obvious that the event portended a change in the character of the war.[12] No one in the Hungarian capital seemed to care about Hanoi's war, about America's role in it, or about the fact that it had become an issue in the American presidential campaign. The general indifference to the presidential campaign was voiced by János Kádár, first secretary of the Hungarian Socialist Workers' party, when he said that Hungary did not care who was elected, Goldwater or Johnson. For Kádár it was the same: they were both imperialists.

Vietnam remained an unimportant issue for the Hungarian government at least until the beginning of the next year. In his annual speech before the United Nations General Assembly on December 22, 1964, Foreign Minister Péter cursorily mentioned Vietnam (together with the Congo crisis), deploring the actions of the colonialist and neo-colonialist powers for preventing a peaceful solution. His mild expressions were watered down by the fact that during his conversation with Secretary Dean Rusk, Vietnam was not discussed at all.

In January 1965, this indifference began to change as a result of Soviet pressure. The new Soviet party chief, L. I. Brezhnev, popped up in Budapest along with Politburo member N. V. Podgorny. They stayed three days in the Hungarian capital in uninterrupted session with Kádár and his Politburo. The Russians outlined their plans for calling together an international consultative meeting of the Communist parties to reestablish unity in the international Communist movement; also they informed the Hungarians that during Premier Kosygin's forthcoming visit to Hanoi and Pyongyang the Russians would attempt to reestablish close cooperation with the Korean and Vietnamese Communists, who had been greatly neglected by Khrushchev. In connection with Vietnam, Brezhnev underlined that the NLF forces had already liberated almost 75 percent of the countryside and units of the People's Army of Vietnam (North Vietnamese army) had joined the guerrillas. But an American intervention might change this favorable situation. Thus the Soviet party Politburo felt it necessary to send Kosygin to Hanoi to conduct an on-the-spot investigation. Naturally Kádár fully endorsed the Kremlin plans and promised cooperation.

On February 7, the day after Kosygin arrived in Hanoi, Viet Cong guerrillas attacked U. S. Army advisers' barracks at Pleiku, killing eight Americans and wounding 126. Twelve hours later American jets hit military targets in North Vietnam. Even as the U. S. planes carried out their bombing mission, Washington assured the Kremlin that Kosygin's visit in Hanoi had no connection with the timing of the reprisal strikes and that no offense to the Russians was intended. The Soviet government, however, chose to adopt a different view. Kosygin angrily pointed out that the situation was fraught with serious implications, that continued American military attacks on Communist countries would gravely jeopardize Washington-Moscow relations. Then, to demonstrate Soviet determination the Kremlin organized a protest movement against the U. S. air attacks and against Washington's Vietnamese intervention in general. British, French, and Italian Communist parties were asked by Moscow to stage an anti-American mass demonstration and all the East Europeans were requested to organize similar protests. On February 12 the Hungarian Parliament, together with the government, condemned "the renewed criminal actions of the United States with deep indignation and anger." The next day Asian and African students studying at Hungarian universities along with 800 hand-picked members of the Hungarian Communist Youth Organization (KISZ) were organized by the Agitation and Proproganda Department (Agitprop) of the party to stage an anti-American protest and break into the U. S. Legation in Budapest. The rioters carried out their assignment in a forty-five minute rampage in which they ripped the seal of the United States off the entrance to the building, threw ink bottles at the walls, smashed windows, and destroyed office furniture until police, who had been standing nearby all the while, moved in and dispersed them.

The American chargé d'affairs, Elim O'Shaughnessy, charged in an oral protest to Hungarian Deputy Foreign Minister Béla Szilágyi that the police had failed in their duties to keep order and had done nothing to prevent the break-in. In Washington, assistant secretary for European Affairs, William R. Tyler, summoned me to the State Department. He called the Budapest demonstration a "staged affair," complained about the inadequate police protection, and protested "this intolerable treatment of the legation." While accepting the protest and promising to pay for the damage, we disclaimed responsibility.

Moscow was satisfied with the result and judged the demonstration as effective as the ones in front of the American missions in Sofia, Bulgaria, and Prague, Czechoslovakia.

But the Russians wanted more than demonstrations. At the highest level, the Kremlin informed East European party leaders of Kosygin's February visit to Hanoi and offered detailed information concerning the situation in North Vietnam. Kosygin's report to the Hungarian party Central Committee was contained in a letter signed by Soviet party leader Leonid Brezhnev. Kosygin noted that he had found Ho Chi Minh and the rest of the Vietnamese Workers' party Politburo united and in good spirits. While Ho had expressed concern about the growing American involvement, he remained confident that with the military help of the North the Viet Cong could expand its influence in the Southern countryside and maintain control of all major highways, at least at night.

What the North badly needed, Kosygin reported, was protection against American air attacks, which were expected to escalate. The Soviet Union had already agreed to send sophisticated material, including ground-to-air missiles, and to train Vietnamese personnel to man the missile batteries and to fly MIG fighters. The Vietnamese had further requested economic assistance and political support, and here, too, the Kremlin had decided to meet Hanoi's needs.

As was customary on such occasions, the Soviet leadership recommended "united action" and to that end proposed that Soviet and Hungarian officials and experts undertake consultations. Soon after this communication was received in Budapest, the Hungarian Politburo decided to contribute an agreed share to assist the Vietnamese Communists. State Minister Jenő Fock, coordinator of governmental economic activities, was in charge of the aid. It was to consist of light armaments, radar and communication equipment, hospital facilities, and pharmaceutical supplies. First Secretary Kádár gave his stamp of approval, but explicitly informed his subordinates that the aid was not to exceed the modest capabilities of the Hungarian economy.

The department of Economic Policy of the Central Committee* was authorized to supervise the implementation of Kádár's directive. The Politburo resolution instructed the foreign minister as well as the Hungarian intelligence community to follow Vietnamese events closely and report their findings. The Hungarian Embassy in Hanoi was charged with arranging technical details of the aid program. The Department of International Relations of the Central Committee was instructed to inform other Communist parties of the Politburo decision and to coordinate future interparty actions. The military shipments were handled by the Soviets.

*The organization which exercises party control over the National Planning Committee and over the ministries of Finance, Foreign Trade, Agriculture and Food, and Heavy and Light Industries.

A New Phase of the Conflict

The first Soviet-made surface-to-air missiles and other Soviet bloc military equipment arrived in Hanoi in April 1965. Soon thereafter, under the direction of Russian technicians, missile sites were built in a fifteen-mile radius around the North Vietnamese capital. As we learned directly from Hanoi, Le Duan and General Giap felt especially reassured by the newly acquired Soviet military hardware and wanted to step up the pace of the "liberation" of South Vietnam. Their proposal was accepted by Ho Chi Minh, and several complete battalion-size regular army units were dispatched to the South as a preparatory measure for the coming 1965 offensive. On the diplomatic front the situation became more and more complex. In the second half of 1964, Canadian International Control Commission delegate, J. Blair Seaborn, was asked by Washington to transmit a warning to the leaders of Hanoi that the guerrilla attacks and other hostile actions in South Vietnam supported and directed by the DRV should ultimately result in the use of American military force against North Vietnam. But Premier Pham Van Dong's answer was unequivocal. He simply stated and restated to the Canadian that the United States must withdraw from Vietnam, that NLF participation in future South Vietnamese governments must be accepted, and that North and South Vietnam must be united without foreign interference.[13]

Seaborn was not the only would-be mediator whose mission remained ineffective. Repeated efforts by various other governments and individuals to bring about a negotiated settlement were similarly unsuccessful for some time thereafter.

In February 1965, the British proposed to the Soviets that the two governments, as co-chairmen of the Geneva Conference, mediate between Washington and Hanoi; both Hanoi and Moscow rejected the proposal. In March, Pakistan President Ayub Khan tried unsuccessfully to persuade the Chinese leaders in Peking to use their influence to end the war. In addition, the chief DRV commercial delegate in Paris, Mai Van Bo, told Quai D'Orsai officials point-blank that while previously "his government had been ready to consider negotiation of some sort, U.S. actions have changed the situation. Negotiations are no longer a matter for consideration at this time."[14] In April, U.N. Secretary General U Thant suggested a temporary (three month) cessation of all overt and covert military activity across the 17th parallel in Vietnam, again to no avail. Also in April, seventeen non-aligned nations, on Yugoslavian President Tito's initiative, issued an appeal for cessation of all hostilities and called for negotiations without preconditions. In rejecting that proposal, Hanoi defiantly insisted that the "Four Points" proposal of Premier Pham Van Dong (stated on April 8) were the "only correct way" to solve the Vietnam problem.* Finally, over the same period Indian President Radhakrishnan proposed a cease-fire along the 17th parallel, supervised by an "Afro-Asian Force," and former United Kingdom Foreign Secretary Patrick Gordon-Walker sought to find a peaceful arrangement, but again without success.

For a change, on May 13, the Americans tried to entice Ho Chi Minh into peace negotiations by informing him that the United States had decided to call a brief halt to the air attacks in North Vietnamese territory. They indicated no precise number of days as to how long the pause would last; however, they made clear the position that a permanent suspension of the bombing could come about only if the armed attacks against South Vietnam were to end, and such a cessation, in the view of the United States government, could be decisively effected from North Vietnam.[15]

This move, like the previous ones, was greeted by the North Vietnamese with deafening silence; the pause failed to produce any contact whatever between Washington and Hanoi. Indeed, the North Vietnamese ambassador in Moscow refused to receive American Ambassador Kohler when he attempted to deliver the message, and later the North Vietnamese Embassy

*According to the "Four Points" the U. S. government "must withdraw from South Vietnam U.S. troops, . . . must stop its acts of war against North Vietnam, . . . the internal affairs of South Vietnam must be settled by the South Vietnamese peoples themselves in accordance with the program of the NFLSV, . . . [and] the peaceful reunification of Vietnam is to be settled by the Vietnamese peoples in both zones, without any foreign interference." (Hanoi Radio, April 13, 1965).

simply dispatched a messenger to return the American note (it was pushed under the door at the entrance of the American Embassy). In addition, Hanoi Radio branded the suspension of the bombing "a worn-out trick of deceit and threat," designed to pave the way for new U.S. acts of war."[16]

Soviet and Chinese reactions were also disconcertingly negative. On the eve of the pause (May 11), Secretary Rusk relayed Johnson's decision to the Soviet ambassador in Washington, Anatoliy F. Dobrynin. The Soviet representative immediately asked whether the halt in bombing meant "any change in the fundamental U. S. position," and Rusk replied with frankness that it did not, and "this should be no surprise." The secretary added that "Hanoi appears to have the impression they may succeed, but the U. S. will not get tired or be affected by very small domestic opposition or by international pressure."[17] Rusk then underscored the importance of avoiding misunderstandings concerning American determination. Dobrynin cooly responded that he saw no danger of misunderstanding, but the problem was to find a way out of the conflict. Following the notification that the pause had begun, the Russians refused the role of intermediary. Soviet Deputy Foreign Minister Firyubin, who met with Ambassador Kohler in the Soviet Foreign Ministry in Moscow, first lectured at length upon the "U. S. misconception of the real nature of the conflict in Vietnam." Then he simply stated that he was not a postman and it was not the Soviet but the United States government's responsibility to find a convenient way of passing the message to Hanoi. Andrei Gromyko, who met with Rusk on May 15 in Vienna, was even more rigid, telling his American collegue that the temporary suspension of bombing was "insulting" and the Soviet Union would continue to support North Vietnam and would do so "decisively."[18] Peking released an official communiqué denouncing the American proposal for talks as a hoax.

At my observation post in Washington, I was following the Vietnamese situation largely from the diplomatic sidelines, quite without expectation of playing any personal role in it. As a routine procedure, my staff studied the everyday major news stories and editorials. We also anlayzed the important speeches of leading American public figures and documents issued by the White House and State Department and sent them to the Foreign Ministry with our comments. As usual, the Hungarian political intelligence service at the legation (under diplomatic cover) commented that President Johnson's offer of unconditional discussion should not be taken seriously since the bombing of the North continued and the American troop build-up in the South had been stepped up. Our intelligence analyst, István Varga, cited long paragraphs from Johnson's April 7 speech at Johns Hopkins University in Baltimore, and added that the American president's plan for economic development for all Southeast Asia was as "deceitful" as the Marshall Plan of 1947.

Personally, I was not so sure that Johnson's approach to negotiation should be dismissed so quickly. I felt in any case that the DRV had nothing to lose by testing the sincerity of the proposal, and I made my views known. My interpretation was considered unrealistic in the Foreign Ministry, but, luckily, a few high officials in the party headquarters agreed with me.

As a diplomat working in Washington, I was naturally greatly interested in finding out future American plans. To be frank, I was not too successful in this respect. My State Department contacts were not helpful. Director Raymond Lisle of the East European Department and his aides, it seemed, knew little about American actions and plans for Vietnam, or at least they were unwilling to engage in meaningful conversation on the subject. Nor did my meetings with colleagues in the diplomatic corps bring any grist to the mill. A good friend, Indian Ambassador B. K. Nehru, told me I should not worry about the Vietnamese situation since the Viet Cong already occupied more than 75 percent of South Vietnam, and he doubted that Johnson could do anything to reverse the trend. "South Vietnam is lost for the Americans," he said, "no matter how many troops the Pentagon sends to Vietnam." His remark was though-provoking, but I felt the need of more factual information. The Indonesian ambassador, Suwito Kvsumowidago, seemed almost totally indifferent to the Vietnam situation—but then he was a sick man who rarely left his residence. I knew there were other Asian diplomats who must have more information—the South Vietnamese, the Filipinos, the South Koreans, for instance—but I had special instructions not to speak to them. The Japanese, with whom we had diplomatic relations, were uncommunicative. I had good personal relations with the Laotian ambassador in Washington, the quiet, peace-loving Khamking Souvanlasy. He often complained that the great powers, with their interventionist policies, were the real cause of the war in Indochina and he only wished his country's neutrality would be observed by all parties. Otherwise he too gave me no specific information he might have gained in the State Department or elsewhere.

Nor were my colleagues in the Soviet bloc at all forthcoming. At the monthly ambassadorial meetings they simply repeated what was in the newspapers. No doubt the Soviet Ambassador Anatoliy F. Dobrynin really had some inside information, but he said little. To all questions from the ambassadors, he would only reply that he could not detect any change in the American approach to the conflict. He then invariably reiterated the well-known Soviet position that the Americans must stop the bombing of the North before any negotiation could start. To the best of his knowledge, he said, Hanoi was holding tight to its "Four Points" and was mainly interested in the withdrawal of the American troops in Vietnam.

Quite unexpectedly, I finally received some truly interesting background information from Ambassador-at-large Jean Paul Boncourt. I had met Boncourt for the first time in 1959 when he represented France in the Hungarian capital. We became friends then, but in the meantime I had lost track of him. In the spring of 1965 Boncourt came for a short personal visit to the United States, and he invited me to his Georgetown residence. In the course of our conversation he seemed genuinely disturbed by the latest developments in Vietnam. He said the war was escalating steadily and "the Americans are fools; every day they get involved deeper and deeper in this jungle war." He expressed exasperation that the Americans apparently had not learned from the French experience. De Gaulle himself had amply warned Johnson of the dangers involved in a land war in South Vietnam. Why had the American president refused to listen? As Boncourt spoke, he gestured with his hands and paced back and forth in the room. When at last he calmed down, he told me that recently the French government had proposed a compromise solution for Indochina. The basic concept was to create a neutralized Vietnam, with the North and the South separated, to be united later. The plan called for evacuation of all American troops from the area. Unfortunately, said the ambassador, Hanoi was not interested, though in his own view it would have been a good way to extricate the United States from the conflict.

Apart from Boncourt's revelation, probably the most useful information we got was that collected by a Hungarian military attaché, Lajos Varga, whose office systematically pieced together news items of a military character from a great number of local newspapers coast-to-coast. He also obtained much sensitive information from covert and overt sources. He spent a small fortune entertaining foreign military attachés stationed in Washington, being particularly attentive to Third World military representatives who administered American aid programs in their own countries and consequently had frequent contacts with Pentagon officials.

After Secretary of Defense Robert McNamara's July 1965 trip to South Vietnam, Varga learned that the Pentagon was deeply disturbed by the shaky situation and the gloomy outlook for South Vietnam and was working feverishly to stabilize the situation. He did not know what the Pentagon plans were, but he speculated that the Americans most probably would take over the direction of the war, as they had in Korea, and drastically increase the number of American combat troops. He discounted the possibility of the use of tactical nuclear weapons.

Varga was not far from the truth. As we know today from the Johnson memoirs, *The Pentagon Papers,* and other sources, indeed the overall situation became extremely critical for the South Vietnamese government in the summer of 1965. The Viet Cong and their Northern supporters had by then succeeded in capturing six district headquarters in the highlands as well as several other strategically important positions. They were able to cut major communiciation lines and isolate cities and villages from the outside world. Moreover, the economic situation worsened, and the Nguyen Cao Ky government was unpopular among the civilians as well as the military. With this in view, McNamara—in accordance with General Earle G.

Wheeler (chief of staff); U.S. ambassador to Saigon, General Maxwell Taylor; Admiral U.S.G. Sharp; and General William C. Westmoreland—recommended an immediate increase in military strength from 15 to 34 battalions (175,000 men) and the call-up of the reserves. Moreover, he forecast that

> the deployment of more men (perhaps 100,000) may be necessary in early 1966, and that the deployment of additional forces thereafter is possible but will depend on developments.[19]

As far as air bombardment of the North was concerned, the secretary of defense still advised the president to avoid air strikes against populated areas and industrial targets not closely connected with the supply of the Viet Cong. He recommended extended strikes at Viet Cong infiltration routes.[20]

Within the small group of the so-called "Vietnam principals," Undersecretary of State George Ball opposed the McNamara plan. Instead of escalation (from 70,000 to 200,000 men) he suggested either outright extrication or a sharp reduction of U. S. defense perimeters in South Vietnam. "This is our last clear chance to make this decision," the under secretary stated. In a companion memorandum to the president he warned:

> The decision you face now, therefore, is crucial. Once large numbers of U. S. troops are committed to direct combat they will begin to take heavy casualties in a war they are ill-equipped to fight in a non-cooperative, if not downright hostile countryside.

And he added:

> Once we suffer large casualties we will have started a well-nigh irreversible process. Our involvement will be so great that we cannot, without national humiliation, stop short of achieving our complete objectives. *Of two possibilities I think humiliation would be more likely than the achievement of our objectives—even after we have paid a terrible cost.*[21]

As I learned much later from Ball himself, his arguments were based on his previous experiences, gained while he was in close contact with French political circles, including De Gaulle, during the Franco-Viet Minh conflict. He had witnessed the fate of the Navarre plan, the Latour plan, and others. He had seen how the French always hoped each plan would bring them miracles—a quick victory over Ho Chi Minh's forces—and finally how they came to realize they had to get out of Vietnam.

Vietnam, Ball maintained, was not the right place to fight communism, and it was, moreover, no place for a Western power to fight a war, cold or hot. Modern arms could not be used in jungle warfare. From the political point of view, he said, South Vietnam was not a state, it was only a half kingdom, with a government the populace did not trust. Diem was not supported; neither was Ky nor later Thieu. On the other hand, in Ball's view, the Hanoi government was well organized, the people well disciplined, the army trained and experienced for battles in the jungles and rice paddies. The future of Vietnam, Ball thought, would not affect American national interests; the United States had no sizable investment in that part of the world and Vietnam's potential was not important economically or strategically. Finally, Ball warned that escalation could lead to direct intervention of Chinese land forces in the war. Peking then could put pressure on the Kremlin to provide assistance. This alone, in Ball's opinion, might heal the Sino-Soviet antagonism on the one hand and might result in a stalemate in the fighting on the other. At this point, the undersecretary reasoned, pressure would grow on the American side for use of at least tactical nuclear weapons—which would inevitably "upset the fragile balance of terror on which much of the world has come to depend for the maintenance of peace."[22]

The president's chief foreign policy adviser, Dean Rusk, was on McNamara's side. He opposed any delay or compromise. Dean Rusk was a veteran of Far Eastern affairs, having been one of the organizers of the South China and Southeast Asia operations in the Second World War. For years he served as assistant secretary for Far Eastern Affairs in the State Department. While he stressed in private and public that the lessons of the 1930s and the post-World War II years should not be lost, he interpreted the American involvement in Vietnam as an effort to contain aggression and prevent another world war. If that had been done when Japan invaded Manchuria and Hitler seized the Ruhr, he argued, World War II might have been avoided. He maintained that the United States had to defend South Vietnam from Northern aggression. He firmly believed that America had to honor its commitment since "the integrity of the U. S. commitment is the principal pillar of peace throughout the world." Accordingly, he emphasized in his July 1 memorandum:

> If that commitment becomes unreliable, the communist world would draw conclusions that would lead to our ruin and almost certainly to a catastrophic war.[23]

President Johnson agreed with Rusk's views and accepted McNamara's recommendation of a troop build-up. But he declined to call up the reserves as the secretary of defense and the Joint Chiefs of Staff had so energetically proposed. He did not want to create the danger of confrontation with the Russians and the Chinese or place his country on a wartime footing. He also did not want to be overly dramatic or cause too great a stir in Congress. As he explained to the members of the National Security Council, "I think we can get our people to support us without having to be too provocative and warlike."[24]

Then on July 28, 1965, at his White House press conference, Johnson made public his decision. He announced the immediate escalation of fighting strength from 75,000 to 125,000 men and a gradual increase in the monthly draft call from 17,000 to 35,000 per month. However, he said,

> After this past week of deliberations, I have concluded that it is not essential to order Reserve units into service now. If that necessity should later be indicated, I will give the matter most careful consideration and I will give the country due and adequate notice before taking such action, but only after full preparations.[25]

He also reiterated that he was ready now, as he had always been, to move from the battlefield to the conference table. Despite his intention to balance escalation with restraint, the troop increase signaled a new phase of the war whereby for the first time American combat troops would clash with Communist forces in the jungle battlefields of the South, and American planes would hit more and more targets in the North.

Insofar as I felt any immediate concern about these events, it was that the escalation of the fighting in the South and the intensified bombing of the North would harm the atmosphere I was trying to create for initiating broad cultural and economic ties between Hungary and the United States. I went back to Budapest on home leave in July (1965) and reported directly to party chief Kádár and leaders in the party apparatus as well as in the Foreign Ministry. The Vietnam War was still a minor topic in Budapest and was generally regarded as a headache because of the diversion of money it was causing under the Moscow-sponsored "united action" concept. Otherwise the outcome of the war, the victory or defeat of Ho Chi Minh, did not yet seem a critical concern to anyone there.

One bit of advice affected me personally, however; I was told that on Soviet request we were to slow the pace of our cultural exchanges with the United States. For this reason we cancelled the second U. S. tour of the Budapest Children's Choir and called off some American artists' performances in Hungary. As Vencel Házi, director of the American and NATO Department in the Hungarian Foreign Ministry, explained, we would "demonstrate our solidarity" with Vietnam by cutting off some of the cultural programs, especially those likely to attract publicity.

At the party headquarters the attitude was far more rigid than in the Ministry. Secretary and Politburo member Zoltán Komocsin reminded me that the Soviets were sending more and more aid to Vietnam; thus we Hungarians and other East Europeans were to demonstrate our solidarity with Vietnam by stopping our cultural exchange with the Americans. There was no use arguing with Komocsin, who was a hardliner and a blind follower of Moscow's orders. It was his earnest belief and greatest fear that expanded contacts between East and West would eventually diminish Russian influence in Eastern Europe and step up "hostile bourgeois ideological penetration" into socialist countries, which would ultimately erode Communist rule in Hungary. He opposed President Johnson's new approach—the famous policy of "bridge building" through trade, travel, and humanitarian assistance to span the gulf that divided the United States from Eastern Europe. He felt it a matter of grave importance that steps be taken to counterbalance or, if necessary, to stop "the negative consequences" of the "loosening up activities" of the Johnson government.

During my stay in Budapest, I had long conversations with the Hungarian ambassador to Hanoi, Gusztáv Gogolyák, who had just returned from three years' service in the North Vietnamese capital. He was a trustworthy man, one of the few diplomats in the service who had the reputation of not glossing over his reports. We exchanged notes, especially on the five-day bombing pause in May. I told him what I had picked up from the *New York Times* and my friends in the Washington press corps. I could not tell him anything about the Rusk-Dobrynin or the Rusk-Gromyko discussions since I did not know about them at the time. Here Gogolyák was better informed since he had been briefed by the DRV Foreign Ministry. The Vietnamese comrades, said the ambassador, interpreted the American action as a ultimatum, a threat of further aggression. That was the reason the Vietnamese ambassador in Moscow refused to speak with Ambassador Kohler. Of course Trinh was aware of the consequences. He had forecast intensification of U. S. bombing but remained confident that the DRV, with the assistance of its socialist friends, could meet the challenge. Gogolyák was less optimistic. The DRV had made a mistake, he felt, or at least a tactical error in not trying to prolong the bombing pause. At the very least they could thereby have gained a breathing period. But, he said, Ho Chi Minh would never negotiate under pressure.

I found Gogolyák's observations reasonable; nevertheless, I ventured to remark that the experienced Ho Chi Minh must know what he was doing. Gogolyák was not so sure about that. He simply repeated again and again that the situation in North Vietnam was not good. The American bombing was hurting, and there was a shortage of food and medicine. The bombed-out industrial compounds had to be abandoned, and the Vietnamese could evacuate only the medium and small industrial plants into the jungle villages. Vulnerable barracks, storage depots, and petroleum dumps had to be dispersed in scattered areas and carefully camouflaged. The morale of the population was low in Hanoi, Haiphong, and some parts of the countryside. Criticism of Ho Chi Minh's decision to resume fighting in the South was growing, and the police had found it necessary to make wide-ranging arrests to stem opposition and prevent disturbances.

The intensified air bombardment, said the ambassador, created other problems too. It became more and more difficult to resupply the troops in the South. The Vietnamese could move men and material only at night and through the crude jungle roads and complex waterways; thousands and thousands of workers and soldiers had to be mobilized to keep this primitive transport system functioning. Gogolyák concluded that the Vietnamese survived only because the socialist countries had substantially increased their aid to the DRV.

As summer turned into fall, we received confirmation of Gogolyák's information and further news on Vietnam from Warsaw, where the Soviet bloc countries held their regular annual coordination meeting before the U. N. General Assembly session started in New York. There the Soviets informed their East European colleagues that the intense American air bombardment in Vietnam had inflicted heavy damage and had badly shaken the morale of the populace. Time was needed, they said, to build air defense systems, to repair communication lines, and to supply the armed forces and the civilian population. They urged socialist delegates at the U. N. to spare no effort to stop the American bombing. Hungarian Deputy Foreign Minister Péter Mod, who attended the Warsaw meeting, told me later that the Russians expressed real anxiety about the Vietnam situation and the bloc countries had resolved unanimously to push for a suspension of the bombing.

The extent to which this topic was on the minds of the Soviet leaders at that time was further demonstrated just before the General Assembly session convened in New York, when Gromyko himself reminded the foreign ministers of the bloc countries of the Warsaw resolution. Lest they had forgotten, they were to see what they could do to set the wheels in motion for another bombing pause.

CHAPTER III

The Pyongyang Visit

By the fall of 1965, Hungarian Foreign Minister János Péter sensed that the Vietnam War might offer an opportunity for mediation and for winning political prestige. This possibility attracted him not only for reasons of personal vanity but because the tenth anniversary of the anti-Communist Hungarian revolt was only a year away. Hungary was in need of prestige and respectability after spending nearly a decade in the purgatory of world opinion, and the role of peacemaker suited this need.

Chance accommodated Péter's desire to involve himself with *realpolitik.* A few weeks before the United Nations General Assembly was scheduled to meet, Péter went to a friendly visit to North Korea. Behind the invitation was the fact that the North Koreans were not satisfied with the manner in which the Outer Mongolian representative to the United Nations had been looking after their interests. They thought that Péter, who had been involved with General Assembly work since 1957, would be a better man to front for them.

Péter was delighted by the invitation of the North Korean government and reported it immediately to the Department of

International Relations of the Central Committee of the Communist party. He also informed the Soviet ambassador, G. A. Denisov. The reply from Moscow came in a matter of days: Foreign Minister Gromyko would gladly meet János Péter while the latter was on his way to Korea, and would look with interest toward an exchange of views after the Korean visit.

Péter's plane left Budapest on September 5, and the next day the Hungarian was sitting in Gromyko's seventh floor office in the Soviet Foreign Ministry at Smolensk Square in Moscow. They reviewed the Korean situation and concluded that for the time being nothing could be done to remove the Americans from South Korea. They also agreed that regardless of how much Premier Kim Il Song wanted to unify Korea under his leadership the international situation did not favor such a move. As far as Kim Il Song's foreign policy was concerned, Gromyko gave Péter the cautious opinion that the North Koreans were beginning to switch from the Chinese line towards friendlier relations with the Russians.

They discussed the Vietnam War and its international ramifications. Gromyko thought the fighting in the South might lead to yet further American intervention and finally to the extension of the conflict—which was precisely what the Chinese wanted. He bitterly remarked that Peking had created all sorts of difficulties to slow Soviet attempts to aid Hanoi. He heaped blame on the Vietnamese too, who often appeared unsure of what they wanted for themselves. Moreover, the port facilities in Haiphong were in such poor shape that the greater bulk of Russian shipments had to be sent overland through China—and the Chinese were demanding hard currency for freight costs and even ransacking the military cargo, mostly looking for missiles. Finally, Gromyko reiterated the Soviet belief that a bombing pause was essential, because this would give time to the Russian specialists working in the DRV to strengthen the air defense system. It would prove, moreover, to Hanoi that, contrary to the Chinese view, diplomacy could be as effective as guns in forcing the Americans out of Vietnam.

Péter, of course, fully agreed with Gromyko and assured him he would do his share in the common effort of the socialist countries to try to stop the American air attacks against North

Vietnam. He also promised that on his way from North Korea he would offer a full account to the Soviet comrades of his findings.

In Pyongyang Péter found the North Korean foreign minister, Pak Song Chol, particularly critical of the Chinese. Naturally Péter was prepared for this; nevertheless, he was surprised by the intensity of Pak's denunciation of China's "sinful error" in hindering the presentation of a united socialist front in Vietnam and of Mao Tse-tung's chauvinistic great-power politics. (Péter was among the first witnesses to this North Korean foreign policy reorientation. Within a few months, the Koreans would switch yet again to exploit the Sino-Soviet differences and adopt a low-key policy of neutrality between Moscow and Peking. But this was to develop after Péter's visit.)

Recalling the recent past, the North Korean foreign minister criticized the policy of the Twentieth Congress of the Soviet Communist party in 1956 on the grounds that it had caused upset and turmoil in the entire international workers' movement. He was bitter in his condemnation of Khrushchev, not only for his revisionist behavior and his de-Stalinization policy, but for his personal manners. To make the last point clear, Pak related that not once, but twice, Marshal Kim Il Song had put aside all differences and invited Khrushchev to Pyongyang; that both times Khrushchev had accepted the invitation, and that on both occasions—after the Korean capital had been decorated with his portraits—Khrushchev had called off the visit at the last moment. But the new Soviet leaders were different, Pak Song Chol said; they had shown themselves ready to give substantial economic aid to the socialist construction of Korea and to lend the support that had been denied by Khrushchev for the modernization of the Korean armed forces. Pak then moved on to state his views of Hanoi. Ho Chi Minh, he declared, had shown extreme political shortsightedness in Vietnam. He should never have gotten into a war with America without first assuring himself of the complete military support of the Soviet Union. It was unthinkable that Ho should continue to listen only to the Chinese, who in terms of military technology were so far behind the Soviets, when the Vietnamese were not prepared for modern warfare and could only fight against the Americans in the way they had fought against the French. Thus did the North Korean foreign minister write off his Vietnamese comrades.

Pak's main interest was, of course, his own country. In several discussions that took place, the Korean explained to Péter how in his view the situation in his country had ripened so that the United States could be forced through the United Nations to withdraw from South Korea, opening the door for Korean unification. By way of concession, North Korea would send an observer to the United Nations General Assembly—on condition that the Assembly would condemn the American role in the Korean War.

Péter, of course, considered this plan unrealistic. In his speech at the United Nations a few weeks later, he simply urged that "an entirely new start should be prepared in the light of the historical realities of Korea."[1] That was his sole contribution to the "holy cause" of Kim Il Song.

The Korean visit had accomplished something more from Péter's point of view, however. It enabled him in his U. N. speech to allude to his recent visit to the Democratic People's Republic of Korea; he had happened to visit Panmunjom, where, under the flag of the United Nations, United States army commanders were discussing frontier incidents with the representatives of North Korea. Péter hoped that Americans in Budapest or Moscow or perhaps in Panmunjom would take note of his Far Eastern trip and conclude that he had traveled not only to North Korea but to North Vietnam as well. (In Panmunjom, for instance, he went to the demarcation line to have his picture taken with North Korean army officers.) Moreover, he endeavored to plant hints through the U. N. press corps that he had discussed the possibility of a negotiated settlement of the war with Ho Chi Minh and others and that, after a bombing pause, a new Geneva Conference might be convened.

Péter was not a professional diplomat. Born in 1910, he studied in Budapest, Paris, and Glasgow, after which he become a pastor of the Hungarian Reformed Church. During World War II, he was chaplain of the Budapest Bethesda Hospital, where in 1944 he concealed fellow clergyman Zoltán Tildy, who was then head of Hungary's conservative Smallholders' party. Two years later Tildy became president of Hungary, and Péter, after a short service in the Foreign Ministry, was named to head his secretariat. Simultaneously, having guessed that the Communists would take over, Péter began working as an undercover agent for the Communist-controlled secret police. The Communists, in fact, did ascend to power in 1948. In the summer of that year Tildy's son-in-law, Victor Csolnoky, was recalled from his post as minister to Cairo and arrested; the following December he was convicted of selling the Hungarian diplomatic code to a Western power. The affair hopelessly compromised President Tildy, who resigned.

It fell to Péter to go abroad and try to persuade Csolnoky's wife to return to Hungary. Although he failed in this, his efforts were appreciated; he was given a seat in Parliament and the bishopric of the Trans-Tibescan Synod in Debrecen, the center of Hungarian Protestantism, where he purged the church of anti-Communist pastors. His urbane, plausible manner made him a useful propagandist in the early 1950s. He first visited the United States in 1954 to represent the Hungarian Reformed Church at the second assembly of the World Council of Churches in Evanston, Illinois, where he was attacked for his pro-Communist stand. Although he was driven out of his church office during the revolution of 1956, he was among the first to declare support for the Kádár government. He toured the nonaligned countries of Asia, as well as Syria, Egypt, and the Sudan, on a goodwill mission with Deputy Foreign Minister Károly Szarka and Foreign Ministry Director Pál Rácz. They attempted to convince the leaders of these countries that the Hungarian revolution in 1956 was nothing but a "fascist counter-revolution instigated by the United States" and that the Soviet intervention had saved "democracy, socialism, and world peace."

In 1957 Péter became the president of the Institute of Cultural Relations (a government agency often used not only to promote international cultural exchanges but also to carry out covert operations of the secret police). In the same year he became a member of the Presidential Council. He was appointed first deputy foreign minister in 1958 and foreign minister in 1961. Only then, at a meeting in the Foreign Ministry party organization, which I attended, did he openly join the Communist party. Around the Foreign Ministry he was called—behind his back—"Father Péter."

Péter's appointment as Hungarian foreign minister gained him the title but not the power of that office. In Hungary, as in all East European Soviet bloc countries, the real power—legislative, executive, judicial—resides in the highest council of the Communist party, the Politburo. Péter was not a member of the Hungarian party Politburo. For several years, the true power in the area of foreign relations had rested with Dezsö Nemes, a party historian, a veteran *apparatchik,* who was a member of the Politburo and one of the secretaries of the Central Committee. Nemes was in charge of Hungary's international relations on the party and state levels and hence the man who determined foreign policy actions. He read all reports and cables that arrived from Hungarian diplomatic missions; he was informed about all discussions between Foreign Ministry officials and foreign diplomats accredited in Budapest. Not only did he supervise the preparation of important diplomatic notes, memorandums, and aide-memoirs; he even scrutinized such routine messages as telegrams of congratulation. Hungarian envoys arriving from posts abroad reported to him first and visited Péter later. In sum, Péter's status, his title notwithstanding, was in effect that of a deputy foreign minister.

The Department of International Relations of the Central Committee also fell under Nemes' direction. The primary function of this party agency was to maintain contact with other Communist parties, but Nemes also used it to control the Foreign Ministry. Nemes' subordinate, the director of the department, Imre Hollai, was technically equal to Péter in rank but in fact enjoyed a good deal more authority by virtue of his frequent contact with the Soviet Communist party Department of International Relations. Hollai also handled sensitive information—policy decisions and action plans in case collaboration was needed—to which Péter seldom had access. Whenever a policy decision arose, both Hollai and Péter were required to go to Nemes for guidance, and Nemes in turn usually placed the matter before the Politburo. If it was a strictly Hungarian concern, the Politburo could decide what to do; if it involved or affected the international interest of the Soviet Union, the Budapest party headquarters coordinated its actions with the Kremlin.

Under such circumstances—and especially having Nemes as his superior—Péter had little chance to exercise personal initiative. Then the situation changed. On June 25, 1965, Nemes, because of his age, was transferred to the Institute of Party History—though he retained his membership in the Politburo—and Kádár appointed Zoltán Komocsin to the Central Committee as the new secretary for International Relations. Komocsin had been a party functionary throughout his whole career: he had served as deputy party secretary in Szeged, the third largest city of Hungary; he had been deputy director of the Agitation and Propaganda department of the Central Committee; for a time he was secretary-general of the Communist youth organization and editor-in-chief of the party's central organ, *Népszabadság*. Now he was faced with the task of dealing with complex international questions without any qualifying training or scholarship, and he was forced to turn to Péter for advice.

As foreign minister, Péter often visited Moscow and established a good relationship with Gromyko. Naturally always supporting the Russian viewpoint, he proved to be useful for the Kremlin in intra-bloc diplomacy. At the Warsaw Pact Political Consultative Committee meetings, where the Pact countries' premiers and foreign ministers discussed international problems, Péter almost scuffled with the independent-minded Rumanian delegates when they refused to cooperate with the Russians.

Péter served in the Communist system long enough to know that if Soviet foreign policy interests were not directly or indirectly involved, he had freedom of action. Accordingly, Péter visited foreign capitals from Warsaw to Cairo, signed bilateral cultural, scientific, and trade agreements, and permitted himself to make occasional surprise statements to demonstrate his "independent tone." He did so, for instance, in January 1965, in Paris, when he told newsmen on his arrival that he hoped "to study the ideas of President Charles De Gaulle for an independent Europe, a European Europe, and an enlarged

Europe." But despite his self-confident outward appearance and growing activities in the international arena, he was an insecure man, afraid of losing the grace of the Hungarian party leadership or Moscow's patronage.[2]

The Meeting Between Foreign Minister Péter and Secretary Dean Rusk

By late September everything was ready to celebrate the jubilee of the second decade of the United Nations General Assembly. Understandably, the special occasion attracted a great number of heads of state and foreign ministers to New York. Hungary was represented by Foreign Minister János Péter. His plane landed in the evening hours of September 19 at the Kennedy Airport, where permanent United Nations delegate Ambassador Károly Csatordai and I were waiting for him.

Inside the United Nations building, the sleekly modern central assembly hall had been completely remodeled to make room for the delegates of newly admitted nations. In the gallery, a staff of interpreters arranged themselves behind the glass windows, ready to begin their work of simultaneous translation into four major languages: French, English, Russian, and Spanish. The Chinese interpreter, in accordance with U. N. regulations, also sat behind a translator's microphone, although he knew his work would not have much practical value: the members of the Nationalist Chinese delegation knew English well and rarely listened to the speeches in their mother tongue. Ambassador Nikolai Federenko, however, the Soviet permanent representative, frequently switched his five-language earphones to Chinese to freshen up his knowledge of the language.

The rest of the building looked like a giant ant-hill. Arab delegates discussed strategy in one corner of the main corridor, while in another corner Africans in national costume chatted amiably. The bartenders in the delegates' lounge busily served thirsty guests, newsmen circulated among the crowd in pursuit of the latest news, and, here and there, knots of diplomats exchanged information and lobbied for votes. There was plenty to dicusss and gossip about, for the provisional agenda of the General Assembly contained more than a hundred items. Members of the Hungarian delegation joined the swarm in the lounge to gather information and misinformation that would arm them for whatever intrigues were to surface in the forthcoming sessions.

Meanwhile, other preparations and discussions were in progress behind closed doors on the third floor of the Hungarian U. N. Mission headquarters in Manhattan. There—in a double-walled conference room, where music blared forth from six or seven loudspeakers to counterbalance the FBI's listening devices—Péter briefed the mission staff. I was present as the head of the Hungarian legation in Washington and also as a "special political adviser" to the Hungarian U. N. delegation. Péter began by observing that the Hungarian Question, which for years had limited our activities, was no longer on the agenda. "We can step out into the arena of world politics and concentrate on strengthening the anti-imperialist front. We must be active particularly among the delegates of the nonaligned nations, so the demand may be sounded for the Americans to cease their bombing of the Democratic Republic of Vietnam." He also casually mentioned that he had recently visited North Korea and noted that in response to the Korean government's request the Hungarian delegation must do whatever it could to force the Americans to evacuate their troops from South Korea.

Péter was followed by Károly Csatordai, who repeated essentially what Péter had said, but in sharper language, his sentences stitched with cliches about "American aggression and atrocities." Csatordai was not overly bright, but he had been stationed in Peking and Hanoi as a diplomatic officer and sincerely believed in the "hard" Peking Communist line, even though the Hungarian government was openly anti-Chinese. Next to Csatordai I took the floor and offered a *tour d'horizont* of the bustling political scene in Washington. Then we discussed organizational matters. Every delegate received his work assignment: in which committee he would be active and on which question he would speak.

The meeting ended around noontime. I went with Péter to have lunch at his favorite restaurant, the Jagerhaus, in the Yorkville section of Manhattan. "You know, I don't trust Csatordai's double-walled, loudspeaker room," he said. "I don't dare discuss serious matters there." Meanwhile, the waiter came, welcomed Péter cheerfully (Péter always gave him generous tips). In turn, Péter inquired about the well-being of the waiter's family. After a minute or two of this fraternization we ordered two Manhattans, and the serious talk began. Péter asked about arrangements for his meeting with Secretary of State Dean Rusk. I could not tell him much news. I reiterated what I had already reported to him a few weeks earlier. I told Péter that I had met Raymond Lisle, the director of the State Department's East European Division, at the Rumanian Embassy reception on August 23. There I suggested to him to set up a meeting between Péter and Rusk, just as it had been organized in 1964. Lisle was not unprepared, I noted. Without thinking twice he pointed out that Secretary Rusk would be "staying in New York during the General Assembly debate and would gladly speak with the Hungarian Foreign Minister if he wished. A reply was requested, however, because the Secretary's New York schedule would be very heavy."

Péter said somewhat pompously that time might be found for the meeting if Secretary Rusk wanted it. "The Politburo and Comrade Kádár personally gave me a free hand to decide on the spot, in New York, whether or not I should take part in a meeting suggested by the Americans," he added. Then, to my surprise, he inquired about the American reaction to his recent Far Eastern trip: "Do they know that I traveled only in North Korea, or do they presume that I was also in Hanoi?"

I could not answer this question, since I simply did not know whether the Americans had even heard of Péter's Korean visit. Péter continued, "The meeting with the Secretary must be set up, but in such a way as to make it appear that it has come about at the initiative of the Americans. We must take into consideration the sensitivity of the North Vietnamese and the influence of the Chinese in Hanoi." Then in a half sentence he noted, "We must get the Americans to stop their bombing of the Democratic Republic of Vietnam . . ."

"I don't understand why the Americans should presume that you were in Hanoi, when you were not," I said.

"You'll see later," Péter replied. "In any event, you must inquire whether Secretary Rusk presumes that I went to Hanoi. You might try without delay to find out from newspapermen and diplomats."

"This can be determined only if I ask them."

"That doesn't matter. You can feel free to ask them."

Péter then reemphasized the form of the reply I was to deliver to the State Department; if the secretary wished to meet with the Hungarian foreign minister, that might come about after appropriate mutual agreement as to timing.

The next day I telephoned Lisle and told him I had conveyed his message to the Hungarian foreign minister. In order to carry out my orders, I added: "Naturally, if Rusk wishes to speak with Foreign Minister Péter . . ."

Mr. Lisle told me that the American side appreciated the reply and recommended October 7 as a date. I reported this to Péter, who gave me permission to accept the date. He added, however, that he would not attend a reception that was to be given by Secretary Rusk for foreign dignitaries attending the U. N. in New York: "That would give the impression that I was pressing unduly for the meeting."

I thought it more likely that Péter's absence would merely give the impression that the Hungarian foreign minister was not acquainted with elementary rules of international courtesy, but I kept my thoughts to myself. I still did not understand why Péter should be so concerned about whether the Americans thought he had been in Hanoi. Nor did I understand why his public behavior had become so ostentatiously strange and secretive of late; he appeared at U. N. headquarters only infrequently, and when there he spoke only with the principal diplomats of the socialist countries.

Péter signed up on the list of persons to speak before the General Assembly on October 6—the day before he was to see Secretary Rusk. He considered the timing extremely important, since he intended to address his remarks not so much to the general audience as to the American delegation.

On October 5, Péter showed the draft of his speech to members of the Hungarian delegation. Károly Csatordai found the tone overly conciliatory; he would have liked the section dealing with Vietnam to sound more bellicose. Other members of the delegation recommended just a few stylistic changes. I recommended no changes; I knew Péter never made any changes. Besides I was interested in improving Hungarian-American relations, and a moderate speech by my foreign minister at the U. N. General Assembly session could be helpful.

Péter's speech was a masterpiece in the art of conveying the message beyond the words; clearly, to a properly conditioned listener, his omissions would be more important than his statements. He made no explicit mention of Hanoi's Four Points or the Viet Cong's Five Points,* which all the spokesmen of the Socialist countries had emphasized. After criticizing the American role in Vietnam in uncommonly moderate tones, he recommended that the Geneva Conference on Indochina be reconvened so that the great powers might eliminate "the most crucial issue of the present deterioration of the world situation." He further announced that he was making this recommendation "with full knowledge of the opinion of the government of the Democratic Republic of Vietnam and that of the National Liberation Front of South Vietnam." If the United States desired to be taken seriously with regard to any peaceful settlement, he said, it must suspend bombing and all manner of aggression against Vietnam.

The speech, as I expected, was well received. American, British, and French diplomats took notes. Nonaligned countries' representatives applauded. Even those veteran U. N. diplomats who, over the years, utilized the General Assembly session to catch up with the news in the daily press put down their papers and paid attention. When representatives of the Com-

*The "Four Points" and the "Five Points," which constituted the public position of Hanoi and the Viet Cong respectively, amounted to the unconditional U.S. withdrawal and "peaceful reunification" of Vietnam without foreign interference.

munist bloc nations approached Péter to offer the congratulations that are customary after U. N. sessions, their expressions, however, were a mixture of forced smiles and raised eyebrows. Federenko of the USSR registered no expression at all.

A few days later Huang Luong, the North Vietnamese ambassador accredited to Budapest, courteously informed one of the high officials in the Hungarian Foreign Ministry that his government had not changed its position: it could enter into discussions with the "American imperialists" only on the basis of the Four Points. He noted with regret that while other friendly socialist foreign ministers had underlined the DRV's Four Points (and the NLF's Five Points) the Hungarian foreign minister had not done so. Péter cabled back to Budapest that the Vietnamese ambassador should not complain. The "Four and Five Points" were all implicit, "nicely wrapped up in the speech."

Péter thus remained confident as he prepared for the October 7 meeting with Secretary of State Rusk. Several leading newspapers in the United States, including the influential *Washington Post,* had reacted as he had hoped, and the word was out that the Viet Cong might no longer insist on withdrawal of all American troops before starting peace negotiations.[3]

Péter was tense as we started out the next day for our early afternoon appointment. While the chauffeur picked his way carefully through New York traffic, Péter talked of the press reaction to his speech. Several papers had put the speech on the front page. "This is a good preparation for the meeting with Secretary Rusk," he said. "The newspapermen will be waiting for me and will besiege me with questions."

"I don't like that," he added, "because newspapermen often ruin everything in the pursuit of sensational stories. In any case I will not talk to them before the meeting. Rusk will surely bring up the Vietnam question . . . I must bring him around to the bombing pause."

I wondered whom this foreign minister sitting next to me was representing—little Hungary or some great power—and I patted the notebook in my pocket to make sure I would have a place to put down every word.

Secretary Rusk met with Péter and me at the United States

Mission to the United Nations in New York.[4] It was Rusk who introduced the subject foremost in the minds of both men: "Your speech of yesterday had quite a large echo in the press."

"Yes," said Péter, "the press is a great power. But the Vietnam question interests not only the press but us. We, for our part, see great danger in this conflict. This is why I would like to hear your opinion as to what way out you can see."

"The policy of the American govenment is clear and unambiguous," the secretary replied. "We are prepared to sit down at the negotiating table without conditions, as President Johnson stated in his Baltimore speech of April 7, but, unfortunately, Hanoi is showing no signs that it would be interested in any kind of negotiated settlement."

"Hanoi cannot show any sign of its willingness to negotiate as long as bombs are falling on the territory of the Vietnamese Democratic Republic," Péter rejoined. "If the United States is truly striving for a settlement, the bombing of North Vietnam must be stopped."

"Day after day in South Vietnam terrorists are exploding bombs, and innocent people are dying," pointed out Rusk. "This, too, is bombing. But beyond this, we have concrete proof that more North Vietnamese military units are operating in South Vietnam. We are speaking not simply of a civil war but of aggression coming from the North. The United States must carry out its commitment made to South Vietnam. We cannot leave our Vietnamese friends in the lurch." At this point the secretary cited the Laotian example. He noted that after the 1962 Geneva Conference on the settlement of the Laotian question the United States, acting in good faith, had withdrawn its military personnel from the territory of Laos. Regular North Vietnamese units, however, had stayed on in areas of Laos under the control of Pathet Lao. Furthermore, returning to the subject of Vietnam, the Viet Cong was demanding that it be the sole representative of the people of South Vietnam—but Buddhists, Catholics, various hill tribes, and others not represented by the Viet Cong lived in the South.

Péter then played his high card. He was in a position to state with complete responsibility that the Democratic Republic of Vietnam was ready for negotiations, but not while the bombing continued. The DRV government could not show weakness, he noted. If the bombing were to cease, he had no doubt this would create the atmosphere necessary for negotiations. In Péter's words, "I can report this to you with the most complete authority. We are in intimate contact with Hanoi. As a matter of fact, I can add that today a Hungarian delegation is arriving at the DRV's capital."[5]

Rusk pondered this disclosure for some time and then started probing for soft spots. "As you know, in May of this year we suspended the bombing of North Vietnam for six days. We informed their embassy in Moscow of this decision in a note. The North Vietnamese simply sent back our note with a messenger who shoved it under the door of the main entrance of the American Embassy. Soviet Foreign Minister Gromyko, as a matter of fact, considered this action as an insult."

"Yes," acknowledged Peter, "the May bombing pause was not effective because it was too short. The bombing must be stopped without threat of a renewal of bombing."

"But what would they do in Hanoi if we began a new bombing pause? Would they sit down at the negotiating table?" asked the secretary of state.

"I am convinced," insisted the Hungarian foreign minister, "that the government of the DRV is ready, under certain conditions, for negotiations. If the United States stops the bombing, this would be the kind of gesture that would convince Hanoi of the good intention of the United States."

"But what is the guarantee?" Rusk asked.

"It is impossible to get any kind of guarantee from the North until after the bombings cease," was the reply.

Rusk furrowed his brow and shot a quick glance at Péter. "We can't proceed on a unilateral basis for very long," he said sternly.

The bombings had begun without announcement, Péter reminded him. They could be halted without announcement, at least for a short while. Besides, if the United States stopped the bombing it would not be a one-sided step, but rather a new beginning in search of a solution.

Rusk now inquired how much time would be required, in the opinion of the Hungarian foreign minister, before Hanoi would enter negotiations after cessation of air attacks. Péter estimated a few weeks, certainly—and that provided the attacks were stopped without threat of renewal. But some reciprocal action was sure to come on the diplomatic level, perhaps in the ground war as well. It was impossible to expect, because of the nature of the conflict, that both sides could move at the same time.

"Why is it necessary for one party to take steps before the other?" the secretary asked. This was not the traditional path of negotiations.

For the first time, Péter appeared to be confused and searching for new arguments. If the United States had no ambitions in Southeast Asia, he said, the points of agreement between the two sides were much closer than they seemed, but it was impossible for Hungary to talk to its friends in North Vietnam about negotiations as long as the bombings continued. Péter then went into a somewhat rambling attempt to differentiate between the air attacks in the North and the ground war in the South, to which the secretary responded that he found it difficult to accept such a distinction. "Nevertheless, the key to the solution," Péter insisted, "is in the hands of the United States."

At this point Rusk suddenly interjected the question, "Mr. Péter, you have perhaps spoken with the leaders in Hanoi?"

Péter's response came after a slight pause. "Everything that I have said to you I can state with the most complete responsibility. We are in intimate contact with Hanoi; we are completely familiar with the intentions of the government of the Democratic Republic of Vietnam."

In spite of himself, Rusk smiled a little. "If you are not in a position to tell me, then I can't force you. But still, what happens if Hanoi is not willing to negotiate?"

"The United States, in that case, will not be risking anything. At the most, it can begin bombing again." This reply came without hesitation.

"If we were to accept your opinion, Mr. Péter, and stopped the bombings, what would you do? Would you be our ally before world opinion?"

Again without hesitation, "I would absolutely be your ally.

But I know that a bombing pause would definitely create the kind of atmosphere which would lead to the conference table."

"For all that, we won't ask the Hungarian Air Force to help us recommence the bombing," the secretary jokingly assured. Then, turning serious, he said he would study Péter's remarks and give the entire subject prayerful consideration, but he made it clear that this statement meant to imply no promise or pledge.

"This is natural," Péter replied.

As the meeting ended Rusk and Péter agreed that they would tell the press only that questions of interest to both countries had been discussed, and in the course of the discussions the subject of Vietnam had come up.

In the hallway of the American Mission, Péter was surrounded by newsmen and deluged with questions. Vietnam was the main interest. Was there a discussion of the Vietnam question? "Certainly," was the answer. Did the Hungarian foreign minister travel to Hanoi? Did he bring a message from Ho Chi Minh to the American government? "No comment," was Péter's reply. When Murray Marder of the *Washington Post* asked whether a halt to the bombing of North Vietnam would produce negotiation, Péter answered that in the judgment of his government "a pause would insure such a situation in which negotiations can be surely reached."[6]

Péter's evasive replies did little to satisfy the representatives of the news media. They next questioned Rusk's press secretary. Did the Hungarian foreign minister bring a message from Hanoi? The secretary replied as previously agreed. The two sides had exchanged views on questions affecting the two countries. They had "discussed" Vietnam. When pressed for more, he disclosed that Péter had brought no message from Hanoi. Neither had he brought any assurance that Hanoi was modifying its insistence on the withdrawal of American troops as a prerequisite to negotiations.

Bleak Prospects

Péter was pleased with the discussion. Though he had not expected the secretary's hard, cautious manner of debating, he thought his own reasoning had struck home. Above all, he felt there was an excellent chance that the secretary would turn to him as the most "optimistic" of the Communist spokesmen. In this respect he was right. There was little encouragement for Péter's course in the Communist camp. To begin with, Gromyko's attitude on Vietnam was rigid, even chilly. In his U. N. speech, the Soviet foreign minister had accused the United States of aggression and violation of the Geneva Agreements of 1954, declared support for Hanoi's Four Points, and discounted as "deceptive" the Johnson administration's efforts to begin talks on the question of Vietnam. His conclusion was, "Stop the aggression completely and without previous conditions."[7]

Nevertheless, the United States secretary of state in private conversations with Gromyko, pressed the matter of Vietnamese objectives to determine what the North Vietnamese leaders would do if the bombing were stopped. Gromyko, clearly reluctant to discuss the issue, merely reiterated his public stand and replied in general terms that, according to his knowledge, Hanoi had no intention of negotiating while the air bombardment continued. Rusk then asked Gromyko to act as a mediator on Vietnam, and Gromyko refused.

Thus no meaningful results came of the Gromyko-Rusk exchange. Significantly, this futile dispute over Vietnam was not allowed to cast a shadow over strictly bilateral Soviet-American relations. Gromyko continued to express interest in new arrangements on the German question, his main concern focusing on West Germany's participation in NATO and American intentions regarding the multilateral nuclear force plan for that alliance. No effort was made to link the European issue to the Vietnamese question.

Rusk also discussed the Vietnamese situation and the prospects for a negotiated settlement with Rumanian Foreign Minister Corneliu Manescu. That discussion, which took place at a dinner party in New York on October 14, was uncluttered by doctrinal pronouncements and posturing, thanks to a relatively good working relationship the two men had developed over the years.

Manescu was an old Communist. As a law student at the University of Bucharest, he had joined the Democratic Student Front and the underground Rumanian Communist party in 1936. During World War II, the Russians organized a division of Rumanian prisoners named after the hero of 1821, Tudor Wladimirescu. These prisoners fought side-by-side with the Russians, and Manescu, a prisoner himself, became an officer of the Tudor Wladimirescu division. After the end of the war he continued his military career and became first head of the Higher Political Department of the army and later deputy minister of the armed forces, with the rank of lieutenant general. He left the service in 1955 and was nominated deputy chairman of the State Planning Committee, a post he held for five years. He was then transferred to the diplomatic service. I met him in Budapest in 1960, where he represented his country's interest as ambassador. He returned to Bucharest unexpectedly in the summer of 1961 to become foreign minister. (He himself told me he did not know beforehand that Rumanian party chief Gheorghiu-Dej had nominated him to this cabinet post.) When Manescu assumed direction of the Rumanian Foreign Ministry, his country took its first step away from the Soviet path to explore more independent, neutral foreign policies. From that time on, every year he was the leader of the Rumanian delegation to the United Nations General Assembly.

In 1964, he was the only East European foreign minister who—despite American involvement in Vietnam—was ready to accept an invitation from Secretary Rusk to tour the United States.[8] Moreover, Manescu's office in the Foreign Ministry was always open to the American ambassador, William A. Crawford—an entrée denied most American diplomats in East European capitals—and he and Crawford frequently discussed the Vietnamese situation. In June 1965, Crawford told Bucharest the United States would welcome any advice or information that it might offer with regard to a settlement in Vietnam. None, however, was forthcoming.

When Manescu met Rusk in October, he also could provide no indication of any North Vietnamese willingness to come to the conference table. On the contrary, he reaffirmed that Hanoi was interested in starting negotiations only on the basis of its Four Points. That condition, of course, was unacceptable to the Johnson administration. In view of the evident impasse, the foreign minister stated, he did not believe Rumania could do much to help resolve the conflict.

For Rusk, Manescu's outlook was a disappointment, especially since he was aware it did not derive from an unwillingness to mediate. Moreover, Rumania's neutrality in the ideological feud between the Chinese and the Soviet parties had won Bucharest the confidence of Peking and Hanoi, an asset that enhanced Manescu's potential as a go-between. Now Manescu was repeating to Rusk what he had told leading East European diplomats at the U. N.—there was little if anything to mediate.[9]

Finally, Secretary Rusk explored the possibilities of a negotiated settlement with the Poles. Polish Vice Foreign Minister Jozef Winievicz, a familiar figure at the U. N., had taken over the duties of ailing Foreign Minister Adam Rapacki in 1965 as head of the delegation to New York. He enjoyed a reputation for sophistication and candor, and was generally regarded as one of the doves in the Polish Foreign Ministry. When Rusk met with him at the United States Mission in New York, however, he was all abrasion and rectitude. He bluntly demanded the withdrawal of all United States forces from South Vietnam and the cessation of bombing in the North; furthermore, acting on special instructions from Polish Party Secretary Wladislaw Gomulka, a hardliner, he launched into a broad-ranging lecture on Vietnam and finished with the pronouncement that the Polish government wholeheartedly supported the Vietnamese Communists' position on ending the war. The ensuing discussion quickly accelerated into a lively debate centering on whether the cessation of bombing had to be considered a precondition for any improvement of the Vietnamese situation. Rusk did not exclude this possibility—he even conceded it might be a constructive position—but he suggested that before making such a move the United States would want some indication that such an initiative would lead to negotiation.

At that point Winievicz changed tactics. He expressed his willingness to forward a message from the secretary to Hanoi. He even ventured to say that a pause in the bombing might indeed positively influence the North Vietnamese, but cautiously added that—through their good offices in Hanoi—the Poles could only try.[10]

On the whole, however, the prospects for peace were bleak. Through the early fall of 1965 Secretary Rusk, viewing Hanoi's position through the glass held up by Gromyko and the other East Europeans, had to consider the situation unchanged. Hanoi still sought the unification of North and South Vietnam under its leadership, and Ho Chi Minh still appeared unwilling to consider diplomatic means to achieve this end. Hence Rusk remained convinced that the North Vietnamese were unwilling to "do something" in return for a bombing halt, even if the halt were permanent and unconditional. It thus had come as a surprise to him and other American leaders when Hungarian Foreign Minister János Péter stepped forward with the optimistic forecast that a few weeks' pause in the bombing would bring about negotiations. Moreover, only Péter held that the United States had the continued option of resuming the bombing if Hanoi were to respond in bad faith to a pause. Finally, it appeared that his attempt to establish credibility as an emissary on the strength of his visit to Korea had, at least in part, succeeded.

Whether Rusk had found the meeting with Péter interesting or entertained a great deal of skepticism, I could not know. But I assumed that the Americans might put out inquires to find out whether Péter really had been in Hanoi. As we know now, the American Legation in Budapest tried to solve the puzzle but learned only that the foreign minister had spent about two weeks abroad during the late summer. Where he had spent this time, they could not discover—but it was concluded that if Péter's destination had, in fact, been North Vietnam, both Hanoi and the Hungarians probably would want to keep it quiet.[11] This advice, however, failed to dispel Rusk's misgivings.

Later in October, Péter spent three days in Washington as my guest. He stayed in my residence off Massachusetts Avenue, and at dinner the first evening I asked whom he wished to see. Should I arrange a dinner with the Soviet ambassador, Anatoliy Dobrynin? Did he want to talk with any Americans? Any newspapermen?

"No," he said. "I would not like to see anybody—except the secretary."

"That is very easy," I said. "I can make a call to the State Department."

"No. Don't make any call. They know that I am here. If they wish to see me, they can invite me." He added that if the State Department did not call, he would like to visit some historical places.

"I would like you to come to the legation and meet with the staff," I said, and Péter grudgingly agreed. (He did visit the legation, but for such a short time—about half an hour—that he left the personnel understandably resentful.)

We took in the usual Washington sights—the Washington Monument, the Lincoln and Jefferson memorials, and, at my suggestion, President Kennedy's grave, where Péter volunteered the opinion that Kennedy was not a great president. "He didn't show any big qualities as a politician. He was not efficient."

"Who," I asked, "in your view, was the greatest American president after the war?"

"Eisenhower."

"Why?"

"Because he didn't intervene in the 1956 Hungarian counter-revolution. He understood that this would lead to nuclear war."

Only once did Péter seem really interested—when he saw the graves of America's Korean war dead, 961 of whom lie in Arlington. "I did not think," he said half to himself, "that so many Americans had died in the Korean War. Now I understand why it was possible to arrange a cease-fire with the Americans."

The second day I took Péter to Williamsburg and Jamestown. On the third day he returned to New York. The State Department never called. I suspected Secretary Rusk and his colleagues were still weighing the question of how much credit to give the statements Péter had made.

On October 20, Péter went back to Budapest. As our group gathered in the V.I.P. lounge of Kennedy International Airport to see him off, I volunteered my theory that, because of the Sino-Soviet divergencies, the Soviet Union could not risk a mediation role in Vietnam, but that Hungary, as a small country, could do so and assume the risk of minor complications. Péter replied, in the tones of a professor lecturing a young student, that the Americans would revert to what he told them because he offered them the most. Gromyko refused to mediate. Vačlav David (the Czechoslovak foreign minister) demanded a suspension of the bombings. The Rumanians did not even discuss the question seriously. Only the Poles were ready to mediate, but they did not hold out any glittering hope, as he had, that a few weeks after the suspension of the bombings Ho Chi Minh would sit down at the conference table. On top of everything else, Péter believed he had succeeded in giving the impression that after his visit to Korea, he had gone to Hanoi.

Csatordai, who was also present, remarked that the Americans didn't want peace or serious negotiations and that they would fail miserably in the Vietnam adventure. He knew the Vietnamese and the Chinese, he said, having spent quite a few years in the Far East, in Peking and Hanoi. If necessary, the Vietnamese could brace themselves for a war of 10 to 15 years, but they would not capitulate to the Americans.

I waited for Péter to remind his U. N. delegate that this was not the way he had presented the question to Secretary of State Rusk, but the foreign minister said nothing, just continued sipping his Manhattan indifferently.

When the hostess appeared in the waiting room and announced that the time for boarding had come, Péter said good-bye to everybody. He stressed to me that I should immediately report to him in the event of some development in the Vietnam affair. I suddenly remembered Rusk's final remark to him: "We will keep Mr. Radványi busy in the future; he will have a lot of things to do."

CHAPTER IV

The Bombing Pause Debate

While Gromyko, Péter, and other Communist bloc diplomats continued in diverse ways to pressure Washington for a bombing halt, Hanoi substantially escalated the fighting. Several new regiment-size North Vietnamese Army units moved down the Ho Chi Minh trail to Viet Cong bases in the South, and the Viet Cong stepped up its recruiting program in the areas it controlled. The total strength of the Communist forces in the South now reached 137 battalions, or about 134,000 men. With this impressive army at his command, Defense Minister Giap shifted from guerrilla warfare to mobile main-force offensives, aiming to drive the Americans and South Vietnamese government troops out of the Central Highlands and split South Vietnam.

Giap's offensive started in mid-October 1965 with an attack against the American Special Forces camp in Plei Me, about 220 miles from Saigon. The heavy assault forced the U. S. command to rush in fresh troops to relieve the beleaguered defenders. Soon the fighting expanded in the Chu Pong mountain area. By mid-November, North Vietnamese regular troops had engaged the U. S. First Airmobile Cavalry Division in four major battles in the narrow Ia Drang River Valley seven miles from the Cambodian border. The Communists used a traditional warfare pattern: first their artillery launched a heavy mortar and rocket barrage on the American positions; then the infantry stormed. The Cavalry Division, supported by South Vietnamese paratroopers, withstood the attacks, although some units had to withdraw to safer positions. Other units were ambushed, and after fierce hand-to-hand fighting broke into small groups. *New York Times* war correspondent Neil Sheehan reported from the battlefield that not since the French-Vietminh war had the highlands seen such bloody battles. The last Ia Drang engagement continued until October 19. The Americans brought in fresh troops and helicopter gunners, B-52 bombers of the Strategic Air Command devastated the North Vietnamese rear base at Chuprong Massif, and finally the Communists decided to withdraw. Casualties on both sides were heavy. Radio Hanoi claimed the South Vietnam Liberation Forces (the Communist forces) had killed 1,700 men of the First Airmobile Cavalry Division. The Americans reported Viet Cong and North Vietnamese losses at over 1,200 killed in action and U. S. losses at over 200.[1]

In Hanoi official propaganda proclaimed the fighting a resounding success and the government organized nationwide victory celebrations. Peking followed suit, and in the great cities in mainland China mass meetings were held to mark the triumph over the American "aggressors."[2] As I learned from our embassy in Hanoi, some East European military observers in the DRV assessed the outcome differently. They considered the offensive badly timed and the heavy losses not worth the psychological victory. They carefully avoided making any critical remarks to their North Vietnamese friends, however; instead they concentrated on learning details about the new American battle tactics, especially the use of helicopter gunners.

Meanwhile, the American press reported that the United States military commander in Vietnam, General W. C. Westmoreland, also claimed unprecedented victories and complimented his troops for the fighting spirit. The general, however, publicly warned of "a certain danger that we will be overwhelmed by certain feelings of optimism and may lose sight of what I consider a true appraisal of the situation. . . . It involves a long conflict," he underlined, "and we must be prepared to accept this."[3] Privately, he then sent a cable to Washington to the effect that the increased North Vietnamese build-up would require almost twice as many American troops as previously planned (200,000 instead of 112,000). McNamara was attending the NATO Defense Ministers' meeting in Paris when he learned of Westmoreland's urgent message. He decided to go straight to Saigon and see for himself why the situation suddenly demanded such drastic action.

Following a two-day conference with Westmoreland on November 28-30, McNamara returned to Washington and reported to President Johnson that his field commander had not exaggerated the seriousness of the situation. Indeed, more troops would be needed, at least 400,000 by the end of 1966 and 200,000 more during 1967, and even this substantial increase of ground forces would not guarantee success. U. S. servicemen killed in action could be expected to reach 1,000 a month or more. Whatever the foreseeable difficulties—and McNamara acknowledged there were many—he believed the best chance of achieving American objectives lay in sending a substantial number of additional troops and gradually intensifying the bombing of the North. But parallel with this move he urged Johnson to declare a long halt in the bombing:

> It is my belief that there should be a three- or four-week pause in the program of the bombing of the North before we either greatly increase our troop deployments to Vietnam or intensify our strikes against the North. . . . The reasons for this belief are, first, that we must lay a foundation in the mind of the American public and in world opinion for such an enlarged phase of war and, second, we should give North Vietnam a face-saving chance to stop the aggression. I am not seriously concerned about the risk of alienating the South Vietnamese, misleading Hanoi, or being "trapped" in a pause: if we take reasonable precautions, we can avoid these pitfalls. I am seriously concerned about embarking on a markedly higher level of war in Vietnam without having tried, through a pause, to end the war or at least having made clear to our people that we did our best to end it.[4]

As the Pentagon Papers attest, this was not the first time

McNamara had urged the desirability of a political settlement rather than a military one. Back in July 1965, he had said it would be necessary not only to heighten military pressure by gradual degrees but at some stage to introduce a pause in the bombing. According to his strategy, any suspension of the bombing should last a substantial period (6 to 8 weeks) to allow for detection of Hanoi's reaction and intentions as well as to allow the opponent time to appraise his situation and to change his course. In a memo to President Johnson at that time, he suggested:

> The program should be designed to make it politically easy for the DRV (North Vietnam) to enter negotiations and to make concessions during negotiations. It may be easier for North Vietnam to accept negotiations and/or to make concessions at a time when bombing of their territory is not currently taking place.[5]

During the next three months, administration officials had argued incessantly about the course of the war. The Joint Chiefs of Staff and General Westmoreland urged further intensification of the air war to include strikes against petroleum supplies, power plants, and other strategically sensitive targets in the Haiphong harbor area.

In early October the idea of a long pause was revived by State Department Soviet specialist, Ambassador Llewellyn Thompson. He reviewed the results of the bombing campaign and warned that an attack on the harbor of Haiphong would force the Russians to send supplies through Chinese territory, making them dependent on the Chinese railroads. Consequently, Chinese influence would grow in Hanoi and the Russian "moderating influence" would diminish. For this reason, the ambassador felt, a pause should be announced as soon as possible with the understanding that bombing would be resumed if negotiation efforts failed.[6] McNamara and George Ball had quickly endorsed the Thompson proposal, and under Ball's direction Assistant Secretary of State William Bundy formulated a memorandum describing steps toward a suspension of the bombing. Like Thompson, Bundy thought the lull should be temporary unless the United States government was satisfied that the DRV had made a response that gave really serious and continuing promise of leading toward a peaceful solution. In addition, he underlined that the American government would not settle merely for a North Vietnamese willingness to negotiate but would look for some responsive military reduction on the other side.

The bombing pause was brought up again by McNamara on November 6 at a policy planning meeting between President Johnson and his closest advisers. McNamara first pointed out that only the large American troop deployments (175,000 men) of the previous months had prevented the Communists from inflicting the serious military defeat that had been threatened. Then he outlined the tentative plan for the next year's troop increase and added that before new troops were deployed it was time for a renewed test of Ho Chi Minh's willingness to talk. A bombing suspension, he contended, would reinforce United States diplomacy and prepare the American public for future escalation; it would deter the Soviets from deeper involvement and permit them to bring moderating arguments to bear; it would minimize the risk of widening the war and the danger of direct Soviet and Chinese involvement finally, it would offer Ho Chi Minh an opportunity to start reasonable negotiations if he felt so inclined.[7]

But there was no indication that Ho Chi Minh would agree to an acceptable settlement, said presidental adviser Clark Clifford, and a pause might well be viewed in Hanoi as a sign of American weakness. Clifford suggested that instead of a bombing halt, Johnson should make a major speech, once more stating the American desire for a peaceful settlement. National security adviser McGeorge Bundy and others felt that a speech alone would not alter the situation. As the debate went on, General Wheeler took the floor and expressed concern that Hanoi would use the pause only to escalate the infiltration of their troops and material.

The president listened and made no comments. He still remained the most important of the skeptics. In his view, the overwhelming evidence suggested that a renewed halt would not bring Hanoi to the barganing table, and in case of failure he was concerned about public reaction to a resumption of bombing. In addition, the nonproductive five-day bombing pause in May continued to be a painful memory for him. In his memoirs he bitterly adjudged that undertaking a total failure: "It produced nothing, and as usual, the critics shifted ground. The trouble, they insisted, was that the pause had been too short. If we had just held off a little longer, we might have obtained results." He also noted that American officials were beginning "to hear the same refrain from Communist governments," whose leaders now asserted that a halt in the bombing would ease the atmosphere and might lead to negotiation.[8]

Now his misgivings concerning a second pause were strengthened by American officials in charge of the war. In a long memorandum from Saigon, Ambassador Henry Cabot Lodge argued that "an end of bombing of the North with no other *quid pro quo* than the opening of negotiations would load the dice in favor of the Communists and demoralize the GVN [government of South Vietnam]." General Westmoreland and Admiral U.S.G. Sharp, Jr., supported Lodge's protestation on military grounds.[9] By sheer coincidence, the Lodge cable was received the same day McNamara was presenting his recommendations for the pause. But the president did not that day commit himself for or against the suspension of the bombing.

Dean Rusk, who did not attend the November 6 policy-planning meeting (he was resting and preparing for a Latin American trip), expressed his views separately in a State Department memorandum a few days later. He too opposed the pause, on the grounds that he could detect no interest on Hanoi's part in a compromise solution to the conflict. It was his contention that a pause should not be undertaken unless the United States had assurance that Hanoi would respond by reciprocal actions leading in the direction of a peaceful settlement. Basic to Rusk's position was the belief that a bombing pause was a card that could not be played too often. Nevertheless in discussions with third parties he had actively searched for signs of moderation in Hanoi's intentions.

As I had seen, in October the secretary of state had stayed in New York during the Twentieth Session of the U. N. General Assembly for just that purpose and had met with most of the leading statesmen attending the session. The prospects for peace were not bright at that time. There was, however, another matter to follow up; the discrepancy between the noncommittal attitude of Soviet Foreign Minister Gromyko and the flexible position of Hungary's foreign minister, János Péter. Gromyko refused to mediate, while Péter came up with the optimistic forecast that a few weeks' pause in the bombing would bring about negotiations. Even in retrospect I think this must have raised a serious question for Rusk: Had the Hungarian acted on his own or with Soviet consent?

Then, in late November, what seemed to be an answer to the puzzle came from the Russian camp. Soviet Ambassador Dobrynin told McGeorge Bundy that if there were to be a pause of "twelve to twenty days" the Americans could be assured there would be "intense diplomatic activity." This time, he said, the Soviet Union would make a real effort if the Americans ordered a suspension; however, he was equally plain in stating that he was not in a position to give assurance of any clear result.[10] As I learned much later, nobody in the administration knew whether this was an official communication from Moscow or merely the ambassador's personal opinion. Nevertheless, Dobrynin's statement seemed in accord with Péter's: one said twenty days was needed; the other had estimated a few weeks. Several days later Secretary Rusk came to the conclusion that a bombing pause might be worth the risk.

International Complexities

Thus by early December Rusk had privately dropped his objection to a pause, but his public stand on Vietnam still appeared as unyielding as ever. Eric Sevareid's article "The Final Troubled Hours of Adlai Stevenson," which appeared in the November 30, 1965, issue of *Look* magazine, and the Fanfani affair, which broke in the news soon afterward, reinforced Rusk's image as a man of no compromise. It was a rather tense period on the American political scene.

A wave of criticism erupted following Sevareid's sensational disclosure that the Johnson administration had spurned a North Vietnamese proposal for bilateral talks worked out by U. N. Secretary General U Thant in the fall of 1964. The administration did not deny that U Thant had told Ambassador Adlai Stevenson he believed, on the basis of information received from a third-party source, that Hanoi was willing to talk to an American emissary. State Department spokesmen contended, however, that there had been no serious intent on the other side to negotiate. Rusk now probed the matter and learned that the secretary general's source was a high-ranking Soviet official at the U. N. Secretariat, Victor Mechislavovich Lessiovsky, a man known to have close connections with the KGB, the Soviet intelligence agency. The question then arose whether the Russian had acted on behalf of that agency or had presented a personal opinion. In view of the rigid discipline under which Soviet officials operate abroad, it seemed likely he had spoken under instruction from his headquarters. And if so, it was likely he hoped—by misleading the Americans—to create confusion and weaken the credibility of the Johnson administration.

Rusk continued checking. He initiated a number of discussions with Foreign Minister Gromyko and Ambassador Dobrynin, only to learn they knew nothing of the message. Moreover, there apparently were no records in Moscow to indicate that the Kremlin had authorized any Russian in New York to make a suggestion to U Thant concerning Hanoi's readiness to negotiate. All in all, it appeared that both U Thant and Adlai Stevenson were badly misled by the Russians.

In the meantime, on November 25, Hanoi issued an official denial that it had suggested any such negotiation. Nevertheless, critics of the administration's Vietnam policy remained convinced that the United States government had let slide a great opportunity for peace negotiation before the bombings began in the North and the fighting escalated.[11]

With the debate around the U Thant affair still raging, the president of the United Nations General Assembly, Foreign Minister Amitori Fanfani of Italy, apprised Washington of another peace feeler, in this case based on conversations between Ho Chi Minh and two Italian professors, Giorgio La Pira and Mario Primiceri. This overture, if it could be called that, again was too ambiguous to indicate a genuine North Vietnamese willingness for negotiation. Ho was reported by La Pira to be interested in peace talks on the basis of a cease-fire, application of the Geneva agreements according to Hanoi's Four Points, and full representation of the National Liberation Front at the negotiating table.

Rusk's reply was cool but not a refusal; he needed clarification on Hanoi's conditions. He was prepared, however, to include the Four Points for consideration in peace talks along with any proposals the United States might wish to advance.[12] On December 18, Hanoi Radio gave the answer: it flatly denounced the offer reported by Fanfani as yet another American peace hoax and insisted that the Four Points as previously laid down must be used as a basis for settlement in Vietnam. Fanfani was forced to conclude there was no substance in the La Pira peace feeler, but not before a great deal of damage was done. The affair created such a storm in Italy and elsewhere that ultimately the foreign minister was forced to resign.

In the midst of these complexities, on December 8, the Viet Cong Liberation Radio announced that its guerrilla forces would observe a twelve-hour truce at Christmas. "The fact that the Front has thought of allowing the enemy to take a rest to celebrate Christmas is really a most noble and beautiful gesture toward the U. S. puppet and satellite troops," commented the radio announcer in Vietnamese.[13] His remark, directed toward soldiers in the field and not toward policy makers in Washington, was regarded by most observers (including East European diplomats in the United States) as simply a repetition of a similar move made the previous year by the Viet Cong. Officials in the White House, the State Department, and the Pentagon generally doubted that the truce would offer an opportunity to start peace talks. Meanwhile, Radio Hanoi repeated the Four Points of the Democratic Republic of Vietnam that Premier Pham Van Dong put forward on April 8, 1965.

On the same day Dean Rusk appeared on the National Education Television network and told his TV audience he saw virtually no room for compromise with the Communists in

South Vietnam. He further indicated that in a future settlement of the conflict the Viet Cong's political organization, the NLF, would be given no political status. Asked whether he excluded any form of coalition government in Saigon, he replied:

> If the South Vietnamese people have a chance in free elections to make their own choices, they will not elect a Communist to power in Saigon. I do not believe that the South Vietnamese people will be the first in history freely to elect a Communist regime.*

The Chinese Factor

While the main influence on Johnson's view concerning the bombing pause came from Rusk and McNamara, there were others—congressional leaders and civilian advisers—who steadily pressed him to support it on the grounds that stepped-up bombing and ground fighting might give China an excuse for massive intervention in Vietnam. Senator Mike Mansfield went one step further and stated that the American air attacks against the North might be healing the split between Moscow and Peking.[14] Ambassador William H. Sullivan was concerned that the mining of Haiphong harbor and other North Vietnamese ports might tip Hanoi away from Moscow and toward Peking. The ambassador felt strongly that eventually China might consider the harbor-mining as tantamount to an invasion of the North and might decide to send ground troops and air power to rescue their Vietnamese comrades. Some below-cabinet-level officials and senior analysts in the State Department voiced the same view; doubtless unaware of the different forces at work, they assumed it was China that would swing the balance.

There was also pressure on Johnson from the ultra-

*The interview was released on December 8, but had been recorded three weeks earlier. The TV network had promised to alter the interview if events warranted, but since seemingly nothing had happened no changes were made.

conservatives. They launched the slogan "No alternative to victory" and warned the president that the Vietnam War would become a major political issue if the administration failed to win it. The spokesman of the conservatives, former Vice President Richard M. Nixon, expressed concern that the United States was getting bogged down in a long and costly ground war and advocated bombing all military targets in the North, including those in the Hanoi area. He doubted that such action would bring the Chinese Communists into the Vietnamese conflict. Without deliverable nuclear weapons and Soviet assistance, he surmised, China was a fourth-rate military power. His view was shared by, among others, Representative L. Mendel Rivers, chairman of the House Armed Services Committee; Senator Richard B. Russell, chariman of the Senate Armed Services Committee; and Representative Gerald R. Ford of Michigan.

President Johnson and his closest advisers stood in the middle. They spent considerable time analyzing and judging the militant Chinese attitudes and actions. Since they were concerned that an abrupt change in the conduct of the war might trigger irresponsible Chinese reactions, they tried to avoid such drastic changes. They calculated that China would not enter the war unless there was an American invasion of the North beyond the 17th parallel or the Hanoi regime was in danger of being toppled. But they showed considerable anxiety in September 1965, when Marshal Lin Piao, the then heir-apparent of Mao, spelled out Chinese plans for world revolution. In an article entitled "Long Live the Victory of the People's War," Lin announced that China, while emphasizing self-reliance in "revolutionary struggle," certainly would encourage the outbreak of revolution among the newly emerging nations. In setting forth how these revolutions would be effected and what would be their outcome, he used the metaphor "encircle the cities from the countryside." North America, Japan, and the Soviet Union were the cities, and the newly emerging nations of Africa, Asia, and Latin America were the countryside. Vietnam was singled out as the most convincing application of the "encircling theory." Undersecretary of State George Ball considered Lin Piao's enunciation a do-it-yourself kit for global revolution. Dean Rusk compared it to Hitler's *Mein Kampf.* President

Johnson pointed out that it confirmed the notion that if Vietnam fell others in Southeast Asia would follow.[15]

Peking, at the time, was also making much of a new "anti-American power axis" that was said to be shaping up between Djakarta, Hanoi, Peking, and Pyongyang. There was no doubt that something like cooperation was developing among Indonesia, North Vietnam, China, and North Korea, but the limited consensus among them was a far cry from an axis. It appeared that the one weak point in the "Chinese menace" was the rivalry between Moscow and Peking, and even that had its sinister implications. For through American eyes China appeared to be the driving force behind North Vietnam's decision to militarize its strategy and resist entering peace negotiations. It was still widely believed in United States government circles that the Soviets were the Communist moderates, the ones favoring a negotiated settlement.

Whatever the potential of a Peking-dominated axis, events quickly overturned prediction. When the Indonesian Communists were implicated in a bloody but abortive coup against the military at the end of September and were thereafter systematically liquidated, Moscow blamed Peking for the adventure and the failure. This disaster for a major Communist party in Southeast Asia was accompanied by an unfavorable reception of Chinese revolutionary pronouncements throughout the Third World, especially in Africa.

Following the Indonesian fiasco and several other major setbacks in foreign affairs, China quietly turned inward and talk of a new Asian axis ceased. American satellite and communications intelligence, mountains of refugee information, and local newspaper and broadcast data from Southeast Asia added up to a picture of a China more concerned with its own institutions and developments than with ventures abroad. Relying on these data, many analysts began a cautious reappraisal of Chinese intentions. China experts outside the State Department—like John Lewis—began to stress the difficulties China would face in making a move to intervene, and to express doubt that Peking would risk American retaliation. Many felt the Korean War did not present an appropriate analogy, mainly because Ho Chi Minh—unlike the North Korean

Communist leader Kim Il Song—seemed reluctant to invite either Chinese or Russian "volunteers" to fight this war. More and more they began to speak of the high threshold the United States would have to reach before the Chinese would feel forced to intervene, and increasingly they urged the notion that Mao Tse-tung was less concerned about a possible war in Southeast Asia than with the grave internal problems that beset his nation and with the ever-growing Soviet pressure against his regime.

Many of the China watchers in the State Department, however—especially those in the office of Research in Far Eastern Affairs and in the intelligence community—disagreed. They strongly believed the United States and China were headed for a collision that neither wanted; they warned not only of direct intervention but of probably Chinese diversionary action in Laos or even India. As the United States intelligence community confirmed that China's armed forces were on the move, these officers took seriously China's threats to intervene, for they were frankly concerned about a self-fulfilling prophecy. But they were also cautious. Most of them—men like James Thomson in the White House and Allen Whiting in the State Department—were not only China analysts but experienced men as well, and each was conditioned to calculate his actions so as to avoid "loss of credibility."

It was in November in this bureaucratic milieu that Asian experts in the State Department, the White House, and elsewhere in the government assessed mounting incoming evidence concerning a change in China's position on the war. Their principal information told of military preparations in South China, a buildup of Chinese forces along the Sino-Vietnamese border, aid inside North Vietnam, and militia conferences in a number of Chinese military districts. The available evidence lent increasing credence to the notion that China was preparing for war. New rail links, roads, and airfields were being built in South China on a priority basis. Air raid trenches and shelters were in preparation, air raid drills against atomic fallout were held, contingency plans were drawn to evacuate non-essential personnel and elderly persons from the cities to the countryside, and large amounts of grain had been purchased from Canada, Australia, and Argentina.

The Chinese also launched an all-out propaganda campaign to ready the population for a U. S. invasion, asserting that the American imperialists were frenziedly widening their aggressive war against Vietnam and the flames of the war had spread to the gates of China. The United States, clamored the Chinese news media, had formed South Korea, Japan, Okinawa, Taiwan, the Philippines, Vietnam, and Thailand into an arc of first line offensive bases and the Bonin Islands, Iwo Jima, and Guam into a second line "to put into execution its plot of encirclement and aggression against China." Not only had the American government unceasingly built up its forces in Vietnam but it had methodically moved troops from the United States to reinforce the military contingents deployed at these bases in preparation for the enlargement of its "sinister, aggressive war" against China. By early December, U. S. intelligence reported that Chinese construction battalions were in North Vietnam working on large-scale bases and that there was a movement of fighter aircraft to South China. In December, Chinese Premier Chou En-lai, speaking at a mass rally in Peking, said that if the United States insisted on "going along the road of war expansion and on having another trial of strength with the Chinese people" the Chinese would "resolutely take up the challenge."[16]

For a brief moment, the cry went out and was echoed throughout Washington and in the press that the Chinese were coming. Allen Whiting of the State Department was so caught up in the furor that years later he was to describe "how we almost went to war with China."[17] Even in retrospect he continues to argue that the threat of a showdown was real and that only U. S. actions to reassure the Chinese prevented a catastrophe:

> The worst did not come. U. S. air attacks remained within essentially the same geographic and target limitations as before. The American Government made public that it knew Chinese troops were in North Vietnam but did not try to cut all supply lines from China. American aircraft attacked Chinese troop positions in North Vietnam, while Chinese gunners shot down U. S. pilots and planes. But neither side publicized its casualties or its kills.

Whiting also stresses China's caution:

> Even the better known danger of American planes overflying China was handled with relative restraint by both governments. Mao's response to accidental violations of China's airspace ran from total passivity through political protest to shootdowns.

But if Whiting was much concerned with the possibility of a Chinese intervention, his superior, Dean Rusk, was not. Although the secretary of state acknowledged increased support and shipments from Peking to North Vietnam in December, he reported nothing "qualitatively different" during the month.

As Washington at the highest level discounted Chinese intervention, Peking's propaganda about a threatened American attack abated. By the end of 1965, Mao Tse-tung was so convinced that the Vietnam conflict would remain inside the geographical limits of South Vietnam that he decided to launch his greatest power struggle since he had consolidated control over the Chinese Communist party in 1942, in which he was now determined to eliminate his internal enemies and counterbalance Soviet pressure (*see* pp. 000-000). In the course of this struggle, which became known as the Great Proletarian Revolution, Mao mobilized millions of youth to destroy Communist party organizations that supported the "revisionist" pro-Soviet Liu Shao-ch'i and his followers. Whereas Stalin had solved similar problems in the 1930s with the help of his secret police and by means of show trials and bloodbaths, Mao relied on his friends in the army and the ancient Chinese method of humiliation. In this life-and-death struggle among Chinese Communist factions, Mao was the ultimate winner, but not before all China had endured three years of a frenzied turmoil that is elsewhere unparalleled in recent history.

In retrospect, and in view of the scope and consequences of the Cultural Revolution, it is highly unlikely that the shrewd and cautious Mao would have begun his purge had he not been convinced the Americans would not attack China.

Final Arguments

Whatever influences were being communicated in December to the president, it is certain that the case for a bombing pause was not made on purely partisan lines. As we have seen, Johnson trusted and actively sought the counsel of his senior advisers in the government and at times relied heavily on the judgment of his ambassador in Saigon and his military advisers, mainly the Joint Chiefs of Staff. Moreover, he sought advice from the legal minds in the judiciary branch and from other lawyers who were his friends. Clearly, he respected the views of George Ball, who regularly drew together the principal dissenting views.

The president's focus concentrated on one central problem: to assure the survival of the South Vietnamese government. Although there were no stipulated constraints on his power to achieve this objective, he was loath to use American might to its fullest extent. His general concept of the American role in the warfare came down to containment of the North, and his model to achieve this was the Korean experience. The bombing of North Vietnam was intended as a retaliatory action as well as one aimed at cutting supply lines; in Korea, both purposes had served to achieve containment. The president was convinced that the bombing had proved safer and less risky than the ground operation and that it had helped insure the survival of the South Vietnamese government. Nevertheless, it had thus far only a limited impact on Hanoi's war machine, and it was becoming obvious that it could not stop the flow of men and supplies from north to south. Arguments for a pause would be persuasive only if they fit into this firmly held picture of the war. Domestic opposition to the war—particularly to the bombing—was growing, and the peace movement had become vocal, but in the final analysis this had almost no impact on the decision. The bombing of the North could be supported on moral grounds just as well as it could be deplored.

On balance, the most persuasive arguments made to the president appear to have been those that stressed the negotiatory character of the aerial bombardment. On December 3, 1965, new arguments were drafted by Assistant Secretary of

State William Bundy for a bombing pause. His memo was sent to high officials in the Department of State, and copies went to McGeorge Bundy in the White House and John McNaughton at the Pentagon. The memorandum began by emphasizing that the Soviet Union was now ready to use its influence in Hanoi to start negotiations. It cited the attempt by Soviet Ambassador Dobrynin to persuade McGeorge Bundy to accept a pause. From there it went on to point out that there were new signs of dissension among the Soviet Union, China, North Vietnam, and the Viet Cong, and that a pause might foster further disagreement in the Communist camp. Moreover, it would make it difficult for Moscow to justify an increase in its military support for Hanoi. Bundy also noted that the American position was somewhat weakened by the fact that Senator Mike Mansfield had told Gromyko during his recent trip to Moscow that the United States might prolong the pause if negotiations were merely begun irrespective of how they developed. As for the domestic political situation, Bundy noted that American casualties were mounting and a halt in the bombing would strengthen the public's confidence in the president's efforts to reach a negotiated settlement. Bundy also referred to the experiences of World War II in making the point that should a resumption of bombing be required it "would be even more painful to the population of North Vietnam than a fairly steady rate of bombing." Furthermore, a resumption would demonstrate U. S. determination to "finish the job."

The assistant secretary then considered arguments against the pause. He noted that if it should fail to lead to meaningful negotiations future American peace-seeking efforts might be compromised or hindered. Hanoi might misread American intentions and view the cessation of the bombing as evidence of weakness. Moreover, a pause could even cause difficulties for the Johnson administration at home: not only would the "doves" disagree with a resumption of the bombing, the "hawks" could be expected to press to have the bombing increased and extended to Hanoi and Haiphong.

The memorandum contained no final recommendations one way or the other, but the arguments for a pause exceeded those against it. On December 6, Bundy and Alexis Johnson prepared another draft of the memorandum, repeating both sides of the arguments. This time, however, they proposed in the name of the State Department that the president "approve a pause as soon as possible this month." Secretary Rusk endorsed the memo and it became a State Department position paper.[18]

The next day Rusk, McNamara, and McGeorge Bundy flew to the president's Texas ranch to present the memorandum. During the two-day discussions they strongly recommended the pause. They maintained that the bombing pause would place the responsibility for continued fighting on Hanoi and on those Communist governments which contended that only the bombardment of the North blocked the road to peace. The weight of the argument was that although Hanoi probably was not ready for peace talks every possible avenue of settlement must be explored before additional military measures could be justified.

But Johnson still was not convinced. He wanted to know how the Congress was viewing the war, the troop increases, escalation of the bombing campaign, and an eventual bombing pause. He wondered whether new congressional action was needed or if a reaffirmation of the Tonkin Gulf Resolution would assure him necessary protection from future congressional critics. For this reason he gave special instructions to Rusk and McNamara to conduct an urgent sounding among the senior members of the two houses of Congress. They found the majority of the fifteen key senators and congressmen wanted further intensification of the air war against North Vietnam. Some liberal Democrats, like Frank Church of Idaho, strongly criticized the president's Vietnam policy, arguing that it lay beyond the power of the United States to impose a Pax Americana upon an unwilling world. But neither he nor the others requested special congressional action to halt the bombing. Mike Mansfield and Robert F. Kennedy, on the other hand, held the view that the United States government and the government of South Vietnam (GSVN) should be prepared to extend the Christmas truce at least until the Vietnamese New Year, which begins January 21. The president, probably influenced by the diversity of opinion, did not pursue the matter and did not ask Congress for approval of his Vietnam policy. Instead, he delayed his bombing pause decision.

Then on December 10, Radio Hanoi quite unexpectedly denounced any future American bombing pause in advance. First, it branded the five-day bombing pause of May 1965 "shameful trickery" equal to "an ultimatum." Second, it observed that Dean Rusk, Ambassador Arthur Goldberg, and others were now talking about another bombing pause, but the "U. S. imperialists" should "harbor no hope that the Vietnamese people would be taken in by such a shopworn trick." This extremely sharp outburst, which closed with the usual demand that the United States accept the DRV Four Points and prove it by concrete acts, was soon followed by an ambiguous private communication from the Soviets. On December 16, Ambassador Dobrynin's trusted deputy, Minister Counsellor Alexander I. Zinchuk told William Bundy that Hanoi almost certainly would not respond this time to a suspension of the bombing unless the United States made a major concession in the South. The Soviet diplomat did not elaborate on what the concession should be, but Bundy got the impression Zinchuk was thinking of stopping further deployment of U. S. troops to South Vietnam.[19]

High officials in Washington were puzzled but could find no explanation. Why was it necessary for Hanoi to denounce a second pause in advance? Was Hanoi inalterably opposed to any negotiation, or had the hardliners merely temporarily prevailed over the doves—if indeed there were doves in North Vietnam? Had the Chinese, who adamantly opposed negotiations, gotten the upper hand in DRV affairs? Or was the propaganda attack perhaps aimed at squeezing more concessions out of Washington? And finally, was Ho Chi Minh stubborn as ever? Was he signaling Washington that no matter what the United States did he would not negotiate? Concerning the Bundy-Zinchuk conversation, these same officials did not know what to think; was Counsellor Zinchuk's remark coordinated with Hanoi's view and should it be regarded as a semi-official statement? Or was he merely expressing a private opinion?

As luck would have it, the themes of the Bundy-Alexis Johnson memo were urged anew on December 15, when the president held private talks at the White House with British Prime Minister Harold Wilson, who had come to Washington to voice his considerable misgivings about America's Vietnam policy. He has written about the occasion:

> I pressed the President hard, as I had in a number of Downing Street-White House exchanges, at least to suspend the bombing to test the sincerity of North Vietnamese hints that there might be a response on their side, possibly leading to negotiations. It was clear that his mind was not closed to this, and we discussed the modalities. At the same time I repeated that if U. S. aircraft were to bomb Hanoi or Haiphong we should be forced publicly to dissociate from that action. It was right that there should be no misunderstanding or subsequent recriminations between us.[20]

Of all foreign opinions on Vietnam other than those of the principals directly involved, Johnson considered British opinion moderately important.

On December 18, 1965, President Johnson met in the Cabinet Room of the White House with Rusk, McNamara, McGeorge Bundy, George Ball, and Alexis Johnson. The close friends of the president, Clark Clifford and Associate Justice Abe Fortas, were also invited to take part in the discussions. The president wanted to review once more all the arguments for and against a suspension of the bombing of North Vietnam.[21]

The representatives of the executive branch unanimously expressed themselves in favor of the pause. As on previous occasions, McNamara and Bundy disagreed with military experts in the field who were fearful that "a month's pause would undo all we've done." McNamara argued that they could resume the bombing at any time. Secretary Rusk pointed out, "It is our deepest national purpose to achieve our goals by peace, not war. If there is one chance in ten, or twenty, that a step of this sort could lead to a settlement on [the basis of] the Geneva Agreements and the 17th Parallel, I would take it."

The two outside civilian consultants were opposed. Justice Fortas argued that the United States would get little credit for trying to find peace and failing. Clark Clifford again felt a halt "could be construed by Hanoi as a sign of weakness on our part."

Johnson was reluctant to overrule the judgment of these old friends; the opposing arguments, however, were strong. In addition there were two pieces of information on his desk that he could not ignore. One was a transcript of the October 7 Péter-Rusk discussion documenting the Hungarian's promise that peace talks with the Vietnamese would commence in a matter of a few weeks if the bombing stopped. The other was a memo on Dobrynin's observation that "intense diplomatic activity" would ensue if the United States suspended bombing for "twelve to twenty days."

Torn by conflicting advice but impressed by Rusk's new stance, the president tilted in the direction of a longer bombing pause. Yet he delayed his final decision. Instead, he agreed to go part way toward an extended pause. He would respond to a Viet Cong offer of a twelve-hour Christmas truce by proposing a thirty-hour cease-fire including a halt in the bombing of the North starting on Christmas Eve 1965. Moreover, he would set no definite date for the resumption of the bombing.

CHAPTER V

Expansion of the Christmas Truce

Although the bombing pause was very much in the air during the weeks before Christmas, the Soviet bloc diplomats in Washington had not the slightest idea that President Johnson's principal advisers, McNamara, Rusk, and McGeorge Bundy, had reached the consensus to support it and had almost brought the president around to the same point of view. Perhaps Soviet Ambassador Anatoliy Dobrynin knew what was going on inside the American administration, but he did not tell us. At our regular monthly ambassadorial meeting in December, the socialist countries' mission chiefs, one after the other, offered their views on the subject.

Petre Bălăceanu of Rumania was extremely critical of Johnson's conduct of the war; he used strong words to condemn the recent extension of the air raids on North Vietnam and said he hoped Hanoi would not enter into negotiations until the Americans accepted Premier Pham Van Dong's Four Point proposal and simultaneously got out of Southeast Asia. Bălăceanu was always the toughest of all the bloc countries' diplomats on the subject of Vietnam. For example, in early July 1966, shortly after the Americans bombed the storage facilities and other military installations in Hanoi and Haiphong for the first time, President Johnson invited the diplomatic corps (including the bloc diplomats) to the presidental yacht *Sequoia* for a boat excursion on the Potomac River. Polish Ambassador Edward Drozniak, Soviet Chargé d'Affairs Alexander Zinchuk, and I were inclined to accept the invitation. The Rumanian, however, objected violently, and there were meetings among ourselves and consultations with our respective capitals. The final decision came back that we should not attend at any level. Some of my colleagues pleaded sick and declined; I quickly informed the State Department I was taking my summer vacation and boarded a plane. Bălăceanu refused the invitation without excuse. Even so, I think, Bălăceanu only pretended to be anti-American, hoping to counteract allegations that Rumania was not wholeheartedly behind the Soviet "United Front" policy in Vietnam.

The Bulgarian ambassador, Luben Guerassimov, a blind supporter of Moscow and a great admirer of Stalin, spoke at the meeting as if he were reading from the dull central organ of the Bulgarian Communist party, the *Rabotnitsestvoja Delo.* The Americans, he said, wanted to compel the Vietnamese people to lay down their arms and give up their legitimate aspirations. Therefore, Hanoi was right when it demanded that the United States stop the bombing, evacuate its troops, and cancel its military alliance with the Saigon regime before any negotiation could take place. To give weight to his remarks, he began to praise the "brilliant success" of the "Washington March for Peace in Vietnam," which had been sponsored by the Committee for a Sane Nuclear Policy in late November, and noted that heavy American casualties, discontented workers, and the progressive elements of America would ultimately force Johnson to give up his Vietnamese adventure.

Our host, Edward Drozniak of Poland, a former director of the Polish National Bank, was mainly interested in expanding trade between his country and the United States and deliberately avoided making any derogatory remarks about the Americans and evinced a clear lack of interest in the whole

Vietnamese affair. The Czechoslovak ambassador, Karel Duda, who was known to have good connections on Capitol Hill, spoke at great length about congressional reaction to the war. He began by remarking that legislative opposition to Johnson's Vietnam policy was slowly but steadily growing as the fighting escalated and casualty reports mounted. He added that criticism from Mike Mansfield, William Fulbright, and Robert Kennedy of Johnson's handling of the war was only a fake opposition: they would do the same if they had presidential power, said Duda. He also mentioned that right-wing pressure on President Johnson was strong; hawks like Nixon were not merely urging an all-out war against the DRV but had even proposed bombing China. This, Duda thought, was absurd, and he expected Johnson would resist such demands. He concluded, however, that the majority of the Congress supported Johnson's Vietnam policy. Concerning the question of a bombing pause, the Czech ambassador cited the recent editorial endorsement in the *New York Times* as the most influential advocacy of the idea that he had seen. He regarded as next in importance the calls for a cessation of bombing by the National Council of Churches, Wayne Morse, and Martin Luther King, Jr. But Duda remained skeptical about the possibility of the suspension. He could not believe Johnson would order a halt unless Hanoi stopped supporting the NLF—and this was, of course, out of the question.

On my part, I was no better informed than my colleagues, though I had picked up a valuable piece of evidence about the ongoing bombing pause debate within the administration without realizing that there was a debate at all. In late November, columnist Charlie Bartlett told me, to my great surprise, that Defense Secretary McNamara was a "dove"; he wanted to negotiate rather than continue the war. I immediately reported Bartlett's remark to Budapest, but nobody there gave it much credence. In fact, I was told quite bluntly that an American secretary of defense simply could not be a "dove." When I repeated my story at the ambassadorial meeting my colleagues' reaction was about the same as that of Budapest. Only Dobrynin found the information worthy of reflection, but he made no mention of the fact that he knew McNamara had promoted the bombing pause behind the scenes. What Dobrynin subsequently said, however, was interesting. First, he reiterated what we all knew, that Hanoi was clinging steadfastly to its Four Points as the only basis of negotiation. Then he stated that the North Vietnamese were unwilling to start negotiations, not only as long as the bombing of the North persisted, but also as long as the United States continued sending troop reinforcements to South Vietnam.

Following the ambassadorial meeting, I rushed to New York to report what I heard from Dobrynin to First Deputy Foreign Minister Péter Mód. Mód was the second man in the Hungarian Foreign Ministry. He had taken over the direction of our U. N. delegation after Péter's departure in late October. Mód quietly responded that Hanoi's demand with respect to American troop deployments clearly reflected a stiffening of Ho's attitude toward negotiations, but in the final analysis it could be viewed as only a slight variation on the DRV's original demands for ending the war.

When I reported the news to Budapest, I received the same answer from Foreign Minister Péter. He added, however, that everything he had said to Dean Rusk concerning the suspension of the bombing remained valid and I should sit tight and wait for the secretary to call us.

I did not have long to wait.

On December 22, I was sipping coffee with a Yugoslav diplomat in the U. N. Delegates' Lounge. The headquarters building of the world organization was filled with a pre-Christmas atmosphere. Delegates were preparing to leave for home, and the heads of delegations had already departed. The 20th General Assembly was holding its closing session, and almost the only persons about in the huge building were members of the U. N. apparatus and the guards. My Yugoslav friend and I were discussing Christmas gifts we had bought and how we planned to spend the holiday when I was called to the telephone. My secretary in Washington informed me in excited tones that Secretary Dean Rusk wanted me to come to the State Department the following day.

I said good-bye to the Yugoslav, left for La Guardia airfield, and returned to Washington on the first plane.

On December 23, at 5 P.M., I presented myself at the State Department. I had brought along a secretary to take notes. At the diplomatic entrance the Hungarian desk officer, Christopher Squire, greeted us and escorted us to Dean Rusk's seventh floor office. The secretary apologized for calling during the Christmas holiday, but, as he explained, the events of the world unfortunately do not always conform to the calendar and frequently it is necessary to work at times when one would prefer to be in one's family circle. He stopped for a second, looked at a piece of paper on his desk, then came directly to the point. "The Hungarian foreign minister," he said, "showed special interest in the Vietnam question during our last meeting in New York, where you were also present. For this very reason let us review the whole problem once more." We lit cigarettes as the secretary resumed talking. "As you well know," he said, "the United States is seriously interested in settling the Vietnam conflict as soon as possible. It is ready, at any time, without preconditons, and anywhere, to begin discussions with representatives of North Vietnam. On my part I am ready to meet, without preconditions, with a competent representative of Hanoi."

Rusk reaffirmed the American position as set forth by President Johnson in his "unconditional discussions" speech at John Hopkins University the preceding April.[1] He added, however, that if this formulation was not satisfactory, the United States was ready to begin discussions on the basis of the so-called declaration of 17 neutral nations, "sent to us and also to Hanoi." (This declaration was an appeal, as mentioned earlier, to start negotiations "without posing any preconditions, . . . and in the spirit of the Geneva Agreements.")

"The Geneva Agreements of 1954 and 1962 may form the basis of future discussions," continued Rusk, "or we can sit down at the negotiating table in the framework of an international conference competent to settle Southeast Asian questions."

"If my understanding is correct," I said, "the American side would consider an appropriate forum not only a meeting based on the 1954 and 1962 [Geneva] Agreements but also a newly convoked conference concerned with Southeast Asia."

"Yes, by all means," was the answer. "At this conference the first question to be discussed could be a cessation of the hostilities in Vietnam. If by chance Hanoi should consider it expedient to discuss this topic in the course of talks preliminary to the conference, we on our part are willing to do this also."

"If I understand [you] correctly," I interrupted, "you spoke of the cessation of hostilities. Would this mean, operationally, discussions aimed at bringing about a truce?"

"Yes, that is what I meant," said Rusk. "But, if North Vietnam should wish to negotiate on the basis of their Four Points . . . we accept that also, but, naturally, along with other points which others might wish to propose." Rusk emphasized that the United States did not want to maintain permanent military bases in Southeast Asia; that it did not want to keep troops in South Vietnam after peace was assured; that it supported free elections in South Vietnam; and if, after free elections, Vietnam should follow the political orientation of non-aligned countries, "we will accept this." And "this also pertains to any country of Southeast Asia whatsoever." He further stressed that on the question of unification "the Vietnamese people will have to decide freely"; finally, he stated, the United States would much prefer to utilize its resources for the economic reconstruction of all of Southeast Asia—including North Vietnam—rather than for war.

"As you can see," the secretary continued, "we have collected everything in a large basket of peace. We accept every form of variation except one: to abandon South Vietnam to aggression."

In the interest of accuracy I went over Rusk's twelve points again, then asked what else I should communicate to János Péter. The secretary thought this over and said: "The belligerents have accepted the thirty-hour Christmas truce. During this period there will be no aerial bombardment either, and perhaps later there may be a new opportunity for further extension of the pause. Therefore, I would now like to ask Mr. Péter what, in light of present circumstances, he could add to what he told me in New York."

I promised the secretary to transmit his message to Budapest without delay.

We exchanged Christmas greetings, then parted. I stopped

for a moment at the door. "What shall we say to the reporters if they show up?" I asked. "It will be best to tell the press," he answered, "only that we discussed questions of mutual interest." I agreed with his suggestion. My hunch was well timed, for a few reporters were waiting outside Rusk's office. Endre Márton of the Associated Press asked me first: "What can you tell us about your meeting with Secretary Rusk?" I answered according to the agreed formula. But he pressed further, "Was it Vietnam, or perhaps you discussed some bilateral question, like Cardinal Mindszenty's departure to Rome?"* I told him and the other reporters that I was indeed sorry but I was not in a position to tell them anything more.

Finally I reached my car. I remember racing across Washington from the State Department to the Hungarian legation. The secretary's message was in János Péter's hand in Budapest in three hours.

That evening I stayed late at my office reflecting on the conversation with Rusk. The first question that came to my mind was, why had Rusk called me and not Dobrynin, with whom he usually discussed vital international matters like a peace proposal in Vietnam? My guess was, and still is, that he probably wanted to avoid putting the Russians on the spot and turned to one of the smaller countries instead. He had decided to speak with me because my country's foreign minister had made the strongest statement of all the East Europeans in favor of a bombing halt. Perhaps Rusk also wanted to test in earnest the validity and efficiency of the Hungarian communication channel. Then I went through the transcript of the conversation. It showed that the secretary had a wide range of diplomatic possibilities in mind. I was of the opinion it might well serve as a good starting point for negotiation if the thirty-hour Christmas truce could be extended. If the United States bombing of North Vietnam should be resumed, what then? On these two points Rusk had said nothing specific. All now depended on my foreign minister, I thought—on how quickly he could act and how convincingly he could make his case in Hanoi.

*There were baseless rumors at the time that the Hungarian and American governments as well as the Vatican had started negotiations to let the self-exiled cardinal leave the U. S. Embassy and retire to Rome.

Filled with uncertainty, I drove over to the Soviet Embassy to inform Dobrynin about the American plan and ask his opinion. This was customary procedure in the Hungarian diplomatic service: everything had to be run past the Soviet Union. The ambassador received me in his soundproof study where we could speak without being bugged by the FBI. Dobrynin was sitting behind his desk when I entered. He had slippers on his feet because his legs were hurting him, he said. He looked tired and nervous, nevertheless he listened attentively to my report and carefully wrote down each of the twelve points. "What do you think about it?" I asked him. The ambassador waited a minute or so, then remarked that he could discover nothing new in Rusk's proposal. He predicted that the North Vietnamese would not view it as a basis for discussion and they "would not move." I was more optimistic. I felt the Americans were ready to negotiate on almost any terms. "Rusk has offered a comprehensive package deal," I said. But Dobrynin remained skeptical.

The next morning I moved my office into the communications room of the legation. Although I was officially out to all calls, the Washington correspondent of the Hungarian news agency managed to get into the communications room and ask some awkward questions before I succeeded in shaking him off. I then spent a few hours in suspenseful waiting. Would I get an answer from Péter in time, before the expiration of the Christmas truce? At 10 A.M. the first message arrived from Budapest, instructing me to contact Secretary of State Dean Rusk and inform him that Foreign Minister Péter thanked him for the twelve-point American plan. Péter had found the plan interesting; he had brought it to the attention of the Hungarian government, and would answer it soon. In the meantime, Péter wanted me to sound out American intentions concerning a possible extension of the Christmas truce.

I saw Rusk at 11 A.M. and delivered the message. He listened closely and took notes. "Perhaps this time it will be possible to reach some result," he remarked. According to the military field reports from South Vietnam, no grave incidents had occurred thus far. To my question concerning the Christmas truce, the secretary indicated that the United States government might consider an extension but it would be easier to move ahead if he knew what Hanoi would do if the bombing were suspended. I said I could not promise anything, and with this my short visit ended. We agreed that we would not inform the press about our meeting at all and Rusk's secretary saw me out after checking for newsmen in the halls. I was shepherded into Rusk's personal elevator and out of the building through the basement.

On Christman Day, in the afternoon, I was at home, off Massachusetts Avenue, chatting and drinking eggnog with my neighbor and eating traditional Hungarian Christmas cakes—poppyseed and walnut rolls. The telephone rang in the other room—it was the secretary on the line. He asked me to inform the Hungarian foreign minister immediately that, for one or two days after Christmas, the United States would not bomb North Vietnam and there would be no ground action initiated by U. S. troops in the South. I passed this message on to Budapest, adding my own opinion that the American side was serious about negotiations and Hanoi should be made aware of that. I further urged Péter to reply promptly since I was convinced the Americans would not suspend the bombing of the North beyond the one or two days indicated unless they detected signs of some encouraging development.

The next day (December 26) I did not hear from Budapest. I was not too concerned, for I was sure Budapest had forwarded the message to Hanoi and Moscow, and, after all, not much time had elapsed.

In the morning hours of December 27, with the deadline nearing for the end of the extended truce, Dean Rusk telephoned to ask whether I had any answer from Péter. I told him I had none, but promised to inform him at the first word from Budapest. He told me he could be reached at any time through the White House switchboard or at his State Department office. I cabled a report of the telephone conversation to Budapest, indicating that time was running out.

That afternoon a cable arrived from Péter. He asked whether Rusk's communication of December 23 meant the United States government was ready or willing to enter negotiation on the twelve-point basis "with the National Liberation Front."

As I translated Péter's cablegram (from Hungarian to English) I was seized by a sense of unease. In view of his conversation in New York with Rusk, why did Péter ask that question? Had he received such an inquiry from Hanoi? If so, why had he not informed me? Or was he trying to squeeze a further concession out of the Americans to facilitate the start of negotiations? I had little time for mediation because I had to see Rusk urgently.

It was 6 P.M. when I called Rusk's office saying that I had another message. I drove to the Department again, directly to the basement garage and was transported by elevator to the seventh floor. This time William Bundy was present when Rusk received me. After I relayed the very precisely phrased message (I had been careful to translate it word for word), Rusk responded snappily: The Vietnam War could be ended within hours if aggression from the North were to stop, if no bombs were to explode in the South, if the NLF would stop kidnapping village teachers and South Vietnamese administrative personnel. The United States armed forces were in South Vietnam only because of the North Vietnamese aggression against the South; hence the American government would have to deal with Hanoi and not the National Liberation Front. "We cannot enter into negotiations with the NLF," Rusk said, "but there would be no insurmountable obstacle for the Viet Cong to make its words heard during the talks with the representatives of Hanoi. Besides, it is a well known fact," said Rusk in a more conciliatory voice, "that many South Vietnamese families of high standing have split in two, some of them occupying key positions in the South Vietnamese government, the others siding with the Viet Cong. But because the traditionally strong family contacts were upheld even so, the NLF could talk to Saigon. Mr. Péter must see this clearly when he talks with his Vietnamese friends."

I could not agree with the secretary's arguments, and I bluntly said so.

Rusk interrupted, "Our impression, on the basis of Mr. Péter's message, is that the Hungarian foreign minister is speaking in the name of Hanoi or the NLF or possibly in the name of both."

I replied cautiously: "I have authorization only to transmit the message."

Rusk then brought up the bombing pause. "We prolonged the Christmas truce bombing pause," he said. "This was a unilateral step on our part. It is necessary for us to know what the other side will do if we suspend the bombings. I would like to know Mr. Péter's opinion."

It was now late afternoon; through the windows I could just make out the contours of the Lincoln Memorial. Rusk had whiskey brought in and began talking in a more relaxed vein. He asked how I felt about finding myself in this affair. I answered that if we were successful it would be worth all the exertion and fatigue. The secretary then remarked that reports from the field in Vietnam indicated fewer truce violations than expected. "Perhaps," he added hopefully, "we will be able somehow to infiltrate peace into South Vietnam."

The Decision

As we know today, Péter's message was reported without delay to the Texas White House. I believe it was not so much the substance of it as the cloud of mystery and deep secrecy surrounding it which impressed President Johnson. Moreover, this message was probably the last piece of information received by Johnson before he made his decision to extend the bombing pause. Only a little earlier that afternoon he had apparently expected that the bombing would start again very soon; he had put through a call from the ranch to McGeorge Bundy's office in Washington and inquired about the schedule for resumption. After checking with McNamara, Bundy replied that no time had been set but that he and the secretary of defense joined in suggesting the halt be extended at least until New Year's Day.[2] Johnson promised to give the matter careful thought. He conferred once more with Rusk, and sometime late that night he decided to extend the halt for a substantial period and to launch a major diplomatic offensive to bring the North Vietnamese to the negotiating table. The time consideration was vital. Obviously it would take a certain amount of time for his emissaries to go around the world to marshal support in foreign capitals. Furthermore, he wanted more time to observe Hanoi's attitude; he hoped above all to avoid creating the impression that the United States was issuing Hanoi an ultimatum.

In the morning hours of December 28, I received a cable from Péter. It contained one sentence: "Tell the secretary that every word of his proposal is under careful study." Precisely what this meant I could only guess. Might it be only a stalling tactic to enable him to coordinate with Moscow and Hanoi? I was considering asking for additional information from Budapest when Rusk telephoned to summon me again to the State Department.

William Bundy was also present when I arrived at Rusk's office. The secretary informed me that the United States government would not resume bombing for several days; then he handed me a written message which, in summary, stated the following:

> There has been no bombing of North Vietnam since December 24. No date has been set for a resumption of bombing. The United States Government hopes that the present standdown might last at least through New Year's Day. If the other side reciprocates by making a serious contribution toward peace, it will have a favorable effect on the possibility of further extending the suspension.

Rusk asked that I relay this information to Budapest promptly. I promised to do so and in turn told him that the Hungarian foreign minister wished to inform him that "every word of your proposal is under careful study." I reasoned then that Rusk must have been very busy because he asked Bundy to write down the message and discuss it. (We know now that Rusk was already making preparations to launch Johnson's worldwide peace offensive.)

Bundy and I left for Bundy's office. Once there, he asked what Péter's message meant. Were only the Hungarians studying the proposal, or were the Vietnamese studying it as well? I did not have the answer, but I knew too much about the decision-making process in a socialist state to imagine that Péter would discuss such a sensitive diplomatic question without prior approval of the Politburo of the Hungarian Communist party and without coordination with the Kremlin. Moreover, I strongly believed that Péter was in touch with Hanoi and acted on their behalf. I expressed my cautious opinion that the phrasing of my message meant that the American proposal was being studied by "someone other than Péter."

Back at the legation I quickly translated Rusk's memorandum into Hungarian, summarized my discussion with Bundy, and sent my cable to Budapest.

Then I sat down, relaxed, and thought to myself: I have made some real progress, the U. S. bombers have been grounded, and the North Vietnamese have received a package deal from Rusk to start negotiation.

The scenario of the pause was quickly transformed into action. Rusk informed the United States Embassy in Saigon of the president's decision to extend the bombing pause for "several more days," and the South Vietnamese government concurred. The secretary also advised U. S. allies in the Pacific, members of the North Atlantic Treaty Organization, and U. N. Secretary General U Thant, who was assured he would be kept abreast of developing military and diplomatic initiatives.

Meanwhile, U. S. Ambassador Llewellyn E. Thompson met in Washington with his Soviet counterpart, Anatoliy Dobrynin, and handed over the same written message Rusk had given me. In the course of their discussions, Thompson quietly reminded Dobrynin that the Americans were expecting Soviet assistance to start things moving in Vietnam. He referred to the Soviet ambassador's remarks to McGeorge Bundy in late November—his suggestion that the Soviet Union would make a real effort toward negotiation in Vietnam if the United States would undertake a good-faith initiative. Dobrynin only nodded. When asked whether he knew about the Hungarian mediation role, however, he answered without hesitation that he had first-hand information and was aware of the exchange of messages between Rusk and Péter.

Finally, the president himself wrote personal letters to many state and government leaders calling attention to the halt in the bombing of the North and making it clear that similar restraint on the part of Hanoi would be viewed with favor in Washington and would influence future American action accordingly.

In the midst of this overheated atmosphere, I had a few days of calm. I received no messages to transmit from Budapest or Washington. I went to see Ambassador Dobrynin and asked whether he had any reaction to the bombing pause from Moscow or Hanoi. He had none. It was too early to expect any reaction, he said. He still doubted that the pause would promote negotiation. Moreover, he thought that the American "peace envoys' missions" imparted a rather theatrical flavor to the suspension of the bombing and predicted that it would do Johnson more harm than good. I agreed with him and noted that President Johnson seemed unaware that only secret diplomacy can produce results. As I recall, I discussed Vietnam with other diplomats in those "quiet days." One of them was the Czechoslovak Ambassador Karel Duda. He was a good friend, and it was difficult for me not to tell him the whole story; yet I was under orders from Budapest not to disclose details, even to friendly countries' diplomats (the exception being the Soviets). After a great deal of fretting, however, I felt I could tell Duda about at least part of my discussions with the Americans. Thus I summarized for him Rusk's "Twelve Points" and told him that Washington had set no deadline for the end of the bombing pause. Duda, grateful for the information, found the Rusk plan attractive and finally promised to forward this sensitive information directly to his foreign minister, Vačlav David.

The counsellor of the French Embassy also got wind of the Hungarian mediation and visited me in the last days of December. He seemed to have some knowledge of my meetings in the State Department because he asked me whether I had transmitted any message from Washington to Hanoi and vice versa. He even inquired whether cease-fire negotiations were going on between the DRV and the United States. He was aware of the content of the Rusk plan. It was somewhat confusing, however, since he spoke of a fourteen-point plan and mine had only twelve. A few days later I learned that two more points had been added to the original list.*

I did not deny having discussed Vietnam with the Americans, but I felt it was not my duty to inform a diplomat from a NATO country about my discussions; therefore, I told him nothing affirmatively. In turn, I tried to get his opinion about the prospect of a negotiated settlement of the Vietnam conflict. He simply replied that I must know more than he did. Without saying so, we both knew that further pressing of the issue on either side would lead nowhere. He finished the cognac I had offered him and departed.

On January 4, I was again busy. I received an early morning

---

*On January 2, 1966, the White House made public the extended version of Rusk's "12 Points" entitled "The Heart of the Matter in Viet Nam," and Presidential Press Secretary Bill D. Moyers underlined that the 3-page paper contained the essence of Johnson's message which the U. S. emissaries had delivered to foreign leaders. It reads as follows:

1. The Geneva Agreements of 1954 and 1962 are an adequate basis for peace in Southeast Asia;
2. We would welcome a conference on Southeast Asia or on any part thereof;
3. We would welcome "negotiations without preconditions" as the 17 nations put it;
4. We would welcome unconditional discussions as President Johnson put it;
5. A cessation of hostilities could be the first order of business at a conference or could be the subject of preliminary discussions;
6. Hanoi's Four Points could be discussed along with other points which others might wish to propose;
7. We want no U. S. bases in Southeast Asia;
8. We do not desire to retain U. S. troops in South Vietnam after peace is assured;
9. We support free elections in South Vietnam to give the South Vietnamese a government of their own choice;
10. The question of reunification of Vietnam should be determined by the Vietnamese through their own free decision;
11. The countries of Southeast Asia can be non-aligned or neutral if that be their option;
12. We would much prefer to use our resources for the economic reconstruction of Southeast Asia than in war. If there is peace, North Vietnam could participate in a regional effort to which we would be prepared to contribute at least one billion dollars;
13. The President has said "The Viet Cong would not have difficulty being presented and having their views represented if for a moment Hanoi decided she wanted to cease aggression. I don't think that would be an unsurmountable problem."
14. We have said publicly and privately that we could stop the bombing of North Vietnam as a step toward peace, although there has not been the slightest hint or suggestion from the other side as to what they would do if the bombing stopped.

Washington's Fourteen Points, January 7, 1966, *Department of State Bulletin* (Washington, February 14, 1966).

cable from Péter directing me to inform Rusk that the Hungarian government considered it possible to arrange a meeting to enable the United States, the Democratic Republic of Vietnam, and the National Liberation Front to exchange opinions. In the second part of his cable, Péter asked Rusk when and where such a meeting could take place. I deemed it prudent to send an urgent cable back to Budapest before I called on Secretary Rusk. I reminded Péter that the Americans had stated they were interested in talking only to Hanoi and pointed out that any insistance on formal representation for the NLF might jeopardize our mediation effort. Might not the question of the NLF's representation be better resolved, I suggested, once Hanoi and Washington started preliminary negotiations? Less than two hours later I received a laconic answer repeating the original instructions.

Rusk received me at noon. William Bundy was again present. Attaché József Kerekes accompanied me for the purpose of taking notes. I relayed Péter's message orally; and, as I expected, Rusk received it with disfavor. Obviously, he read this message as another attempt to smuggle the NLF into the negotiations as the representative of South Vietnam. He made it clear again that the United States rejected forthwith the idea of entering into negotiations with the Viet Cong.

With this point disposed of, the secretary relaxed his attitude and regarded me appraisingly, holding one earpiece of his spectacles to the right edge of his lips. He pondered a minute or two, then began talking, choosing his words carefully: "Hanoi moves with great difficulty, but there is still some hope. Your foreign minister certainly knows from his North Vietnamese comrades that this time we were successful in passing our statement [the twelve-point proposal under study in Budapest] to the North Vietnamese consul general in Rangoon. This time . . . ," he paused, "the North Vietnamese did not send it back as they did during the short May pause."

I sent off my report of the meeting that night, and the following morning I had a reply from Péter: Rusk's answer leaves the impression that he misunderstood "the first part of our message."

Péter insisted he was not asking for a meeting like the one

that had taken place in Rangoon; no, no: "We are speaking of the type of meeting at which the official representatives of the two governments negotiate directly and an exchange takes place between them about their ideas. We are asking you whether the United States government is ready to participate in that type of meeting. On the basis of careful examination, we are of the opinion that the possibility of that type of meeting exists."

I was glad. It looked as though Hanoi had accepted the advice I offered in my first cable of the preceding day. For the first time the NLF was not mentioned; instead, the possibility of direct talks between Hanoi and Washington was actually stressed.

Rusk thought a long time about this message. When he finally spoke, he said: "This sounds different. The Hungarians should realize that the Rangoon contact was brought into existence by our ambassador in Burma and that he, in turn, handed our official communication to the representative of Hanoi. There was no doubt as to the official nature of the exchange. But," he added, "I must discuss the matter further with my colleagues. I'll let you know our answer shortly." I did not want to ask, but I felt sure Rusk was going to the White House.

A few hours later William Bundy gave me the answer: "We have examined the latest message carefully, and our response is that our ambassador in Rangoon is available for any kind of discussions the Hungarian government has in mind with appropriate North Vietnamese representatives. If Mr. Péter has suggestions about another location for such discussions, we would be ready to consider them."

For the sake of accuracy I asked directly whether, in effect, the American reply was "yes."

"Certainly affirmative," said Bundy. He then urged upon me the necessity for requesting a prompt reply, since there was—as he put it—some urgency in the matter.

I returned to the legation filled with enthusiasm. I cabled the good news, emphasizing the need for haste, and then set myself to wait for a reply, privately hoping that the negotiations might take place in Budapest, not Rangoon. But my optimistic expectation was cut short when Endre Szluka, the head of the political intelligence service at the legation, a hardliner who had opposed my mediation effort right from the beginning, rushed into my office and with a self-satisfied, ironic smile showed me an angry statement of the DRV Foreign Ministry issued the previous day. It called the American peace effort a "large-scale deceptive peace swindle" and branded the suspension of the air attacks on North Vietnam a "trick." It claimed that the United States policy remained unchanged; Washington was sabotaging the 1954 Geneva Agreements on Vietnam; it supported a "puppet regime" in Saigon and refused to recognize the South Vietnam National Front for Liberation as the sole genuine representative of the people of South Vietnam. Moreover, the spokesman of Hanoi maintained that every time the United States wanted to intensify their "aggressive war" they talked more glibly about peace, that the real purpose of the peace drive was to carry out negotiations from a position of strength and force the Vietnamese people to accept the American terms. The statement finally ended with the warning: "A political settlement of the Vietnam problem can be envisaged only when the United States government has accepted the Four Point stand of the Democratic Republic of Vietnam, has proved this by actual deeds, has stopped unconditionally and for good its air raids and all other acts of war against the DRV."[3]

I read the statement again and again. Basically it did not contain new elements, and its harsh wording was not unusual either. As a matter of fact, Hanoi Radio had broadcast similar blows just before the bombing pause was announced. But this denunciation was not merely a news item, it was an official statement of the DRV's Foreign Ministry. Significantly, the statement coincided with Péter's proposal to Rusk that "representatives of the two governments [Washington and Hanoi] negotiate directly. For a moment a disturbing question flashed through my mind: why had Péter raised false hopes that the possibility of negotiation existed? Perhaps there was a misunderstanding between Budapest and Hanoi? I quickly asked Budapest for explanation. But Budapest did not reply. It transmitted no more messages on the subject—not that day, nor the next, nor the next. There would be no more messages—not even an explanation for the silence. I grew more and more nervous, and was confused when Soviet Ambassador Dobrynin asked me on what basis the Hungarian foreign minister suggested an exchange of ideas between the Americans and the North Vietnamese? Did the DRV government request this of Budapest? I did not know. The ambassador shook his head in disapproval but did not ask any more questions.

CHAPTER VI

The Harriman Mission

Following the December 27 decision to extend the bombing pause for an unspecified length of time, President Johnson initiated vigorous action to probe the prospects for a settlement in Vietnam. The American government was in touch with virtually all the governments in the world, in many cases through special emissaries. Ambassador Arthur Goldberg carried a presidential message to Rome, Paris, and London. Assistant Secretary of State G. Mennen Williams visited fourteen African countries. The State Department's top Latin American specialist, Thomas Mann, traveled to South and Central America. McGeorge Bundy flew to Ottawa. Everywhere these emissaries called attention to the bombing pause and stressed that the United States was ready to start negotiations with Hanoi without prior conditions. Ignoring the sneers of critics who branded the campaign an improvised Madison Avenue publicity operation, the president remained resolute. As he pointed out in his memoirs, he wanted the world informed. He wanted international pressures brought to bear on Hanoi, and he wanted congressional cooperation at home.

The winter peace offensive of 1965-66 took veteran Ambassador Averell Harriman, one of the most experienced and effective of President Johnson's special emissaries, to Eastern Europe. Harriman had not participated in the earlier attempts to start negotiations with the North Vietnamese, but now Johnson decided to make use of his expertise and his high-level contacts in the Communist world. On December 28, the ambassador was in his State Department office when he received a call from the Texas White House. The President asked him to leave at once to see all his "East European friends" and find out "what they'll do."[1]

The ambassador conferred first with Dean Rusk, who summarized for him the pertinent facts of the Fourteen-Point plan on Vietnam, which the secretary was personally preparing for the presidential emissaries on the eve of their departure. Besides this, Harriman did not get much encouragement. Rusk was clearly not enthusiastic about Johnson's worldwide peace offensive. He preferred behind-the-scenes discussions rather than open diplomacy. Then Harriman called McNamara at the ranch for more information. The defense secretary told him the president wanted him to see as many people as possible who had communication with the North Vietnamese and to explain that the bombing had been suspended in the hope of getting negotiations started. There was little time for meditation, and Harriman decided his chances for success would be greatest in Poland, Hungary, and Yugoslavia. He excluded Moscow from his itinerary because he did not want to give Peking a new opportunity to accuse the Soviet leadership of conspiring with the United States.

As a member of the International Control Commission for Indo-China (together with India and Canada), Poland was charged with enforcing the provisions of the 1954 Geneva accord, which guaranteed the independence of Laos, Cambodia, and Vietnam. But the Poles had in fact hampered implementation of the treaty by ignoring the military build-up in the Democratic Republic of Vietnam and the infiltration of North Vietnamese regular troops into the South; nevertheless Harriman felt that Warsaw would be a useful intermediary precisely because it enjoyed Ho Chi Minh's confidence.[2]

Hungary was chosen largely on the strength of Foreign

Minister János Péter's insinuations that he spoke for Hanoi when he predicted that a bombing halt would produce negotiations. Moreover, the new American peace proposal to Hanoi had been forwarded only a few days before through Hungarian channels.

Yugoslavia was included in the itinerary mainly because Ambassador Harriman had a sufficiently close personal relationship with Marshal Tito to know that he would be receptive to the American initiative. (The Ambassador had been instrumental in helping Tito get American economic and military support in 1948, when Stalin excluded him from the Communist camp, put heavy military pressure on Yugoslavia, and blockaded it economically.) Moreover, in April 1965, Yugoslavia had joined with seventeen nonaligned nations in calling for a Vietnam peace negotiation without preconditions.

Assistant Secretary of State William Bundy called me late in the afternoon of December 28 to tell me that Harriman was flying to Warsaw on a peace mission for President Johnson. From there, if the Hungarians so desired, he would visit Budapest to clarify any questions that might have arisen since the last exchange of messages.

I quickly relayed this message to Péter. His response—this time through the American chargé in Budapest—was that the ambassador's appearance in the Hungarian capital at this time would reveal his and Foreign Minister Péter's active role in the mediation; thus it would seem more appropriate if Harriman did not stop at Budapest. The ambassador accepted this explanation since he knew that Rusk wished to deal personally with the Hungarians.

As he hastened aboard a special Boeing 707 presidential jet on December 28, Harriman had with him two aides: a State Department specialist on Chinese and Far Eastern affairs, David Dean, and the Hungarian desk officer, Christopher A. Squire, who had been present when the secretary of state discussed his twelve-point package deal with me. (I learned later from Harriman that he selected Squire to accompany him because of his general experience, not because he was at that time the Hungarian desk officer.) While the plane cruised toward Europe, the State Department instructed the American Embassy in Warsaw to get the necessary landing permits and arrange for a meeting the next day between Harriman and Polish Foreign Minister Adam Rapacki.

The news that Harriman's plane was on its way to Warsaw reached John A. Gronouski, United States ambassador to Poland, at the Poznan trade fair about midnight of the same day (December 28). Gronouski had to hurry to catch the 4:00 A.M. train that would return him to Warsaw in time to meet Harriman at the airport. Meanwhile, his deputy at the embassy in Warsaw, Albert W. Sherer, Jr., contacted Mieczyslaw Sieradski, the deputy director of the North American department of the Polish Foreign Ministry, to clear the landing permit. The American request was immediately forwarded to Rapacki, who got in touch with Polish Workers party chief, Wladyslaw Gomulka, who in turn made certain that Moscow was informed. It was not long before a high-level decision was reached that Poland would receive the special envoy and see what he had to say. The rest was routine procedure: the Air Control Command granted a landing permit, and the Polish Foreign Ministry informed the United States Embassy that Rapacki awaited Harriman.

Harriman and his party landed in Warsaw at 9:30 in the morning and proceeded at once to the American Embassy, where Harriman quickly briefed Gronouski about his mission. By 10:00 Harriman and Gronouski were seated with the foreign minister in Rapacki's office. Also present were two Polish vice foreign ministers: Jozef Winiewicz, who was in charge of U.N. and U.S. affairs in the Ministry; and Jerzy Michalowski, who had previously served on the Indo-China International Control Commission and in 1965 directed and controlled Poland's day-to-day diplomatic activities in Southeast Asia.

These three high-ranking foreign service officials added up to an interesting combination. Rapacki represented the cautious statesman-diplomat; he well knew he had to follow the Soviet foreign policy line to the letter if he wanted to keep his job, and he was prepared to act independently only insofar as he did not disturb Soviet interests.[3] He was a member of the Polish party Politburo, an unusually high position for a foreign minister in a Communist country; among his counterparts elsewhere in the Soviet bloc, János Péter of Hungary, Corneliu Manescu of Rumania, and others were only members of their respective central committees. Privately Rapacki was a great admirer of Ho Chi Minh's independent policy line; when asked which party had greater influence in Hanoi, the Chinese or the Soviet Communist party, he used to answer, "the Vietnamese Workers [Communist] party." As for the outcome of the Vietnam conflict he had the usual East European Communist view. He was convinced that sooner or later the Americans would be driven out. He felt, however, that this objective could be achieved faster through a combined military and diplomatic effort than through protracted guerrilla warfare. Moreover, he was convinced the United States was looking for a face-saving formula to extricate itself from the war, and like his Hungarian counterpart he doubtlessly hoped that he might be the one to come up with this formula.

Vice Foreign Minister Winiewicz and Michalowski were certainly lesser figures in the decision-making process than Rapacki, but they were not without influence. Both were members of the Collegium of the Polish Foreign Ministry, which dealt chiefly with important foreign policy matters and had often participated in Politburo sessions as expert advisers. The two men, however, were quite different in character and personality. By Western standards, Winiewicz appeared reasonable and circumspect and was known for his relatively flexible line; Michalowski, on the other hand, was considered somewhat two-faced, maintaining friendly relations with American and Western diplomats while in reality remaining a consistent hardliner.

At the morning meeting, Harriman and Rapacki quickly dispensed with pleasantries and moved directly to the subject of Vietnam. Rapacki sailed into a castigation of the United States for its heavy bombing of the North, then parried Harriman's reminder that the United States had stopped the bombing indefinitely with the accusation that the United States was acting as an aggressor assisting a puppet government in Saigon. Irritated, Harriman interrupted to say that he had come to Warsaw to discuss serious matters, not propaganda. His government, he said, meant business when it halted the bombing.

Furthermore, the president was willing to withdraw American troops from South Vietnam if the other side would do the same or would sit down at the conference table to find a compromise solution. Then basing his statement on Rusk's Fourteen Points, Harriman presented a general outline of the American position and, point by point, explained the views of the president in detail. Through most of this explanation Rapacki, when he spoke, maintained his rigid line (the usual Polish method of negotiation), emphasizing that Poland stood as a firm ally of the DRV. Finally, however, he expressed willingness to forward the proposal that negotiations between Washington and Hanoi might start in ten days. He did not elaborate on his plans for carrying out this assignment, but Harriman and Gronouski felt confident he would indeed take some action. After all, it was clear that the Polish government had some interest in ending the war, if only because it would then be relieved of the burden of the Kremlin-imposed "United Action for Vietnam" program of supplying the DRV with food and arms. Besides, while the Polish foreign minister wanted to act in cooperation with Moscow, he also wanted to be the one to squeeze more concessions from the Americans and to gauge Ho Chi Minh's reactions.

There was still one important technical problem to be resolved in the Harriman-Rapacki negotiations. Rapacki demanded that the American proposal be tendered in writing. Harriman acceded, but expressed the feeling that the Americans would retain greater maneuverability if the Poles were to compose the text. After long debate, Michalowski was directed to draft a Polish interpretation of the American proposals, to be revised, if need be, in conference with the Americans. At another meeting that evening at Gronouski's residence Michalowski presented a "Five Point" draft the Polish government intended to forward to Hanoi as its interpretation of the United States position for starting negotiations. It was accepted after only a short discussion.

Meanwhile, as it turned out, Rapacki had reserved the whole day for his American guest, and the day was still young. Over luncheon the conferees spun out their conversations on Vietnam and touched upon other international issues, including the German question and the state of Polish-American relations.

When talk began to dwindle, Gronouski suggested that Harriman request a session with Wladislaw Gomulka. He felt that it was important that Gomulka be convinced of Washington's sincerity. Besides, the new U.S. ambassador to Poland had not yet met with the Polish party chief (Gomulka tended to shun all American diplomats), and Harriman's presence would afford a splendid entree.

Harriman and Gomulka had known each other for years. They had first established contact during World War II in Moscow, where Harriman was U.S. ambassador and Gomulka took a leading part in organizing the Polish Workers party as successor to the Polish Communist party, which had been dissolved in 1938 and decimated by the Stalinist purges.[4] In 1960 in New York they met again at Harriman's home, when Gomulka, Khrushchev, and other Communist leaders attended the U.N. General Assembly session.

Meeting with Harriman now in Warsaw, Gomulka appeared committed to a tough, critical, hard-line stance on just about every issue involving United States foreign policy. He attacked the Johnson administration for its "aggression" in Vietnam, accused the Americans of helping to revive "German militarism," and assailed the United States foreign aid program as a form of "neocolonialism." He also proudly asserted that the Polish people were successfully rebuilding their war-ravaged economy despite discriminatory American trade policy.

For about fifteen minutes Harriman suffered this onslaught without saying a word; indeed, the onlookers in the conference room—Gronouski, Vice Foreign Minister Marian Naszkowski, and the interpreter—had almost concluded he was half asleep. But suddenly he broke into an angry rejection of Gomulka's accusations and asked ironically if everything the United States had done in the postwar period was wrong. He pointed to the success of the Marshall Plan in rebuilding Europe and reminded his host of Stalin's refusal to allow Poland to participate in that program. Then, in vitriolic tones, he loosed his own torrent of accusations: if the people of Poland really supported a Communist regime, as Gomulka had so often claimed, why were they so carefully shielded from a broader representation of different views? Why were they not allowed a multi-party system? Why could they not vote in free elections?

Now, in an atmosphere cold with tension, the Polish leader hammered at the charge that President Johnson was to blame for military escalation in Vietnam and repeatedly demanded that the United States stop the bombing of the North without threat of renewal, and withdraw all its troops from the South. Harriman, for his part, doggedly stressed the seriousness of the president's interest in de-escalation and a peaceful settlement, but all he was saying seemed to fall on deaf ears. The Polish party chief began a stubborn reiteration of the theme that the issue of war and peace depended on whether "common sense or political blindness to contemporary realities" was to guide American policy. If the meaning behind this assertion was somewhat ambiguous to his listeners, there was no mistaking the hostility of his manner.

Then, just as it appeared that the exchange had reached a complete impasse, Gomulka abruptly altered his tone of voice and changed the subject. He referred in a friendly and interested way to Harriman's prior meeting with Rapacki, and in a manner implying approval of the Polish mediation. To Harriman, the experienced diplomat, this seemed sufficient guarantee that the Poles would forward the message to Hanoi, and he left Warsaw with a sense of satisfaction and cautious optimism.[5]

Rapacki kept his promise. After obtaining the formal consent of his Politburo, he and his deputy Jerzy Michalowski made a secret trip to Moscow to confer with Gromyko on what to do next. Hungarian Foreign Minister János Péter, who had kept abreast of the evolving situation (he and Rapacki exchanged information right from the beginning of the bombing pause), joined the Poles in Moscow to see what further "useful" role he could play in the affair.

The Polish Initiative

The Rapacki plan was simple. Rapacki wanted his deputy, Michalowski, to go to Hanoi and convey the American proposal. For this he needed Russian endorsement and support. In this respect, however, the situation was somewhat complicated. A high-level Soviet party and government delegation headed by Presidium-member Shelepin was scheduled to visit Hanoi at the same time the Michalowski trip was planned. Naturally the Poles had to find out whether Michalowski's presence in the North Vietnamese capital would interfere with any Kremlin plan.

The three East Europeans had several long sessions with Gromyko, despite the fact that in those days the Soviet foreign minister was even busier than usual. In three days' time, Gromyko, Premier Kosygin, and Defense Minister Rodion Malinovski were to play host to the president of Pakistan and the prime minister of India at a meeting in Tashkent, where attempts would be made to resolve the armed conflict that had broken out over the litigation of Kashmir. From Tashkent, Gromyko was slated to fly to Ulan Bator to support party chief Brezhnev in discussions concerning the prolongation of the Soviet-Mongol mutual defense pact, the deployment of Soviet troops to the Chinese-Mongolian frontier, and Soviet aid. Certainly the foreign minister was heavily involved in the preparations for this trip. In addition, complications over the departure of the Shelepin delegation had him shuttling back and forth all day between the Foreign Ministry and the Kremlin offices of Brezhnev, Kosygin, and Shelepin. He had also to wait for final instructions from Yurii Andropov and Boris N. Ponomarev, the two secretaries of the Central Committee who directed and controlled the execution of party decisions in the field of foreign relations. And finally, there were the usual endless meetings with his own operational directorate—his council of vice ministers. Thus for the moment the Soviet foreign minister had little time to confer with foreign diplomats. Rapacki and Péter, however, posed an exceptional case.

During their discussions Gromyko expressed skepticism about the possibility of some response from Hanoi. Péter and

Rapacki were not as negative as their Russian colleague. Péter proposed that he might try to extract further concessions from the Americans by pressing the old issue of the NLF participation in future conferences. If Washington would agree to allow the representatives of the NLF at the negotiating table, he reasoned, he could go back to Hanoi with a "new" proposal. Gromyko doubted that this was a real possibility but agreed that it was worth a try. Rapacki expressed the opinion that the North Vietnamese and the NLF could not win the war militarily and the time was right to encourage the DRV government to start negotiation with Washington. According to him, Poland, a member of the International Control Commission for Indochina, was well suited to convey this opinion to Ho Chi Minh's leadership. Gromyko was still not convinced. All information he had from his ambassador in Hanoi, Ilya Shcherbakov, indicated that the DRV leadership was not interested in negotiation. In addition, Harriman's proposal and the Twelve-Point proposal Rusk had handed over to the Hungarians were virtually identical, and since Hanoi had already rejected the Hungarian version he could see little reason for Michalowski to go to Vietnam. Yet he did not stop him. In the first place, it was clear that Michalowski's go-between role would in no way disrupt the purposes of the Shelepin mission. In the second place, the Polish initiative might well help to stretch out the badly needed bombing pause, for it was unlikely that Washington would resume air bombardment as long as Michalowski was in Hanoi. And in the third place he did not want to irritate the sensitive Poles. Thus, it was finally agreed that Michalowski would be dispatched to Hanoi to see if there could be any response.

Michalowski proceeded from Moscow via Irkutsk-Ulan Bator to a brief stopover in Peking. He was forced to stay three days in the Chinese capital because bad weather had delayed all civilian flights to Hanoi. While in Peking he paid a courtesy visit to his counterpart, Deputy Foreign Minister Wang Ping-nan, and conferred with the Chinese ambassador to Poland, Wang Kuo-chuan, who had arrived from Warsaw to give his government a first-hand evaluation of the American position on Vietnam.[6]

The Chinese received Michalowski coldly. They made it clear

that Peking favored the continuation of the war and foresaw the likelihood of a full defeat for the United States in Vietnam. Any effort to stop Ho Chi Minh from pushing on to victory, they contended, was a betrayal of the Vietnamese cause, and the Polish willingness to forward the American proposal to Hanoi would be viewed accordingly. In spite of the harsh words, however, Wang Ping-nan treated his guest to the usual thirty-eight course dinner with the 98-proof Chinese rice brandy, the Mao Dai that was required by protocol in the Chinese capital.

Michalowski arrived in Hanoi on January 4 to begin a two-week effort at carrying out his mission. He brought in his attaché case two letters—a personal letter from Gomulka to the aging North Vietnamese party boss Ho Chi Minh and a formal letter from the Central Committee of the Polish United Workers' party to the leadership of the Vietnamese Workers' party. Both letters stressed that the Polish Communists fully shared the views of their Vietnamese comrades on a settlement of the Vietnam problem, but that they also thought political means could be used to achieve victory.

Michalowski conferred most frequently with the Politburo member and foreign minister, Nguyen Duy Trinh. They had known each other since the time Michalowski had served as Polish representative on the International Control Commission. Trinh was known to be a reasonable man and one who was open to suggestion. The Polish version of the American proposal (the "Five Point" proposal) did not, however, win his approval. Like Gromyko in Moscow, he realized that there was no essential difference between the proposal forwarded by the Hungarians and the one proffered by his guest. Nevertheless, he was willing to promise that he would study the Polish position further and discuss it with his colleagues.

Michalowski next met with Prime Minister Pham Van Dong, the chief administrator of the North Vietnam regime and a seasoned statesman whose features seemed perennially composed in a mysterious smile. Dong was one of the closest collaborators of "Uncle Ho"; he was a hard-core Communist and a founder of the Communist party of Indochina. He had hated the French colonialists, and he hated the Americans. Now, at sixty years of age, he was sometimes portrayed as the "dove" in Hanoi, but that was not true. He firmly believed the fortunes of war were on the side of the North Vietnamese simply because, in his view, the United States had no experience in conducting jungle warfare. In explaining this opinion to Michalowski, he asserted that the Americans could send another 100,000 or 150,000 men and they would still be defeated. He further asserted that the American president knew this to be true, which was why Johnson was trying to negotiate—to try to win at the conference table what he knew could not be won on the battlefield. Thus, in Dong's view, peace talks would not be in Hanoi's best interests—at least not at this time.

Michalowski then called on his old friends in the Defense Department. Colonel Ha Van Lau, the head of the North Vietnamese Liaison Office to the International Control Commission, simply dismissed the American proposal as a smokescreen to conceal preparations for further military escalation. Nor was defense minister, General Giap, interested in immediate negotiation; he was convinced that Hanoi could talk to Washington only after the "Liberation Forces" scored a decisive military victory over the Americans and their South Vietnamese puppets, like the one at Dien Bien Phu over the French.

Other North Vietnamese leaders the Polish diplomat visited repeated the same theme with little variation. Some expressed suspicion of President Johnson's intentions or questioned the authority of Harriman to speak for him. Many simply stated that the United States was not yet aware that it was fighting a lost cause, and if Hanoi agreed to sit down to negotiate it would only weaken its own position to no purpose. It was also characteristic that even while discounting the possibility of negotiations, the Vietnamese pressed for more Polish economic and military aid.

On January 7, the Shelepin delegation arrived in Hanoi, and Russo-Vietnamese negotiations, mass meetings, and various social programs absorbed the attention of the DRV leadership. Thereafter, Michalowksi's continued presence in Hanoi went almost unnoticed except when he appeared at diplomatic receptions. For instance, on January 11, at a party given by Ambassador Shcherbakov, Michalowski had an opportunity to converse briefly with Ho Chi Minh. At that time Ho appeared realistic. He was aware that the United States as a major world power would have serious difficulties withdrawing from South Vietnam, and therefore, he said, Hanoi should make no demands that would cause a loss of American prestige. (He added, playfully, that indeed he would roll out the red carpet for the Americans when they left.)

Whatever vacillating hopes Michalowski still entertained for the success of his mission were dashed when he learned from Shcherbakov that Shelepin had offered substantial new military aid to Hanoi and had abstained from recommending negotiations. After that, it was clear to the Polish vice minister that any further attempts to press his cause would be useless. Sore at heart, he packed and left the capital of North Vietnam with the realization that he had accomplished only what Gromyko had expected him to, and no more: he had stayed in Hanoi as long as Shelepin was there, and his presence there had indeed helped to extend the bombing pause. Ho Chi Minh had not moved an inch closer to the conference table.[7]

While Michalowski pursued his disheartening course in Hanoi, Ambassador Harriman was visiting various capitals of the world in a further attempt to carry out his mission for President Johnson. Harriman was empowered to decide for himself where to go, with whom to speak, and how to go about effecting his objective.

From Poland he went to see Tito in his hunting lodge at Brdo, where the Yugoslav leader expressed benevolent interest but offered little effective support: although he sincerely believed the Americans wanted to end the war, he could only urge Moscow through the Soviet ambassador in Belgrade to exert influence in favor of a negotiated settlement. As far as the Chinese were concerned, Tito clearly stated that he could not help at all since the Peking leaders considered him a "revisionist bandit," which was worse than an "American imperialist bandit." Then Harriman hurried on to New Delhi and Peshawar to see Indian Prime Minister Lal Bahadur Shastri and Pakistan President Mohammed Ayub Khan before they left for the Tashkent meeting with Soviet Premier Kosygin. He asked each of them to try at Tashkent to induce Kosygin to use some influence to start negotiations. The ambassador then conferred in Cairo with Nasser, who told him China was adamantly opposed to negotiations but the Soviet Union was more moderate and wanted a peaceful solution. Nasser had a photo of Chou En-lai in his study where the two met, and the ambassador jokingly asked the Egyptian to have their picture taken with Chou's photograph in the background. Finally Nasser promised to speak to both the Russians and the Chinese, but Harriman never heard any results of such an exchange from either of them. In addition, friendly officials in Iran, Thailand, Japan, Australia, Laos, South Vietnam, and the Philippines received Harriman and were informed of America's intentions.

The roving ambassador visited a total of twelve capitals in twenty-two days to carry out his mission for President Johnson. The Fourteen Point peace initiative was widely welcomed, and all the governments and heads of state, after receiving first-hand information from him about American intentions, offered cooperation in one way or the other. It seemed all this earnest effort, this broad-based assurance of good will and cooperation, ought to have produced positive results. However, it did not. For the North Vietnamese were not interested in negotiation; they hoped for a military victory.

On January 13, Michalowski popped up in Vientiane and almost crossed paths with Harriman, who chanced to be in the Laotian captial on the same day. While paying a protocol visit to Premier Prince Souvanna Phouma, Michalowski learned that Harriman was due at the palace in an hour. He departed hurriedly to avoid an embarrassing encounter.[8]

Three days later Michalowski returned to Warsaw. At the airport, by another accident, he bumped into the British ambassador, George Clutton. Without thinking twice, the British diplomat asked him how the North Vietnamese had received Harriman's proposals. At first the surprised Pole did not know what to say. When he found words, however, he admitted his failure in bringing a favorable response from Ho Chi Minh—but the reason for that failure, he claimed, was the strong Chinese influence in Hanoi. His remark was quickly forwarded to Ambassador Gronouski, and any hope Washington might have attached to the Polish mediation vanished.

The Humphrey-Kosygin Meeting

While Harriman tried to reach Hanoi through the East European and Third World countries, Vice President Hubert H. Humphrey, Johnson's top-ranking peace envoy, hoped to sound out the possibilities of ending the Vietnam conflict by soliciting Soviet Premier Kosygin's good offices for mediation. As did other emissaries, he carried with him Dean Rusk's Fourteen Point Plan for a negotiated settlement of the war.

Humphrey's first stop was Japan on December 28–29. There, despite widespread local criticism of the American involvement in Vietnam, he was able to secure the support of Premier Eisaku Sato and Foreign Minister Etsusaboro Shiina. They agreed that Shiina, during an upcoming visit to Moscow, would press the Soviet leaders to exert a moderating influence in Southeast Asia in order to bring Hanoi to the conference table.[9] In Manila, Humphrey had attended the inauguration of Philippine President Ferdinand Marcos and participated in what he felt was a productive exchange of views concerning world problems, particularly those in Southeast Asia. Humphrey genuinely impressed Marcos by telling him that the Johnson administration was committed to utilizing the Asian Development Bank's resources for rebuilding Vietnam as well as the rest of Asia. Humphrey then flew to Taiwan, there to confront the aging leader, Kuomintang President Chiang Kai-shek. Chiang voiced strong opposition to the American containment policy in Vietnam; he was convinced the best way to save South Vietnam was to uproot the strongest supporter of Ho Chi Minh, Mao Tse-tung—and coincidentally, like the Kremlin, he believed 1965 was the year to do it, while the Chinese Communists' atomic weapons system was still in an embryonic stage. To this end he was ready to invade the mainland with his half-million troops, which he said were well trained and well equipped. He needed only American logistic support for the undertaking, but whenever he urged military intervention the Americans turned him down.[10] Concerning the success of Johnson's peace plan, the Nationalist Chinese demonstrated skepticism. There was no point in Humphrey's wasting further time in Taiwan. All he could do was to pledge, once again, the safety and integrity of the island nation. He did that, and left the same day he arrived (January 1).

The last leg of his trip was to Seoul, South Korea. Here, the vice president had to be specific in assuring President Park Chung-hee and his cabinet that while President Johnson was earnestly seeking peace in Vietnam he was not prepared to purchase it with appeasement.[11] The South Koreans still remembered the negative effects of the protracted truce negotiations at Panmunjom in the days of the Korean War. Moreover, Korea had a full army division and a special unit in South Vietnam, a combined force of some 20,000 men, and was expected to send additional troops if the peace overture failed.

Back in Washington, Humphrey reported the results of his mission to the president and his chief advisers. He called together a news conference to inform the news media that he had found no evidence on his tour that the Communists were willing to sit down at the conference table. It looked as if the vice president's direct involvement in the "peace offensive" had come to an end. But Humphrey stayed only a few days in Washington. On January 12, he and Dean Rusk boarded a military jetliner to attend the state funeral of Indian Premier Shastri. That sad occasion provided more than one opportunity for the Americans to speak with Soviet Premier Kosygin, who was also present at Delhi.

Humphrey and Kosygin were seated next to each other at the funeral ceremony. They met again on an early morning walk in the garden of the Redstone Presidential Palace, where both were staying. Finally, they had a long conversation at the residence of Soviet Ambassador Ivan A. Benediktov. Kosygin was willing to discuss general questions ranging from mutual concerns affecting the relations of the two superpowers to the whole scope of affairs in the troubled world. He was decidedly reluctant, however, to speak about Vietnam. In the first place, he never liked to discuss matters for which he was not well prepared, for apparently he had secured neither specific directives concerning Vietnam from party boss Brezhnev nor authorization from the Politburo to discuss the issue. Humphrey nonetheless conveyed the congratulations of his own government for the recently signed Tashkent accord (*see* pp. 174-176) and expressed hope that the same spirit might be extended to other troubled areas of the world. He called Kosygin's attention to the long halt in the bombing of the North and made it clear that corresponding evidence of restraint on the part of Hanoi would be welcomed in Washington and would influence future American actions. Rusk outlined his Fourteen Points peace proposal and repeated his offer to consider Pham Van Dong's Four Points along with the American proposals.

But Kosygin remained inflexible. In addition to continuing the bombing pause, he said, the United States should not introduce new troops. On the contrary, it must withdraw all its troops from South Vietnam; those were the preconditions to any negotiations with the DRV. He even asserted that he had reason to believe the United States was planning to expand the war to Laos and Cambodia, and, he added, the war in Vietnam had cast a shadow over relations between Moscow and Washington. In any case, there was no point in the Soviet Union's attempting to assume an intermediary role in the Vietnamese conflict, he concluded, because Hanoi clearly was not interested in the latest American proposal.

The talks passed without unusual emotional outbursts. Sources close to Chester Bowles, the American ambassador in New Delhi, observed that the conversations were at all times candid and diplomatically polite in tone. They yielded no meaningful results even so; for the wary Kosygin dared not concede any point that might jeopardize Soviet influence in Hanoi or lessen the effectiveness of his country's campaign against its number one enemy, Communist China.

The Byroade Channel

Parallel with their wide-open peace offensive, the Americans attempted to make use of secret diplomacy to bring about negotiations. According to a Pentagon study, the establishment of a direct and unpublicized line of communication seemed necessary "since all the intermediaries (i.e., the Hungarians, the Poles, and the neutral powers), in one way or another, had a definite interest in the success of their role; all transmission from them had to be viewed with some skepticism."[12] Moreover Dean Rusk was convinced by long experience with Communist negotiators that Hanoi would take seriously only those offers that were made in secret.

Henry A. Byroade, United States ambassador to Burma, was the man chosen to initiate this action. The administration must have decided that neutral Burma was a promising place to open up a channel for delicate behind-the-scenes negotiations. The unique position enjoyed by the American ambassador in Rangoon also doubtlessly contributed to the decision.

Byroade was an old hand in Far Eastern affairs. He had served in the Fourteenth Air Force and Air Service Command in the China-Burma-India theater during World War II. After the war, a much-decorated officer, he was the first military attaché accredited to Chiang Kai-shek's China. From that post he was sent to Washington, where he was attached to the general staff of the army as an intelligence officer.

When the Truman administration established the Office of German Affairs as an agency of the War Department in 1949, Byroade was asked to head the new agency. The choice proved a fortunate one until a dispute erupted between Secretary of State Dean Acheson and Secretary of Defense Louis Johnson over plans for the future of NATO and the extent of German participation in it. Polemics in this dispute soon reached such proportions that Secretary Johnson forbade officials in the Pentagon even to speak with their counterparts in the State Department without his prior knowledge. Byroade, meanwhile, had managed to preserve independence in the quarrel and was able to serve as a liaison between the two departments.[13]

In 1952, Byroade switched from military to diplomatic service and became first an assistant secretary of state and later an ambassador. In 1963, he was glad to return to Burma, for many of his old wartime friends were now the leaders of this relatively quiet Asian country, and he liked the land and its people. One of his friends in Burma was General Ne Win, the prime minister, who had equally good relations with leaders in the West and the East and maintained contacts with Chou En-lai and Ho Chi Minh. These circumstances particularly favored the ambassador as a condidate to undertake a sensitive mission for his government.

The action started on December 29, 1965, when Byroade received a cable-instruction from Dean Rusk. He was to seek a meeting with the North Vietnamese ambassador in Rangoon and notify him about the bombing halt:

> As you are no doubt aware, there has been no bombing in North Vietnam since December 24 although some reconnaissance flights have continued. No decision has been made regarding a resumption of bombing and unless there is a major provocation we would hope that the present stand-down, which is in its fifth day, could extend beyond New Year.[14]

Byroade was also asked to say: "If your government will now reciprocate [the American initiative] by making a serious contribution toward peace, it would obviously have a favorable effect on the possibility of further extending the suspension."

Furthermore he was authorized to state that Washington was willing to start negotiations on the basis of the Geneva Agreements of 1954 and 1962; to propose the conclusions of a cease fire; and to discuss Hanoi's Four Points along with the United States proposals. The State Department message pointed out that the United States was ready to withdraw its forces from Vietnam after peace was assured, and stressed that the United States was not seeking military bases in Southeast Asia. The Johnson administration would support free elections and was pledged to leave the question of reunification of North and South Vietnam to the free decision of the Vietnamese people. Finally, the United States offered economic aid to North Vietnam as well as to South Vietnam. In other words, the ambassador was to forward a message summing up the American position along the lines of Rusk's Fourteen Points package.

In his instruction the secretary added that those key Communist governments who were in touch with Hanoi had received the same communication (Rusk obviously alluded to the Hungarian, Polish, and the Soviet governments). Nevertheless, he attributed great importance to having his message forwarded directly to the DRV government.

Byroade quickly contacted the DRV Embassy in Rangoon. The ambassador was unavailable, but he managed to contact Consul General Vu Huu Binh and advise him that he wished to deliver a message. A few hours later (the consul general apparently either had to wait for instructions from his headquarters or needed time for himself to decide), Byroade received an answer: the North Vietnamese would gladly speak with him.

It was 3 P.M. of the same day when the two met in the consul general's office. After friendly handshakes and an exchange of diplomatic niceties, Byroade handed over the written message. Vu Huu Binh studied the document with his English translator for a short time, then promised to transmit it to his superiors.

The two diplomats agreed to get together if an answer was forthcoming from Hanoi and to keep the matter in strict confidence. As a matter of international courtesy, Byroade was to inform his host country's foreign minister, U Thi Han of Burma, and his deputy U Soe Tin about his meeting with the Vietnamese. The next day the ambassador learned from U Thi Han that Vu had indeed forwarded the message to his government. This in itself was good news for the American, the more so since this time the consul general did not ask his Chinese colleague in Rangoon to forward the message, as he usually did, but used the regular Burmese commercial cable service to communicate with his headquarters.

The prospect of a face-to-face meeting between the American and North Vietnamese representatives raised hopes in Washington. Recalling the experience of the previous May, Rusk considered it a positive sign that the North Vietnamese representative had not preemptorily returned the American communication. What is more, he and his aides were convinced that if Hanoi really meant to take up serious contact with Washington and start direct negotiations, the Rangoon message would give Ho Chi Minh every reason to do so.

But Ho Chi Minh chose otherwise. On January 4, his Foreign Ministry issued a statement flatly rejecting the peace overture. Then the Hanoi officials fell silent and two weeks elapsed without any indication of their intentions. On January 21 when

Byroade again met his North Vietnamese contact and pressed for an answer, Vu Huu Binh told the ambassador that he had not yet received instructions from his government to reply officially but was ready to offer his personal views. First, he had found in the tone and the content of the American message an ultimatum—and, he added, the DRV Foreign Ministry's statement of January 4 indicated the same position. Second, he complained that the United States had not kept the Rangoon contact confidential. Finally, he charged that the American president clearly was not sincere, since 4,000 new U. S. troops had landed in South Vietnam during the bombing pause and more arrivals were expected. If Ambassador Byroade still had any doubts about Hanoi's real intentions, they were quickly dispelled when, three days later, Vu sent an aide-memoire to his American colleague repeating word for word what he had elaborated as his private opinion.

Then in the middle of January the Americans forwarded a second message to the DRV Embassy, this time in Moscow. Again Washington urged Hanoi to enter into private and direct talks to work out a peaceful settlement. But United States Ambassador Kohler was told by his Vietnamese counterpart that the Americans should communicate only with the DRV consul general in Rangoon. Consequently, on January 27, Byroade asked Vu once more whether he had any instruction from his government; Vu had none then, but four days later he had Hanoi's answer. Once and for all the Fourteen Point American proposal was rejected, and once more it was underlined that there could be no settlement in Vietnam until "the United States Government has accepted the 'Four Point' stand of the Government of the Democratic Republic of Vietnam, has proved this by actual deeds, has stopped unconditionally and for good its air raids and all other acts of war against the Democratic Republic of Vietnam."[15]

The Resumption of the Bombing

While the Byroade-Vu dialogue was running its rather unproductive course, Washington was buzzing like a behive. Public opinion was divided. Richard Cardinal Cushing, archbishop of Boston, civil rights leader Reverend Dr. Martin Luther King, Jr., Reverend Dr. Eugene Carson Blake of the United Presbyterian Church, and Rabbi Jacob Weinstein were among the influential personalities who called on President Johnson to make him aware of the swelling consensus across the United States against the war and to pressure him not to resume the bombing.

The Congress also was split. An Associated Press poll conducted among fifty senators demonstrated that twenty-five favored and twenty-five opposed resumption of bombing North Vietnam. Armed Services Committee Chairman Richard B. Russell of Georgia and Senator John Stennis of Mississippi wanted immediate resumption; Senate Foreign Relations Committee Chairman J. W. Fulbright, Mike Mansfield of Montana, and Robert F. Kennedy of New York argued for the prolongation of the lull. In a speech on the floor of the Senate, John Sherman Cooper of Kentucky suggested that President Johnson should clarify that negotiations could include the Viet Cong because neither negotiation nor settlement was possible without their inclusion. Senator Joseph S. Clark of Pennsylvania maintained that President Johnson should have complete freedom to play out the string for peace. A resolute critic of the war, Senator Ernest Gruening, Democrat from Alaska, proposed amendments to pending bills that would prohibit sending draftees to combat duty in Vietnam. In opposition to these doves, Senator Bourke B. Hickenlooper of Iowa thought it would be a mistake to stop the pressure on North Vietnam, and Representative L. Mendel Rivers of South Carolina favored not only the resumption of the bombing but demanded a free hand for the military command in conducting the war. House Minority Leader Gerald R. Ford of Michigan echoed the Republican theme that "there is no substitute for victory." Finally, Senator

Stuart Symington of Missouri, who had just returned from a Vietnam tour, urged the President to make a final decision either to win the war or get out of it.

High officials in the administration had differing views also as to what should be done next about Vietnam. The military, who from the very beginning had strongly objected to the suspension of the bombing, now requested an immediate resumption. General Westmoreland cabled the Pentagon on December 27:

> Considering the course of the war in South Vietnam and the capability which has been built up here by the PAVN/VC forces [People's Army of (North) Vietnam and Viet Cong]—the full impact of which we have not yet felt—the curtailment of operations in North Vietnam is unsound from the military standpoint. Indeed we should now step up our effort to higher levels.[16]

Ambassador Lodge backed Westmoreland's recommendation, and Admiral Sharp angrily added: "the armed forces of the United States should not be required to fight this war with one arm tied behind their backs." The Joint Chiefs of Staff fully agreed with them and recommended the resumption of the bombing with a dramatically sharper blow on major targets, including petroleum depots and electric power plants, and the mining of the ports of North Vietnam. In addition, they pressed for the elimination of the so-called sanctuaries around Hanoi, Haiphong, and the North Vietnamese-Chinese border and asked permission to destroy the Soviet-built surface-to-air missles "to prevent interference with planned air operation."[17]

The proposal of the military, however, was not endorsed by McNamara. In his memorandum to the president on January 24, 1966, he did not even bring up the Chiefs' recommendations at all. Instead he suggested that for 1966 the bombing program against North Vietnam should be limited to 4,000 attack sorties per month; around-the-clock armed reconnaissance against rail and road targets and petroleum storage sites should continue; and the present sanctuaries should be preserved.[18]

The same line of thinking emerged from William Bundy's memorandum of January 15. He strongly suggested that:

> Resumed bombing should not begin with a dramatic strike that was

even at the margin of past practice (such as the power plant in December). For a period of two-three weeks at least, while the world is digesting and assessing the pause, we should do as little as possible to lend fuel to the charge—which will doubtless be the main theme of Communist progaganda—that the pause was intended all along as a prelude to more drastic action.[19]

On January 25 George Ball joined the debate by raising his voice against the renewal of the air strikes. He came up with the grim forecast that sustained bombing of North Vietnam would more than likely lead the United States into war with Red China—probably in six to nine months—and could trigger at least a limited war with the Soviet Union. The mining of Haiphong harbor, he predicted, could bring Soviet retaliation in the form of increased aid, even perhaps the sending of Russian volunteers to North Vietnam. The bombing of the airfield would force the North Vietnamese to use Chinese air bases, which in turn would lead to a direct Washington-Peking confrontation. From all these he concluded, "If the war is to be won—it must be won in the South" and "the bombing of the North cannot win the war, only enlarge it."[20]

The warning of George Ball, however, was ignored. The same day his memorandum reached the president's desk, Johnson called a joint White House meeting of the National Security Council and a bipartisan group of Congressional leaders. There McNamara presented a detailed intelligence report on North Vietnamese infiltration activities, pointing out that Hanoi had used the bombing pause to increase its shipments of war supplies to the Viet Cong through the Ho Chi Minh Trail and also accelerated sending its regular troops from north to south.[21] Then Dean Rusk added to the picture by telling the group that not only the public statements of the North Vietnamese government but also the behind-the-scenes diplomatic negotiations with Hanoi had revealed that Ho Chi Minh was interested in starting negotiations only on his own terms, and for the time being he seemed to be convinced he could best achieve his objectives through military means. The president fully agreed with his advisers' presentation and assessment and left little doubt that the one-month-old suspension of the bombing was drawing rapidly to a close.

Following the White House meeting, official sources in Washington disclosed that American diplomats had received instructions from the State Department to notify those governments which had been consulted during Johnson's "peace offensive" that the bombing halt had created great danger for American ground troops in South Vietnam and could not be maintained much longer. In Washington, Ambassador Thompson contacted Russian Ambassador Dobrynin and asked whether the Soviet diplomatic activities promised in late November had produced any progress in bringing the DRV closer to the conference table. Dobrynin could give him no encouraging news. On January 28, I received a telephone call from Secretary Rusk. The secretary asked whether I had any new word from Foreign Minister János Péter. I had to give a negative answer but promised to check with my headquarters. I sent an urgent cable to Budapest, suggesting that Hanoi be alerted to the danger of a resumption of the bombing and asking for an immediate answer concerning the results of the intervention because, in my opinion, a resumption of the bombing was only hours away. I received no reply.

The same day I sent my warning to Budapest, Hanoi Radio broadcast the text of a letter President Ho Chi Minh had sent four days earlier to Peking, Moscow, Budapest, Warsaw, and the other Communist capitals as well as to world leaders "interested in the Vietnam situation." Ho denounced the American offer of unconditional peace talks as "an effort to fool public opinion," and called on "all peace-loving governments and peoples the world over to resolutely stay the hands of the U. S. war criminals." He then repeated his contention that the National Front for the Liberation of South Vietnam must be accepted as the "sole genuine representative of the people of South Vietnam," and if the United States wanted peace it must engage in negotiations with the NLF. In conclusion he stated point-blank:

> So long as the U. S. army of aggression still remains on our soil, our people will resolutely fight against it. If the U. S. Government really wants a peaceful settlement, it must accept the four-point stand of the DRV and prove this by actual deeds. It must end unconditionally and for good all bombing raids and other war acts against the DRV. Only

in this way can a political solution to the Vietnam problem be envisaged.[22]

After this direct challenge, hardly anyone believed Johnson would maintain the bombing pause. Only Poland's foreign minister, Adam Rapacki, thought otherwise. Throughout the entire period of the pause he, his deputy Michalowski, and other high ranking officials in the Polish Foreign Ministry tried to warn the Americans of the grave consequences of an eventual resumption of bombing. On the other hand, of course, their efforts to prepare the way for negotiations had failed. On January 29, Rapacki decided to make a last minute attempt to prolong the lull. He summoned the British ambassador and the American chargé to his office in quick succession and told them that the Polish government had trusted information that President Johnson was soon to order the resumption of bombing and in his opinion this would be a fatal mistake. He claimed that Ho Chi Minh's letter had revealed an important change in the Vietnamese position, a change that was obscured by an unfortunate translation error. Rapacki cited the key sentence of the letter: "If the U. S. Government really wants a peaceful settlement, it must *accept* the four-point stand of the DRV," and added that in the original French text Ho demanded the United States "recognize" not "accept" his four points. For this reason the foreign minister was asking for an extension of the pause and offering his good offices to clarify the translation error in Hanoi. Not fully trusting the diplomats, Rapacki contacted the influential newspaper editor Norman Cousins in New York. Explaining to him the "error" in the translation, he asked Cousins to intervene with his friends in the American government on behalf of the postponement of the bombing. The editor promptly forwarded the message to the State Department.

The American Embassy in Warsaw, not wanting to let the Poles off the hook, proposed to explore this last minute offer. Rusk, considering the situation, asked the British to double-check the differences in the translation. London, in turn, ordered its Embassy in Moscow to contact the Vietnamese diplomatic mission there. The British Ambassador Thomas Brimelow quickly executed the inquiry and the North Vietnamese representative flatly stated that the difference in translation was sheer nonsense.[23] The Foreign Office conveyed the answer to Washington, and Johnson, after consulting once more with Congressional leaders and the National Security Council, made the decision to resume the air strikes against North Vietnam on January 31.

The Budapest File

I learned a great deal more about the behind-the-scenes actions connected with the December–January bombing pause the following summer in Budapest. First and foremost, it became clear to me that Hungary's foreign minister, János Péter, who had presented himself to the United States government as an "honest broker" for a peaceful settlement of the Vietnam War, acted on the basis of knowledge he did not have.

I had long working sessions with my immediate superior, the director of the U. S. and NATO countries in the Ministry, Ambassador Vencel Házi. I conferred with Deputy Foreign Minister Béla Szilágyi and Foreign Minister Péter. I spent days at the party headquarters, where I was briefed and debriefed by the staff of the Central Committee Department of International Relations. I visited several members of the Politburo and the government; and perhaps what was the most interesting, I was able to see the Foreign Ministry's entire Vietnam file for the period of the long bombing pause.

From my conversations and from the file itself, it was absolutely clear that Péter at no time had any message or authorization from Hanoi. On the contrary, he acted against Hanoi's wishes. When the Hungarian chargé d'affaires informed North Vietnamese officials of Rusk's Twelve Point proposal, the director of European affairs in the DRV Foreign Ministry told him flatly that his government did not consider the situation ripe for negotiations. The American ground troops were posing fewer problems for them than had the French expeditionary forces, he claimed, and the aerial bombing had not seriously affected the transport of supplies. Furthermore, all North Vietnam was asking from the socialist countries was that they increase their military and economic assistance; otherwise the DRV could handle the situation unaided. Finally, the Hungarian was asked whether Péter really supported Hanoi's Four Points and whether he perhaps did not understand "the peace trickery of American imperialists." To make certain there remained no misinterpretation whatever, the DRV ambassador in Budapest, Huang Luong, called on Péter and told him in plain words: the American proposal does not appeal to the comrades in Hanoi, least of all to Ho Chi Minh. The only correct solution to the Vietnam question must be one based on the well-known Four Points of the government of the Democratic Republic of Vietnam.

Péter, of course, did not give up easily. He argued that Hungary was sincere in extending diplomatic support, just as it was ready to offer economic and military assistance to the DRV. When I was in Budapest that summer, the North Vietnamese in Hanoi and in Budapest were still exceedingly cool toward Péter for what he had done via my intermediary role. By way of explaining their position, they stated that during the Franco-Vietminh war they had talked to the French while the fighting was still going on; they would know how to go about talking with the Americans in similar conditions if ever it should appear that the time was right.

I then asked a high official in the Foreign Ministry on what basis Péter had presumed to mediate between the DRV and the Americans. "Properly speaking," he said, "the whole move was without any basis, because our Vietnamese friends were not interested in discussions. Péter does such things; he wants to be a great statesman."

"However," my informant added amicably, "it would be best if you do not poke your nose into the affair because you will only end up in trouble. Meanwhile, we should be grateful that we managed to get out of this Vietnam pickle."

It was a sound piece of advice, for sharp disagreements had arisen within the Hungarian Politburo when Péter continued to play his go-between role in the face of Hanoi's explicit disapproval. Several members of the Politburo, including such important men as Administrative Secretary Béla Biszku (the number two man in the party), ideologue Dezsö Nemes, and Defense Minister Lajos Czinege, were strongly critical. The Vietnamese comrades had rejected the foreign minister's mediation once, they kept saying, and unless they changed their minds Hungary should not pry further into the affair. The rest of the Politburo either remained neutral or went along with Péter's "idea": to "make the Americans show their cards." Premier Gyula Kállai, Secretary Zoltán Komocsin, and others argued that Péter's actions certainly could not hurt the interests of the DRV, and might ultimately extend the bombing pause by keeping alive the belief in Washington that a conference on Vietnam was feasible.

The Hungarian "mediation" also stirred up controversy between the foreign minister and Frigyes Puja, the influential director of the Central Committee Department of International Relations. Puja, who was a combination party functionary and political realist, had joined the Communist party in 1944 and started his political career as a village party secretary in his home town, Battonya, in southern Hungary. Since then his star had been steadily on the rise. He first became an instructor on the county party committee of Baja, then desk officer at the party headquarters' mass organization department in Budapest. In the period of the great purges (1949-1953), when the Hungarian Stalinist satrap Mátyás Rákosi liquidated or imprisoned thousands of Communists, Puja was not yet prominent enough to be persecuted. The "Department of Cadres" (the personnel department of the party headquarters) sent him to the two-year Higher Party School. In 1953 Puja was transferred to the Foreign Ministry.

He was not to stay long in home service, however; he soon became Hungarian minister in Stockholm. In 1955, he was appointed to head the Hungarian Legation in Vienna, where he promptly became a participant in the perennially intense East-West diplomatic thrust-and-parry of that neutral capital, and a keen observer of the complex espionage activities of various Communist and Western intelligence agencies working there. He maintained friendly relations with the Soviet ambassador during the turbulent weeks of the 1956 Revolution, a time when most Hungarian diplomats assiduously avoided appearing in public with their Russian colleagues. In 1959 he was promoted to the post of vice foreign minister. Thereafter he made a number of trips to Moscow and had the opportunity to study the organization and management of the Soviet Foreign Ministry. Back in Budapest, he was to apply this newly acquired knowledge to a reorganization of the Hungarian Foreign Office.

Puja and his wife found ready social acceptance in the highest party circles in Hungary, and it was not long before First Secretary Kádár, a devotee of chess, discovered his new vice foreign minister was an apt and willing player. In December 1963, when Kádár reshuffled his cabinet and the central party apparatus, he nominated Puja to succeed the inefficient and vain Imre Hollai as director of the Department of International Relations of the Central Committee. This important promotion not only expanded the scope of his duties greatly but also enabled him to treat the foreign minister from then on as his equal. In addition, his daily contacts with Hungarian party leaders and his close cooperation with the departments of international relations of other Communist parties gave him a vantage point in the center of events.

In 1966, the Kremlin launched a worldwide drive to bring over Communist parties in Asia and elsewhere from the Chinese side to the Soviet bloc as a first step toward organizing a new international "unity" conference of Communist leaders. All East European party headquarters were asked to aid in the task, and it was Puja's responsibility to oversee the Hungarian contribution to Soviet policy. It was in this connection that Péter's dealings with the Americans created problems for him. As Puja told his close associates more than once, his main concern was that unwanted Hungarian mediation would only irritate the Vietnamese Communists and provide grist for Peking's anti-Soviet propaganda mill.[24]

The debate over the wisdom and propriety of Péter's actions descended into limbo when Budapest learned that Shelepin had signed a new aid agreement in Hanoi on January 12, 1966, and had furthermore promised increased Soviet aid to Ho Chi Minh and the National Liberation Front. The members of the Hungarian Politburo, as well as Puja and Péter, were quick to see that, far from fostering negotiations, Moscow was intent on making the Vietnamese leadership as dependent as possible on future Soviet deliveries of sophisticated new weaponry.

Interestingly enough, Budapest apparently was not at all concerned about what might happen to Hungary's international reputation while her foreign minister pursued his dubious game. What is more, although the leaders in the party worried about Vietnamese and Chinese reactions, nobody seemed disturbed at the knowledge that the Americans would sooner or later discover Péter's deception. They rationalized that if the Hungarian efforts resulted only in the bombing being suspended for a few more days, this at least saved a few hundred North Vietnamese lives.

When I had a chance to speak with Péter about it, I asked, "What can I say to Rusk and Bundy?"

"It is not necessary to say anything," was his reply. "Anyhow, the Americans think the Chinese stopped our action at the last minute."

I returned to the United States in a depressed mood.

CHAPTER VII

The Kremlin's Two-Front Battle

Throughout the thirty-seven-day bombing pause there had been no visible change in basic Soviet foreign policy. The main problems remained: how to wage cold war against the "dogmatist, adventurist, and phrase-mongering" Chinese Communists and how to pursue most effectively the "anti-imperialist struggle" against the United States. In both cases the attention of Soviet policy-makers centered around the war in Vietnam.

Interestingly enough, the slowly unfolding Great Proletarian Cultural Revolution in China had little noticeable impact on the Kremlin's attitudes at that time. Certainly there was no dearth of bitter remarks to be heard in the Soviet capital about the "hostile Chinese"; but that was not unusual. Moreover, Brezhnev and his close associates displayed no symptoms of new concern; they seemed content to reiterate criticisms they had already aired many times before. As an instrument of foreign policy, the new Chinese movement was seen as but another manifestation of Chinese great-power nationalism, the cutting edge of which was directed against the Soviet Union. It did indeed look as though Mao Tse-tung was also bent on suppressing resistance inside China, but how far he intended to carry that suppression was not at all clear. Soviet leaders were still hopeful that anti-Mao forces in the Chinese party and government, as well as in the army, would survive to change the situation for the better. And although nobody mentioned Liu Shao-ch'i's name, it was an open secret among high officials in Eastern Europe that Liu was the Kremlin's favorite to succeed the aging Mao.

Meanwhile, while Mao still held the reins of power in China, the Communist party of the Soviet Union wanted to do everything possible to eliminate Peking as another center of world communism. To this end, Moscow had first charged Mao Tse-tung and his adherents with betrayal of Marxist-Leninist principles, citing as an example the well-known article by Lin Piao—"Long Live the Victory of the People's War." Soviet ideologues contended that the concept of world revolution set forth in that article—an encirclement of the city by the village[1]—was a complete revision of the Marxist doctrine of historical mission and the leading role of the working class in the revolution. Of course, neither the denial of the "historical role" nor the negation of the "vanguard role" caused real alarm in Moscow. What really mattered was that Lin Piao preached "people's war" and advertised "encirclement" not only against the advanced capitalist countries but against the Soviet Union as well.

Soviet ideologues also sharply criticized the Chinese party leaders for their disruptive agitation in the international Communist movement and assailed Peking's organization of anti-Moscow factional party groups in some thirty countries. By supporting these groups, Moscow charged, the Chinese were not only interfering with the internal affairs of other Communist parties but were also attempting to force "putschist" tactics upon them. Moscow further blamed Peking for the abortive Communist coup and resulting disaster to the party in Indonesia and suggested that such Peking-inspired ventures could only imperil the leadership and the activists of a number of other Communist parties.

All this of course was not a new policy. As director of the

Asian Division of the Foreign Ministry from 1959–61, I obtained information of this policy and continued to follow Asian events thereafter. Originally the anti-Chinese campaign had been initiated when Khrushchev had attempted to pressure China by economic means, control her militarily (through a "unified nuclear command" where only the Russians had access to the atomic warheads), isolate Mao internationally, and finally encourage Marshal P'eng Teh-huai to overthrow the ailing and aged Mao. But Khrushchev's effort failed. The Russian economic pressure counted for nothing, Chairman Mao's influence in the international Communist movement gathered strength, Chinese scientists developed the atomic bomb, and reportedly Marshal P'eng Teh-huai was sent to a "reform through labor" camp to be "reeducated."

Following Khrushchev's ouster from power, the new leadership in the Kremlin seemingly changed tactics. It suspended the anti-Chinese propaganda assaults and invited a high level Chinese party and government delegation to the 1964 October Revolution celebration in Moscow.

The Chinese, obviously interested in finding out what change, if any, the Russians planned to introduce in their overall policy and in Sino-Soviet relations in particular, sent Chou En-lai to the Soviet capital. He traveled with his old friend Marshal Ho Lung, the vice premier of the State Council and a Politburo member; K'ang Sheng, an alternate member of the Politburo, who in the Secretariat of the Central Committee was in charge of supervising inter-party relations; Liu Hsiao, deputy foreign minister; Wu Hsiu-ch'uan, a Soviet specialist of the Central Committee's International Department; and other experts who had participated in previous Sino-Soviet negotiations.

At first the outlook for Sino-Soviet reconciliation looked promising. In his celebration speech, Brezhnev appealed to the Chinese to improve interstate relations and to tolerate differences in methods of socialist construction, with effectiveness being the test of correctness. The Chinese press reprinted the Brezhnev speech, and *Jen-min Jih-pao* published an editorial on this occasion, making reference only to temporary Sino-Soviet difficulties that could be gradually dissolved.[2] On November

13, 1964, Brezhnev, Kosygin, Mikoyan, Podgorny, Ponomarev, and Gromyko conferred with their Chinese guests in the Kremlin. According to a *Tass* communiqué, the discussion was held in a frank atmosphere of camaraderie. Two days later Chou En-lai flew back home. At the Peking airport he was greeted by Mao Tse-tung, whose presence underlined the importance the Chinese attached to Chou En-lai's mission.

There were other signs hinting that a Sino-Soviet reconciliation was in the making. For instance, at the January 19–20 (1965) Warsaw meeting of the Warsaw Pact Political Consultative Committee, Brezhnev assured Peking that the Warsaw Pact supported the Chinese idea of calling a World Leaders Summit Conference where the complete ban of nuclear arms could be discussed.[3] True, the Russians were not willing to go as far as to comply with what Peking really wanted: renunciation of the already existing nuclear test ban treaty. Nevertheless the "gesture" was considered by some East European leaders as a significant step toward the elimination of Soviet-Chinese differences. Meanwhile, the Soviet party propaganda apparatus made considerable efforts to convince fraternal Communist parties that Moscow had no intention of excommunicating the Chinese Communist party or others from the Communist movement. All it wanted was to reestablish cohesion and unity in the movement. Along the same lines, Soviet diplomats in Washington and elsewhere indicated in private that they hoped for a gradual improvement in Sino-Soviet state relations. Gromyko, who attended the yearly United Nations General Assembly meeting, told Soviet bloc diplomats that he thought the split was something that should be reduced if possible.

But behind the scenes, the Soviets acted differently. On November 24, 1964, the Soviet party Central Committee sent out a circular letter calling together a consultative meeting of thirty-six Communist parties for March 1, 1965, a project which Chou En-lai had strongly opposed during his stay in Moscow. To lessen Peking's influence in North Korea and North Vietnam, Premier Kosygin personally visited Pyongyang and Hanoi and during lengthy negotiations promised to renew the flow of economic and military aid to both governments which had been cut off by Khrushchev.

To meet these challenges, the Chinese resumed their anti-Soviet propaganda campaign, this time under the slogan "Khrushchevism without Khrushchev." They bluntly stated that there was no shade of difference between Brezhnev and Khrushchev on the questions of the international Communist movement and relations with China. They charged that Moscow, at Washington's request, had used its influence to persuade Hanoi to stop sending military supplies to the Viet Cong and to have the Viet Cong halt its attacks on South Vietnamese urban areas. Moreover, they presented Kosygin's visit to Hanoi as one of "betrayal of the South Vietnamese people." "When Kosygin . . . passed through Peking on his visit to Vietnam in February 1965 and exchanged views with Chinese leaders," stated Peking, "[Kosygin] . . . stressed the need to help the United States find a way out of Vietnam."[4]

Naturally the Soviets counterattacked, rebuffing the charges as utterly groundless and slanderous, provocative fabrications permeated with a spirit of hostility toward the Soviet people and toward the Communist party of the Soviet Union. They claimed that although Premier Kosygin had stopped in Peking he had not advocated any negotiated settlement of the war. Moreover, according to Moscow, Peking turned down Kosygin's proposal for normalizing Soviet-Chinese state relations through greatly extended trade; scientific, technical, and cultural cooperation; and foreign policy coordination.

Following Kosygin's visit in Peking, the Chinese used all kinds of strategems to discredit the Soviets. For example, on March 4, when Soviet authorities organized a "spontaneous" demonstration of foreign students at the American Embassy in Moscow, the Chinese students, who were also asked by the Russians to participate, unexpectedly doublecrossed their hosts. In the middle of the demonstration, on a given signal, they attacked the security guard who protected the embassy compound, shouted anti-Soviet slogans, used sticks, iron rods, and stones, and injured several militiamen. After the initial confusion, special riot troops of the Ministry of Internal Affairs had to be called in to quell the unusual upheaval. Two days later the Chinese Foreign Ministry lodged a protest with the Soviet government against the brutal treatment of Chinese students by the Moscow police. Together with the diplomatic move, students in Peking staged an anti-Soviet demonstration in front of the Soviet Embassy. In turn, the Soviet Ministry of Foreign Affairs called the Chinese students "provocative elements" and the incident a "campaign of provocation" against the USSR that had been inflated in China. The Chinese sent one more protest note to the Soviet Embassy in Peking; the Chinese students, who had been expelled from the Soviet Union, received a hero's welcome in Peking.[5]

By summer that incident was closed, but Sino-Soviet relations had grown even more tense. It was clear that the Kremlin's new Vietnam policy was creating exacerbating frictions with China. There were also mounting complaints from Soviet diplomats about difficulties caused by Peking's obstruction of Soviet attempts to get help to Hanoi. According to the Russians, the Vietnamese, impressed by the Maoist doctrine that man is more effective than machines or weapons, had been persuaded to store in caves the electronic equipment sent by the Soviets for air defense batteries.

Moscow also "disclosed" that Peking had refused to permit Soviet transport planes loaded with weapons to fly over Chinese territory. The Chinese quickly denied all charges of obstructionism and declared that China was adhering to agreements worked out with the Soviet Union and the DRV in a secret protocol on March 30. By agreement, the Chinese railways transported all Russian supplies and personnel by special express military consignment; but the Russians were not permitted to open an air corridor over China between the USSR and the DRV or to "occupy and operate" airfields in southwestern China.[6]

Significantly, as the anti-Chinese campaign intensified, the Soviets had less and less to say about the pernicious role of Radio Free Europe and the Voice of America in undermining world social order and the Soviet state, and more and more to say about Radio Peking, which allegedly was beaming direct appeals to various strata of the Soviet people and encouraging them to rebel. Moreover, the Chinese leadership was blamed for propagating the potentiality of military strife between China and the Soviet Union. According to the Russians, the

Chinese on the one hand provoked border conflicts in increasing numbers and on the other refused to resume the border negotiations that had been suspended in May 1964.

The Soviets hit hardest of all on the issue of Vietnam. Here it was pointed out that although the Communist party of the Soviet Union had repeatedly urged joint action by all socialist countries in support of North Vietnam, the Chinese had flatly and obdurately rejected any such proposal. From this, Moscow affected to deduce that the Chinese leaders were trying to prolong the Vietnam War in order to perpetuate international tension and sustain the image of China as a besieged fortress. In addition, the Brezhnev leadership asserted one of the goals of the Chinese leadership with respect to Vietnam was "to originate a military conflict between the USSR and the United States . . . so that they may, as they say themselves, sit on the mountain and watch the fight of the tigers."[7] One outcome of this policy evaluation *cum* persecution complex was that Soviet and Warsaw Pact intelligence agencies were directed to gather evidence of secret "Chinese-American collaboration."

Not surprisingly, the Chinese Communists rejected these Soviet charges one by one and produced counter charges. They accused the Brezhnev leadership of "actively plotting new deals" with the United States, among others the prevention of nuclear proliferation and similar disarmament measures. They charged the Soviet Union was in alliance against China "with the Indian reactionaries" and denounced the Russians together with the Americans for using the United Nations as a tool for opposing revolutionary forces in the Congo (Leopoldville) and in the Dominican Republic. In addition, they blamed the "Soviet Revisionists" for whipping up hysteria against China and heaped reproach on the Soviets for entering into an anti-Chinese conspiracy with the Americans to secure ultimate world domination. Concerning the ideological breach between the CCP and the CPSU, the Chinese ideologues came out with the thesis that "what exists is what causes differences, and that which should be common is missing." Naturally, they threw the responsibility for the existing state of affairs upon the Soviet party leadership. According to Peking, the Soviets were the ones who by then were carrying on great-power chauvinism and a policy of schism in the international Communist movement. As for Vietnam, not only was Moscow's "united action" plan rejected as an attempt to "deceive the world," but the Soviet leadership was accused of trying to tie the socialist countries to "the chariot of Soviet-United States collaboration" for world domination, to use the question of Vietnam as "an important counter" in their bargaining with the United States, and to isolate, encircle, and attack China.

The worsening Sino-Soviet relationship was nakedly and sharply revealed to the world with the publication on November 11 of the *Jen-min Jih-pao* editorial, "Refutation of the New Leaders of the CPSU on 'United Action,' " a prompt Soviet reply entitled "The International Duty of the Communists of All Countries," and an extremely harsh exchange of articles and historical accounts of the controversy. The Chinese bluntly stated that "on all fundamental issues of the present epoch the [Sino-Soviet] relation is one of sharp opposition; there are things that divide us and nothing that unites us, things that are antagonistic and nothing that is common." The Soviets rebuffed by stating: "The CPSU has stood and continues to stand firmly for ensuring the solidarity of the Communist ranks, of all revolutionary forces. It has striven for such solidarity on the principled basis of Marxism-Leninism, regarding as of paramount importance the interest of the common struggle against imperialism and its policy of reaction and aggression, for the triumph of the cause of communism."[8] As in the past, it was almost impossible for an outside observer to establish the facts since the Russians and the Chinese gave diametrically conflicting versions of the various exchanges between Peking and Moscow.

Meanwhile, through the mounting rancor of the Sino-Soviet dispute, the Soviet press continued its steady castigation of the United States' role in Southeast Asia and endorsed North Vietnam's war aims and its conditions for ending the war. Leading Soviet political figures used every occasion that came their way to promise support for the DRV and the NLF and repeatedly declared that the Soviet Union was fully prepared to develop better relations between the United States and the USSR if only the United States would abandon its policy of aggression in

Vietnam. On December 8, 1965, Premier Alexei Kosygin launched one of the sharpest attacks against the Americans since Khrushchev's ouster from the Kremlin the year before. In an unusual interview with James Reston of the *New York Times,* the premier bluntly stated: "I cannot agree that you have the right to kill the weak." He then reportedly asserted that military considerations dictated American foreign policy, and it would not be feasible for him to meet with President Johnson while the Vietnam War continued. In rebuttal, Reston said Kosygin's remarks amounted to a monstrous distortion of the facts. Kosygin, he said, had begun not with Communist actions but with American reactions, with the assumption that it was all right for the USSR to help the Communists achieve political control in Vietnam. What Kosygin was saying, Reston concluded, was that if the Communist side used force it was for self-defense and liberation, but if the United States used force it was aggression.

From Kosygin's vantage point, of course, the whole matter looked different. He was addressing himself simultaneously to the readers of the *Times* and the rulers of China, the DRV, and the rest of the Communist world. His statements therefore were intended not merely to clarify the Soviet stand on Vietnam to the Western World but also to enlist domestic and East European support for the Kremlin's assistance in this Southeast Asian war. In sum, what he said had to accord with his country's effort to create a Soviet-sponsored united front against the United States.

On the Soviet domestic front, meanwhile, the Agitprop department of the Central Committee of the CPSU was busy organizing protest meetings in Moscow, Baku, Kharkov, Voronezh, and other cities, at which demonstrators carried placards with the slogans "Hands off Vietnam," "Yankees, Get Out of Vietnam," and "We Support the Heroic Vietnamese People." Speakers at a mass meeting in Moscow repeatedly warned that the Soviet government would not abandon the Vietnamese people to an American-dictated fate and would continue to render material and political aid to repel the aggressors. (As customary during such meetings, selected groups also delivered protest resolutions to the American Embassy.)

On December 9, 1965, the domestic propaganda campaign

was intensified to coincide with the meeting of the USSR Supreme Soviet. Here Gromyko reported that the Soviet delegation at the Twentieth Session of the United Nations General Assembly had proclaimed its steadfast support for Hanoi's Four Points, and he had represented the same position in numerous discussions with the United States representatives in New York.[9]

To one who read these statements and nothing more, it might have appeared that Soviet-American relations had reached a hopeless impasse. That, of course, was not the case, for in spite of all its fulminations, the Brezhnev leadership was heavily involved in all manner of negotiations with the Americans, and during President Johnson's five years in the White House, Moscow and Washington reached agreements on a series of vital defense issues. The signing of a non-proliferation pact was a milestone in the struggle to reduce the nuclear arms race; an Outer Space Treaty prohibited the placement of nuclear weapons on the moon, the planets, and in space; the agreement on a mutual cut-back in the production of fissionable materials was also achieved. Inasmuch as every one of these settlements was completely in accord with the Soviet national interest, the events in Vietnam were not considered a hindrance.

The Soviets and Americans also reached agreements on lesser issues. The regular two-year Russo-American cultural agreement was renewed; a United States-USSR Civil Air Agreement and a Consular Convention were signed while the war went on in Southeast Asia. In these cases, Vietnamese interests could be disregarded because the Soviet leadership simply adopted the view that carefully selected cultural exchanges, especially in science-oriented programs, were advantageous to the Soviet Union. The Soviet intelligence community, in fact, insisted on the continuation of the cultural programs since they had proved such a useful cover for espionage operations. What is more, there were high officials in the Soviet Foreign Ministry—"doves" like Kornienko, the head of the American Department, and Soviet Ambassador Dobrynin in Washington—who felt that one day the Vietnam War would end and Moscow would then be in a more favorable bargaining position if it continued to have some ties with Washington. This school nevertheless endorsed continued Soviet economic and military support of North Vietnam.

For window-dressing purposes and lest it be thought too yielding, the Kremlin took a few steps to demonstrate its solidarity with Vietnam. For instance, it cancelled a scheduled presentation of the musical comedy *Hello Dolly* in the Soviet capital and called off a tour of an American basketball team. Meanwhile, for propaganda purposes, it stressed that until the Americans stopped "their aggression" in Vietnam, East-West exchanges could not be broadened.

Economic Aid for the DRV

If the war in Vietnam did little to upset existing Soviet diplomatic dealings with the United States, the U.S.-USSR agreements and negotiations did nothing to prevent the Kremlin from extending substantial economic and military assistance to North Vietnam. To be sure, the Russian aid program seemed only a drop in the ocean in comparison to the astronomical sums spent by the Americans on the war; however, together with Chinese assistance, it was enough to support Hanoi's war effort effectively. In 1965 alone, the Soviet Union placed at the disposal of the armed forces of North Vietnam weapons and war materials worth about 500 million rubles (550 million dollars). This contribution included rocket installations, antiaircraft artillery, airplanes, tanks, coastal guns, warships, and other items of military hardware. The DRV also received support in the training of pilots, rocket personnel, tank drivers, and artillerymen. Furthermore, the USSR routed extensive military and domestic supplies through Hanoi to the National Liberation Front of South Vietnam.[10]

The toll of the war, however, was always greater than the supply, and by the end of 1965 the North Vietnamese leadership began pressing for stepped-up assistance. Knowing the complexity of the Soviet power structure, Hanoi adopted a double-pronged approach. The North Vietnamese named one or two of their own Politburo members to head special delegations to Moscow to discuss military and economic aid programs; in addition, they invited Soviet party and government delegations to Hanoi to discuss the growing needs of the Vietnamese and NLF armies. Hanoi was aware that where the Soviets were concerned, vital questions would be discussed and meaningful decisions made *only* at the party Presidium level, where all power in the Soviet Union ultimately rests. They were aware, too, of the significance of the division of responsibility within the Soviet party Presidium.

The Presidium was headed in 1965, as it is today, by CPSU First Secretary Leonid Brezhnev, and was composed of eleven members and eight alternate members.[11] It met regularly every other week (or at any time in case of emergency) to discuss questions of major importance—including outstanding intra-party and foreign policy matters, decisions being reached by simple majority vote. Within the Presidium the ultimate authority rested with First Secretary Brezhnev; his opinion always prevailed. In case of dissent he would settle the controversy through compromise, or he would postpone the decision until unanimity could be achieved. Moreover, he was empowered to make personal decisions without consulting anyone, but in practice he rarely exercised that power—inasmuch as the current trend was toward collective leadership. Obviously, this form of government required a well-defined division of responsibility within the Presidium. In 1965 each Presidium member directed and supervised a certain segment of administration, production, or other state-controlled activity. The first secretary controlled the so-called inner circle, the Secretariat, which dealt with Presidium concerns on a day-to-day basis. To implement their decisions, the Presidium members had at their disposal not only the state administration but a well-organized, sophisticated, and highly centralized party apparatus. By these means they could extend their control to all levels of Soviet life. For example, Alexsei N. Kosygin, Presidium member and chairman of the Council of the Ministers, was responsible for the overall economic policy of the Soviet Union. He directed the central management of the Soviet economy and supervised the activities of the State Planning Committee and the economic ministries. He maintained offices in both the party headquarters and the government administration. Kosygin's specified sphere of competence, however, did not extend to the armaments industry; this vital sector was entrusted to Dmitri F. Ustinov, an alternate member of the Presidium and a member of the Secretariat. At Ustinov's disposal was a specialized section of the party apparatus that was charged with overseeing the implementation of Presidium decisions relative to the armaments industry. In addition, a deputy chairman of the State Planning Committee, a deputy minister of heavy industry, and other civilian and military managers involved in the production of armaments reported directly to Ustinov.

Cognizant of these power relationships, three high-level North Vietnamese delegations were dispatched to Moscow in 1965. Politburo-member and First Secretary Le Duan (the second man in the Hanoi Politburo) and Defense Minister General Giap headed the first delegation. They conferred secretly for more than a week in April with Brezhnev, Shelepin, and Kosygin and were able to assure a sizable military assistance. They arranged, moreover, for a Soviet party and government delegation to visit Hanoi in order to discuss the evolving military situation and to conduct an on the spot review of the military aid program.[12] The second Vietnamese delegation to Moscow was led by Hanoi's chief economic expert, Politburo member and Vice Premier Le Thanh Nghi. It arrived in June and the resulting agreements from the negotiations provided additional assistance to the development of key industrial projects closely connected with Hanoi's war efforts.

The third Vietnamese delegation of 1965, again headed by Le Thanh Nghi, popped up in the Soviet capital on December 6. As Nghi had done in June, he first paid a courtesy visit to party chief Brezhnev. He then proceeded to party headquarters to discuss the broad outlines of new economic aid with Kosygin. From there he progressed to working sessions with the Soviet government expert on international economic matters, Deputy Premier Vladimir Novikov. In nearly three weeks of discussions, the Vietnamese delegation worked out six new agreements with their Soviet counterparts. According to an official communiqué issued at the close of the talks, the Soviet Union had granted additional economic aid to North Vietnam in the form of "supplementing technical assistance" and "additional free economic assistance." The nature of the technical assistance was not specified; the economic aid would entail new loans and postponed repayment on earlier loans. The two sides also signed a renewed bilateral trade agreement for 1966, and the USSR guaranteed that there would be no price increases on Soviet goods exported to the Democratic Republic of Vietnam during the next year. As is customary in Soviet practice, neither the amount of the new aid program nor the volume of the trade agreement was disclosed; however, the promised economic aid—on the basis of the second agreement in six months—was believed to be sizable.

According to customary Soviet protocol, there was a signing ceremony in the Kremlin followed by a luncheon in honor of the DRV delegation. On this occasion Novikov, the chief Soviet negotiator, stressed to his listeners that the talks with Vice Premier Le Thanh Nghi had been extremely warm and friendly and assured his guest that the Soviet Union would go on rendering support to the DRV. Le Thanh Nghi for his part politely acknowledged that Soviet support was helping not only "in building socialism" but "in increasing the military and economic potential of the Republic."[13]

The Shelepin Mission

Soon after Le Thanh Nghi left the Soviet Union to collect more economic aid in East European capitals and in Peking, Shelepin left Moscow at the head of a group of high-ranking Soviet military and political experts. Their destination was Hanoi, and the news of their departure was announced by the official press agency *Tass,* on December 28. The fifty-six word announcement gave no details on the aims of the mission; it stated only that they were going at the invitation of the DRV government and the Vietnamese Workers' party.

The Shelepin delegation was to be the most important Soviet group to visit North Vietnam since Premier Kosygin's trip to Hanoi the preceding February. Shelepin at that time was considered the rising star of the younger generation of Soviet political figures. A graduate of the Moscow Institute of History, Philosophy, and Literature, he had joined the Communist party in 1940 at the age of twenty-two. Later he had worked in the Moscow Komsomol, or Communist youth organization, and from 1943 to 1952 he was secretary of the Komsomol Central Committee. During his years in the Soviet youth movement he came into close contact with the Soviet intelligence community, especially after he was elected a vice-chairman of the World Federation of Democratic Youth (the international Communist youth front organization). In 1952 Shelepin reached a turning point in his life, for in that year Stalin promoted him to the post of first secretary of the Komsomol and he became a member of the CPSU Central Committee. From then on Shelepin was in the mainstream of Soviet political life. While still in his high post in the youth movement, he was entrusted to supervise Khrushchev's scheme for the decentralization of industry. Next he was named to head the Department of Cadres, and thus to propose dismissals from key positions and suggest new appointments. In December 1958, he replaced Serov as head of the secret police when the new post-Stalin Kremlin leadership appointed him chairman of the Committee of the State Security (KGB), a move that was designed to demonstrate the party's control of the powerful police apparatus.

In his new position Shelepin did everything possible to prove that he, with party background, was more efficient than his predecessors with professional police background. He launched a series of actions to liquidate anti-Soviet resistance movements. He organized the assassination of the Ukrainian nationalist leader Bendera and of other anti-Communist leaders living in exile in West Germany and elsewhere. In October 1961, at the Twenty-second Congress, Shelepin stood firmly behind Khrushchev and vigorously attacked the "anti-party group" led by Molotov and Malenkov. On that occasion he testified that the archives of the KGB contained numerous documents proving the culpability of Stalin and the "group" leaders in the mass arrests and executions of the 1930s. He revealed, further, that Molotov's and Voroshilov's initials appeared on numerous orders directing the execution of leading military figures during the Moscow purges. After the Twenty-second Congress, Shelepin handed over leadership of the secret police to another Komsomol secretary, Vladimir V. Semichasty, and gained entrance into the inner circle of the party leadership, the ten-member Secretariat of the Central Committee. He also acceded to a high position in the state apparatus, becoming deputy chairman of the Council of Ministers, and was entrusted with the direction of the newly created Commission of Party-State Control, an agency designed to follow up on reported infractions by officials at all levels of the party and state apparatus.

In October 1964, Shelepin evidently wielded some influence in the conspiracy to overthrow Khrushchev. There were indications that Brezhnev and his colleagues procured through Semichasty, who was known to be Shelepin's minion, KGB support in the palace revolt. In any case, when Khrushchev was removed from the leadership, Shelepin became a full member of the Presidium, and his elevation was considered by many to be a reward for his role in the ouster of his erstwhile patron. In the Brezhnev-led Presidium, Shelepin emerged as a hardliner who not only blamed Khrushchev for the 1956 Hungarian uprising, the Cuban fiasco, and the Sino-Soviet rift, but vigorously supported all-out Soviet aid to North Vietnam. In his new position he also built a reputation as a trouble-shooter for the Kremlin in the international Communist movement. He is credited with bringing Korean party chief Kim Il Song closer to Moscow and enhancing Soviet influence in the Mongolian People's Republic.

At the December 1965 plenum of the CPSU Central Committee, Shelepin was relieved of his government duties in order to work full time in the party as a member of the Presidium and as the Central Committee secretary responsible for the supervision of military affairs and security matters of the Soviet Union. At the time he was selected to go to Hanoi, he was one of the most influential members in the Soviet Presidium.[14]

In addition to Shelepin, the delegation was composed of several top-ranking Soviet officials, further demonstrating the importance the Kremlin attached to the talks in Hanoi in early 1966. Second to Shelepin was the powerful alternate Politburo member Dmitri Ustinov, who, as mentioned earlier, was in charge of the entire defense sector of the Soviet economy.

Konstantin Rusakov, the third man in the delegation, had been Soviet ambassador to Mongolia in 1962–63—at the height of the ideological dispute between Moscow and Peking—and was one of those instrumental in securing Soviet influence in Ulan-Bator. Later, as deputy head of the Department of International Relations of the Central Committee, he was in charge of inter-party relations between the CPSU and Asian Communist parties, including the Vietnamese. His presence indicated that the Soviet delegation would discuss important party matters.

Anatoliy Chistyakov was the delegate from the Soviet Foreign Ministry. He headed the Southeast Asia Department and was regarded as an old hand in Soviet-Far Eastern affairs and for the duration of the trip to Hanoi was to serve as Shelepin's foreign policy adviser. Another diplomat, Soviet ambassador to the DRV, Ilya Shcherbakov, was to join the delegation in the North Vietnamese capital.

Colonel General Vladimir Tolubko was the Soviet armed forces representative in the delegation. He held the important post of first deputy commander-in-chief of the Strategic Rocket Troops and was one of the top artillery and missile experts in the Soviet Union. His presence indicated the nature of the military aid program the USSR was prepared to grant North Vietnam and served as a warning to the Americans that the Soviets might install bases in North Vietnam for surface-to-surface medium- and intermediate-range ballistic missiles of the same type they had sent to Cuba in 1962. These deadly accurate nuclear warhead missiles could reach a target (for example, an American battleship in the Tonkin Gulf or an American military base in South Vietnam) in less than three minutes when fired from a distance of from 1,100 to 2,200 statute miles. To back up the threat, Radio Moscow reported an attitude of "deep concern" in the Soviet capital over suggestions by U. S. leaders that the Vietnamese War might be extended to other Indochinese countries if Washington's dictates were rejected.[15]

When the trip was announced, the Soviet delegation was expected to reach Hanoi before the New Year; instead, the special aircraft carrying Shelepin and the others touched down at Hanoi a week later. There was no official explanation for the delay, but vague rumors circulated among East European diplomats in Moscow that the Chinese had attempted to head off the visit at the last minute. Although these rumors were never confirmed or denied, it is true that Chinese news media began assailing the visit before Shelepin's arrival in Hanoi, linking the mission to Johnson's decision to send out roving peace envoys and implying that Shelepin would pressure the DRV leadership into accepting the American offer of peace talks. Reports of the cordial reception accorded the delegation in Hanoi, however, and of unusually friendly protocol ceremonies tended to dispell the Chinese charges.

Moreover there was nothing in Shelepin's public statements during his week-long visit to suggest that he urged negotiations on any terms other than those set by North Vietnam. On the contrary, he seemed to be stimulating rather than discouraging the aggressiveness of the North Vietnamese as again and again he denounced "the odious war crimes of the United States" and promised full support "against United States military aggression." He voiced firm support of the January 4, 1966, statement of the DRV Foreign Ministry, flatly rejecting the Johnson administration's quest for peace, which he dismissed as "hypocritical." He demanded the withdrawal of United States troops from South Vietnam before talks could begin. He repeatedly declared that peace could come only when the United States finally and unconditionally halted bombing of the DRV. He stated that the only lawful representative of the South Vietnamese people was the National Liberation Front, added that the United States must prove words with deeds by accepting Hanoi's peace proposals, and even warned against a widening of the war into Laos and Cambodia. In sum, Shelepin publicly and unequivocally endorsed the Four Points of the DRV and the Five Points of the NLFSV.[16]

Behind closed doors there was likewise complete agreement between the Soviet and Vietnamese negotiators regarding the American peace proposal. When this question came up during negotiations, Ho Chi Minh explained on behalf of his Politburo that the military situation in the South was not yet considered favorable for a start of negotiations with the Americans. He did not discount the possibility of future negotiations: he viewed diplomatic maneuverings as but another form of revolutionary fighting, one which had been used in the past against the French colonialists, and he hinted that possibly in two or three years the DRV might be ready to repeat these tactics and start negotiations. Shelepin made no attempt to modify the Vietnamese position. His mission was to strengthen party ties with Hanoi, not to weaken them by argumentation, and in any case as a hardliner he completely agreed with Ho. Hence he readily signed a new agreement assuring additional weapons and other forms of assistance for the armed forces of North Vietnam and the guerrillas of the NLFSV.

When it came to convincing Ho Chi Minh that his loyalty should be directed toward Moscow rather than Peking, however, Shelepin encountered some difficulty; after all, North Vietnam was drawing substantial aid from Communist China. As in the past, the Vietnamese deplored the dissensions that divided the international Communist movement and expressed concern for the tensions they created. But when Premier Pham Van Dong thanked the Soviets for their generous and steadily increasing support, he expressed gratitude for Communist China's great assistance as well; and when Shelepin proposed sending Tolubko's special rocket forces to back up Soviet missiles, Ho Chi Minh politely turned down the offer, as much to avoid the introduction of Chinese ground troops in Vietnam as to sidestep the Soviet presence. Finally, when Shelepin extended an invitation to the Twenty-third Congress of the CPSU in March 1966, the Vietnamese agreed to attend even though they knew the Chinese Communist party would probably boycott the meeting. In short, the Vietnamese were able to produce cleverly formulated and well-balanced statements of gratitude and fraternal solidarity all around and at the same time to preserve their options for independent action. Yet

Shelepin must have been satisfied with the mission. He had talked Hanoi into sending a high-level delegation to the Twenty-third Congress, and this success alone would tend to strain Chinese Communist relations with the Vietnamese Workers' party and thus further the aims of the Soviet leadership.[17]

On January 13, the Kremlin's delegation left Hanoi and headed for Peking where, at the invitation of the Chinese, they were to spend twenty-four hours. Presumably, the Chinese wanted to meet and speak with Shelepin, the Communist hardliner considered in many quarters to be a potential future leader of the Communist party of the Soviet Union. The Chinese received the delegation correctly. Politburo member and Secretary of the Central Committee Li Hsien-nien was among the officials who greeted the Russians at the Peking airport; so were the director of the Department of International Relations of the Central Committee, Chao I-min; Deputy Foreign Minister Wan Bin-nanh; the director of the Soviet and East European Affairs, Yu Chan; and other Chinese officials. Also on hand were the Soviet ambassador to China, S. G. Lapin; the North Vietnamese chargé d'affaires; the representative of the NFLSV; and the East European diplomats accredited in Peking. Li Hsien-nien gave a dinner for the delegation in the Forbidden City, and afterward the guests attended a Chinese acrobatic performance.

There was nothing new in the way the Soviet guests were entertained. Just a year before, Chou En-lai had accorded much the same treatment to Kosygin when the Soviet premier was on his way home from Hanoi. But just as the Kosygin-Chou exchange of views had failed to bridge the gap between the two Communist rivals, the Shelepin-Li discussion solved no outstanding issues. Clearly neither side was ready for compromise, despite the fact that both had gone on record in support of the DRV four-point program and both had demanded the withdrawal of all American and allied troops from the territory of Vietnam. There were no differences between Moscow and Peking in formulating and setting the ultimate goals in Vietnam; the differences emerged over the means by which these goals were to be attained.

According to information we had received at that time from Moscow, Shelepin once more held out the olive branch to Peking by proposing the normalization of Soviet-Chinese relations at both party and state levels, and once again the Chinese turned away. Then the Soviet envoy proposed a plan of joint Sino-Soviet cooperation to assist Vietnam. Without discussing the details, Li rejected the proposal and in turn asked that Moscow consider putting military pressure on the Americans in Berlin and West Germany. Shelepin pronounced the Chinese suggestion unrealistic.

Officially, the Chinese never substantiated the Soviet version of the Shelepin-Li conversation. But what Li Hsien-nien supposedly said in private, his countrymen repeated in public. Their assertion was that the Soviet Union was pursuing a policy of appeasement in Europe so that United States troops could be released from West Germany and transferred to South Vietnam. The Chinese campaign for a "second front in Europe" was introduced in Peking on December 20, 1965, at the celebration of the fifth anniversary of the National Liberation Front of South Vietnam. It was intensified at the Tri-Continental Conference in Havana in January 1966, where Chinese delegate Wu Hsueh-tsien asked: "Why is Yankee imperialism allowed to live in peace on the Western Front?" And a few days before Shelepin arrived in Peking, Chinese foreign minister and Politburo member, Ch'en Yi, scoffed at Soviet aid to Vietnam and declared that if the Soviet Union really wanted to help the Vietnamese people it would try to immobilize more American forces.[18]

In the meantime, the Americans were still in the dark regarding Shelepin's mission. Perhaps the Soviet leadership had taken the suspension of the bombing raids more seriously than Hanoi. After all, on November 24, Ambassador Dobrynin had promised McGeorge Bundy "intense diplomatic activity" if the United States were to stop bombing for twelve to fourteen days. Did the Shelepin visit in Hanoi mean that the Soviets were putting pressure on Ho Chi Minh to pursue his objectives by diplomatic means? Was the Russian Politburo member quietly suggesting to Hanoi that it could get its way best by starting negotiatons with the Americans and in the meantime getting the bombing stopped—that in the end this would work out to North Vietnam's advantage? Certainly Shelepin's public statement and the joint Soviet-DRV communiqué issued at the close of negotiations gave little cause for optimism; but perhaps the militant Soviet tone was intended primarily to refute Chinese charges of "collusion" with the United States. On the other hand, it looked as though the main purpose of Shelepin's visit to the North Vietnamese capital was to solidify the Vietnamese Workers' party loyalty to Moscow; if indeed that was the case, it seemed unlikely, in the midst of the bitter Sino-Soviet dispute, that the Kremlin would attempt to mediate between Washington and Hanoi.

The White House, the State Department, and other United States governmental agencies of course were busy analyzing all available information and tracking down every clue that might help them interpret Soviet behavior. Ambassador Foy Kohler's talk with Soviet Foreign Minister Gromyko in Moscow on December 22, 1965, produced nothing new to consider. Similarly, his courtesy call on the new chairman of the Supreme Soviet, Nikolai Podgorny, resulted in a polite, short talk that yielded little information.

Then, on January 27, just three days before the resumption of the bombing of North Vietnam, the State Department received a vital piece of information from Paris. A contact of the American Embassy (a left-to-center French journalist) reported a long and confidential conversation he had with Mai Van Bo, head of the DRV delegation in Paris. While trying to discover some of the details about the Shelepin visit in Hanoi, the Frenchman had received some interesting answers. First, he asked if Hanoi was satisified with the Russian assistance. Bo replied at once that Hanoi was very satisfied since the Soviet Union had substantially increased its material and military aid. Then the journalist inquired whether Shelepin had attempted to influence Ho Chi Minh to adopt a more moderate attitude toward negotiation. The North Vietnamese diplomat categorically stated: "I can only repeat to you that officially and privately, in the name and in the fact, the Russians approve of our struggle, back it, and are increasingly with us."[19] If nothing else, this proved that indeed the Shelepin visit to Hanoi had damaged the chances of the American peace offensive.

Apart from Bo's revelation, there was another move the Soviet government made that indirectly displayed its real intentions. On January 10 it presented a protest note to the British government in which the United States was accused of planning to extend the war in Southeast Asia to Laos and Cambodia. According to the note, the United States was shipping a great quantity of arms and other war materials into Laos and hastily rebuilding Laotian airfields. The note was sent to Britain as co-chairman of the Geneva Conference on Indochina, and Britain was asked to inform the other members of the Conference of its contents. London forwarded a copy to Washington. This was not an "intense diplomatic action" nor even a spectacular one; possibly it was only a routine gesture to add credence to the Kremlin's militant posture against the United States. But by dint of its timing, the presentation was a convincing sign that the Soviet leadership had little desire to help in the American peace offensive.

"The Tashkent Spirit"

While Shelepin was preoccupied with luring the North Vietnamese to the Soviet side, Premier Kosygin made a major foreign policy move to advance the Russian diplomatic position over that of the Chinese on the Indian subcontinent: he offered his good offices to India and Pakistan in 1966 when those two countries concluded their short, bloody war with a shaky cease-fire.

The India-Pakistan conflict grew out of the partition of the province of Kashmir back in the early days of Indian independence in 1947. At that time both India and Pakistan laid claim to this piece of land, with its rich natural resources and mixed Moslem and Hindu population; the dispute was settled by a division of the territory which left neither side satisfied, and thereafter both sides maneuvered to gain complete possession. In 1957, India appeared to have won out when the Constituent Assembly of Kashmir—which had close ties with India's Jawaharlal Nehru—voted in favor of Kashmir's formal accession to India. Pakistan, however, was unwilling to accept the loss, and sent agents into the disputed land to keep the population in a state of tension. In August 1965, Pakistani army units infiltrated Kashmir. The Indians not only fought back in Kashmir but launched an offensive aimed at Lahore, the capital of West Pakistan. China fully supported Pakistan, and for various reasons the Soviet leadership tended to be more sympathetic toward India. The United States stayed out of the conflict. President Johnson suspended deliveries of military equipment to both India and Pakistan and refrained from making new commitments of economic assistance to either.

By September it appeared that the subcontinent might well become engulfed in an all-out armed conflict that would go far beyond the Kashmir controversy. Then, in a combined effort, the United States, Great Britain, and the Soviet Union brought enough pressure on the belligerents to force a cease-fire through the United Nations. The hostilities gave way to a tense no-war, no-peace stalemate that existed for the next three months.

Throughout the crisis the Soviet party Presidium was well supplied with relevant information about the developments which appeared to affect so many vital Soviet interests. The Soviet embassies in Delhi, Karachi, Peking, London, and Washington forwarded short daily cables and monthly reports to the Foreign Ministry in Moscow. On Soviet request the Hungarians and presumably the other East European Communist embassies in these capitals followed the same pattern. The reports from India and Pakistan described and assessed the evolving political and military situation; the embassies in China, Great Britain, and the United States were mainly interested in detecting the reactions of officials in the host countries.

As I understand it, the Soviet pattern of reporting was as follows. The Soviet ambassadors reported directly to the foreign minister or to one of the deputy foreign ministers by means of so-called "personal letters to the minister." These letters contained, in addition to more general information, the observations and evaluations of the reporting ambassador, and sometimes his suggestions. Theoretically, the range of an ambassador's initiative in proposing courses of action was unlimited, but in practice they acted with great caution. In Moscow, a special evaluation team working within the Secretariat of Foreign Minister Gromyko collected all reports on a given subject, extracted and emphasized the similar and contradictory points, and reduced the mountains of material to manageable proportions. Then they sent the most sensitive material—including extracts of the "personal letters" of the ambassadors—to all members of the party Presidium and to the two Central Committee department heads dealing with international matters.

Additional information was provided by intelligence officers working for the External Service of the State Security Committee—better known as the KGB. Disguised as diplomats, these persons operated from centers called *residenturas* that were located in the Soviet embassies and were engaged in the overt and clandestine gathering of political information. Through carefully placed secret agents they also collected classified data and other material from foreign politicians and foreign government officials. What went on in the *residenturas* was sealed off from the rest of the embassy; only the ambassador saw their reports. The agents communicated with their own center, where an Evaluation and Review Department digested their information and incorporated it in the Daily Intelligence Report prepared for the members of the party Presidium. In addition, the KGB received valuable intelligence reports through Soviet advisers who were assigned to direct and control the intelligence services of the East European countries.[20]

The other branch of the Soviet intelligence community, military intelligence, supplied the party headquarters with reports of a military character and only to a lesser extent with political information. The army, air force, and navy attachés' offices were completely separate from the embassies, though often members of the diplomatic staff were recruited to work for one or another branch of armed forces intelligence. Like their counterparts in State Security, the military intelligence attachés reported directly to their own headquarters—the director of military, air force, and navy intelligence in Moscow. Occasionally, military intelligence made use of the data and reports offered by military attachés from the other Warsaw Pact countries' personnel, whose activities were financed by the Soviet Union and coordinated by the office of Marshal A. A. Grechko, first deputy defense minister of the USSR and commander-in-chief of the Warsaw Treaty Organization.

By and large, the separate reporting by the foreign service, the KGB, and military intelligence was a useful practice. It facilitated cross-checking of information and afforded a range of points of view. Not uncommonly, however, personal intrigues, institutional rivalries, and jealousies in the Soviet missions abroad undermined the authenticity of the dispatches and led to a distortion of facts. Moreover, the agencies in Moscow were always jockeying for positions of control over one another, and each element in the Kremlin bureaucracy wanted its voice heard at the sessions of the Presidium. Sometimes valuable information was lost in the push and pull and shuffle. But that is true in almost any big power bureaucracy and it is always the decision makers who have to discount the distorted views.

In addition to the government agencies' reports, the Soviet party Presidium had sources of information that were more specialized and closer to home. Two members of the powerful Secretariat of the Central Committee, Yurii V. Andropov and Boris N. Ponomarev, were aggressively engaged in obtaining material from other Communist parties, especially those in New Delhi and Karachi. Andropov dealt specifically with the Communist and workers' parties of all the socialist countries, and Ponomarev was in touch with nonruling Communist parties; both were experts in their fields and both had at their disposal a sizable department fully staffed with specialists. Taken together, with all their evaluation groups, administrative staff members, courier and liaison services, the two departments amounted to a smaller size foreign ministry, which received, on a regular basis, an enormous flow of documents and information gathered by the fraternal parties.

Ponomarev was especially well qualified for his job. He was an old hand in Soviet underground diplomacy and had proven himself an able and merciless *apparatchik* (party bureaucrat). He served on the Executive Committee of the Communist International from 1937 to 1943—the years in which Stalin's homicidal fury decimated the Comintern central apparatus—and managed not only to survive but to rise in the hierarchy. In 1946 he was named to head the Soviet Information Bureau and in that capacity supplied Stalin with "ideological justification" for the expulsion of the Yugoslav Communist party from the Cominform. Thanks largely to the patronage of Mikhail Suslov, an influential member of the Presidium, Ponomarev in 1953 became head of the Central Committee department that was concerned with foreign Communist parties outside the Soviet orbit. Finally, in 1961, he joined the inner circle of CPSU decision makers, the Secretariat.

Andropov was a less controversial figure. Most of his career had been spent in the Karelian Autonomous Soviet Socialist Republic, where he became first secretary of the Republic's Komsomol (Youth Organization) in 1940. Under the auspices of the veteran Finnish Communist O.V. Kuusinen, Andropov worked his way upward rapidly, and by 1950 he was secretary of the Communist party of Karelia. Transferred to the diplomatic service, he served as Soviet ambassador in Hungary during the Hungarian Revolution of 1956 and was instrumental in crushing the revolt. The next year he returned to Moscow and took over the Central Committee department in charge of relations with Communist parties in power. He entered the Secretariat in 1962.[21]

As consultants in the decision-making process, Ponomarev and Andropov, together with the foreign minister, were always on hand when the Presidium discussed international matters. From time to time one or the other of them initiated foreign policy actions and prepared proposals for consideration by the Presidium, and often the two acted jointly. If they needed government assistance in the execution of the action, the foreign minister was automatically drawn into the preparatory work. Gromyko, to be sure, was also in a position to originate diplomatic action, but he was supposed to consult with Ponomarev and Andropov before he presented any plan to the Presidium. Finally, there were instances in which the three foreign policy specialists prepared a joint proposal, and the

India-Pakistan conflict fell clearly into this category. No matter who initiated the action in their sphere, however, it had to be coordinated with Administrative Secretary A. N. Shelepin, the Presidium member who represented the interests and viewpoint of the civilian and military intelligence; moreover, it had to be discussed with Suslov, who synchronized any actions directed against China. After all these preliminaries were satisfied, the Presidium was ready to take up the question, and as subsequent events demonstrated the proposal for Soviet mediation over Kashmir was accepted because it fitted neatly into the Presidium's general estimate and evaluation of Soviet national interests.

Exactly when the Presidium made the Kashmir resolution was not revealed. But it is known that in January 1966 Russian Premier Kosygin stepped forward to offer his services as an intermediary between Pakistani President Ayub Khan and Indian Premier Shastri. At Kosygin's invitation, the interested parties met in Tashkent, the capital of the Uzbek Soviet Socialist Republic, on January 4–10, and with Soviet assistance worked out a form of compromise. The politico-military accord that was reached at the conference—the Tashkent Declaration, as it was called—included provisions for withdrawal of Indian and Pakistani troops to boundaries existing before the conflict started in 1965; it also set forth provisions for the exchange of war prisoners. Both nations reaffirmed their obligations under the United Nations Charter to avoid recourse to force and pledged to settle future disputes by peaceful means.

At first it looked as though the Tashkent compromise might have paved the way for a significant, if gradual, reduction of militant feelings. The troops were called back on both sides, and Foreign Ministers Swaran Singh of India and Zulfikar Ali Bhutto of Pakistan met in Rawalpindi, Pakistan, in an effort to normalize relations between the two countries. It soon became apparent, however, that despite the auspicious beginning, the situation remained explosive. Students launched demonstrations in West Pakistani cities, protesting the agreement and demanding that New Delhi agree to a Kashmir plebiscite. The Pakistani government arrested some of the protest leaders as they were about to address public meetings, and President

Ayub Khan broadcast an appeal for national unity. (Two months later, Ayub would himself express the opinion that the Tashkent Declaration was merely a "document of intent" and did not diminish the Pakistanis' resolve to defend the sovereignty of Kashmir.) Foreign Minister Ali Bhutto openly declared that the terms of the pact were unfair to Pakistan.

The Tashkent Declaration was further weakened by the death of Indian Prime Minister Shastri, who succumbed to a heart attack on January 11, just a few hours after he and Ayub had signed the Declaration. Although the new premier of India, Indira Gandhi, pledged that her country would honor the provisions of the agreement as a first step toward peace, other important Indian public figures expressed strong opposition. Rehabilitation Minister Mahavir Tyagi resigned his cabinet post in protest. Jan Sangh, the head of the executive committee of the right-wing Hindu party, pushed through a resolution assailing the Tashkent Declaration as detrimental to the national interests and derogatory to national honor. India's ambassador in Washington, B. K. Nehru, and others privately voiced to me the view that it had been a great mistake for India to stop fighting before final victory and that New Delhi should have heeded the advice of neither Washington nor Moscow.

The West, for its part, lauded the Soviet role, pointing out that in this instance, at least, the Kremlin had preferred to help overcome difficulties between two non-Communist states rather than inflame the situation and assist the Communists to gain power.

Peking swiftly and forcefully attacked the Tashkent agreement as one facet of an American-Soviet plan to encircle China. To emphasize Chinese outrage, Mao Tse-tung sent several MIG-19 jet fighters and T-59 medium tanks to the Pakistani army and assured Ayub Khan that 650 million Chinese would stand unswervingly on his side when he fought the "Indian aggressors."

Not surprisingly, the Soviet news media praised Kosygin's mediation as a "new phenomenon of great international significance." But even as the press sang praises, the Soviet military attaché in New Delhi discussed with Indian defense officials the resumption of arms delivery to India. The United States also resumed arms shipments and economic aid to both Pakistan and India.

Certainly Moscow was well aware that the Tashkent Declaration could not iron out the manifold difficulties between India and Pakistan, that no hastily devised declaration, however solemn, would end the racial hatred and the spirit of revenge that had built up between these two embattled neighbors. But neither Kosygin nor the rest of the Soviet party Presidium showed undue concern about the foreseeable new disputes that might arise in the area. On the contrary, a fluid situation there perfectly suited Soviet plans, for above all, Soviet diplomacy was fully deployed to expand the Soviet sphere of influence. Luring India away from the free world had been a constant goal, and now the weakening of China's ally—Pakistan—had become an important objective. But more important than either of these considerations was the interest in containing the rapidly growing Chinese influence on the Indian subcontinent, which the Soviets saw as a major threat to their own national interests. To that end, the diplomatic intervention in Tashkent had proved a useful device to advance the Soviet cause: on the one hand, it had temporarily weakened China's influence in Pakistan and at the same time had increased tensions between China and India; on the other hand, it had helped Moscow gain a foothold in Rawalpindi, lent a large boost to Soviet-Indian relations, and, by extension, facilitated the expansion of Soviet naval power into the Indian Ocean.

The Mongol Interlude

In the wake of the Kosygin accord in Tashkent, and the Shelepin agreement in Hanoi, party chief Leonid I. Brezhnev visited Ulan Bator and signed a new Mongolian-Soviet friendship and mutual aid agreement. To observers the Mongolian tour at first looked simply like another Brezhnev visit to a Communist bloc country. But it soon became clear that the Soviet aim was much more than a routine prestige-building maneuver in Asia: it was an action that constituted a dramatic assertion of Soviet military presence in the Mongol buffer zone, sandwiched between Siberia and Communist China, at a time when tension between the two Communist giants was mounting toward a point of no return.

Brezhnev started his personal inter-party diplomacy on January 7, 1966. He left Moscow's Yaroslav train station for a visit to Russia's remote Asian ally, the People's Republic of Mongolia. It took him four days to reach the Soviet-Mongol border. Apparently the Soviet leader enjoyed the long journey, as he liked to travel, especially in his deluxe special train, looking out the windows at the rich farmland along the Trans-Siberian railway. This landscape may have reminded him of his youth, when, after his studies in land management, he had held a number of posts in that field in the Urals. At stopovers in Omsk, Novosibirsk, and Irkutsk he would leave the train and find welcome among local party and administrative dignitaries; he would mingle with the waiting crowd, in spite of his security chief's beseeching look.

While the train was rolling, Brezhnev was not cut off from the world. A sort of portable Kremlin was attached to the train. He had his secretariat with him, complete with an administrative staff and communication facilities. He had special telephone lines to the Kremlin; he could speak directly to the East European Communist capitals. In case of emergency he was able to reach Washington through the hot line. Three senior members of the Politburo—Gennady I. Voronov, Nikolai V. Podgorny, and Mikhail A. Suslov—remained on duty in Moscow, while Shelepin from Hanoi and Kosygin from Tashkent kept him posted. Two of the five-member mission, Deputy Premier Kirill T. Mazurov and Secretary of the Central Committee Yuri Andropov, travelled with him. The presence of Andropov was obvious since he was the secretary in the Secretariat responsible for the relations with Communist parties in power. The selection of Mazurov was also understandable. He was a trusted economic expert of the Kremlin. Because Brezhnev had no government position, Mazurov also fulfilled the requirement of Soviet protocol that at least a deputy premier be present in the delegation to represent the government.

Mazurov was a newcomer to the collective leadership, having spent all his earlier career in Byelorussia. As a Komsomol secretary during World War II, he directed the operations of partisan forces against the Germans in the dense forests and swamps of his homeland. When the war was over he remained in Byelorussia and served first as the secretary of the Minsk Urban Committee, then as chairman of Byelorussia's Council of Ministers. In 1956 Khrushchev appointed him a member of the Byelorussian Central Committee, and a year later he was nominated to the important post of first secretary of the party organization of Byelorussia. Because of his new position, he automatically became an alternate member of the party Presidium. As a Khrushchev appointee, he participated in the attacks against Stalin and the Malenkov-Molotov "anti-party group" at the Twenty-second Congress of the CPSU. In 1963, however, he turned against his patron and joined forces with Brezhnev. Following Khrushchev's downfall he was promoted to full membership in the new party Presidium and became first deputy premier in the government apparatus. In his new function he was charged with carrying out the moderate industrial reform which the Brezhnev-Kosygin team introduced to supplant Khrushchev's all-out economic reorganization.[22] It was not surprising that as Kosygin's alter-ego in economic matters, Mazurov now also blamed Khrushchev for subjectivism and for ignorance of the economic laws of socialism.[23]

In the delegation, Mazurov had the task of negotiating economic matters with the Mongols. This was difficult and often unpleasant since the Mongols traditionally wasted and neglected modern equipment and installations and were forever requesting new supplies from the Soviets. In the 1960s, for example, they almost ruined the livestock sector of the Mongol economy, on which the growing population of Siberia and the Soviet Far East depended.

According to the original plan, two other members of the Soviet delegation—Defense Minister Malinovski and Foreign Minister Gromyko—were scheduled to join the first secretary somewhere on the way to Ulan Bator. They were assisting Premier Kosygin in the peace-making attempt between India and Pakistan. The discussions, however, dragged on, and they had to catch a plane in order to reach the Mongolian capital before Brezhnev's arrival. The fifth member of the mission, the Soviet ambassador to Mongolia, Soloviev, joined the party at Nauski, the Soviet border station.

On the other side of the border, at Sukhe Bator, the train station was fully decorated with Soviet and Mongolian flags. A reception committee headed by the second man of the Mongolian regime, Politburo member D. Molomjats, and Deputy Prime Minister Gombojav, together with representatives of the local party and government organizations, greeted the guests warmly. Then a brass band played the Soviet and Mongol national anthems, and Brezhnev accepted a salute from a border guard unit that served as a guard of honor.

The next stop was the capital, Ulan Bator. There a grandiose welcome was accorded the illustrious guests. The first secretary of the Mongolian People's Revolutionary party and prime minister, Yumzhagin Tsedenbal, came forth to greet them. The entire Mongol Politburo, the president of the Great Khural (supreme council), J. Sambu, and a large battery of top-level members of the government were also on hand, not to mention a generous delegation of army and air force generals and diplomats.

Mongolia, like the other Peoples' Republics, had well-defined protocol procedures for all occasions. One was designed for high-level party delegations, another for visits from heads of state, a third for combined party and government delegations. Although the Brezhnev-led delegation fit into the last category, the visit still could hardly be handled in the ordinary way: this, after all, was the first time such a high-level Soviet official had come to Mongolia. Stalin and Khrushchev never cared to see how Mongolia lived or what it looked like. Thus the occasion required a special red carpet treatment, and indeed the whole of Ulan Bator turned out to do it justice. Flags fluttered everywhere; pictures of Brezhnev and Tsedenbal adorned the facades of buildings; huge posters proclaimed eternal Soviet-Mongol friendship; the central party newspaper, *Unen,* praised Brezhnev's merits in a front-page editorial; the entire population of the city was massed in the big square before the railway station and along the avenues where the Soviet motorcade passed. As usual, for security reasons, schoolchildren wearing Pioneer red neckties and waving little flags were put in the front rows.[24]

The four-day Brezhnev program included a wreath-laying ceremony at the Sukhe Bator-Choilbalsan Mausoleum, a visit to the war monument commemorating Soviet victories over Japan in 1939 and 1945, a friendship rally in the chamber of the Great Khural, and a full schedule of social events: a banquet hosted by Tsedenbal, a reception given by the Soviet ambassador, some local sightseeing tours, and a gala performance of the famous Mongol wrestlers. In addition, Brezhnev, accompanied by Tsedenbal, spent one whole day in the first "socialist town," Darkhan, visiting the huge thermal plant built by Soviet, Czech, and Polish engineers, and addressing a mass meeting organized in his honor.

Time was reserved for negotiations as well. Reportedly the negotiators considered the possibilities of enlarging Soviet-Mongol economic cooperation and reviewed the latest developments in the international Communist and workers' movement. The two leaders and the members of the delegations had additional informal talks to discuss relevant questions at greater length.[25]

As far as the new twenty-year friendship, cooperation, and mutual assistance treaty was concerned, there was not too much to negotiate. The political groundwork had been laid during the 1965 visit of Tsedenbal in Moscow, and at that time a decision had been reached at the highest level that a new friendship and mutual assistance treaty should be concluded. Thereafter the experts in the two foreign ministries got together and worked out the political and legal framework of the treaty. The military experts were also busily drafting a protocol similar in scope and intent to the bilateral status-of-forces agreements concluded between the USSR and the various Warsaw Pact countries over the past ten years. This projected agreement not only defined the number of Soviet troops and the location of the Russian military bases in Mongolia, but determined the communication lines and the terms of payment for transit of troops and military shipments through Mongolian territory. As a substantial new element, the maintenance expenses and transport of the Soviet troops were to be covered by the Soviet government.

In accordance with the procedure set up by the Soviet state and party bureaucracy, Foreign Minister Gromyko and Defense Minister Malinovski were the first to supervise the draft treaty and the protocol; then Andropov and Shepilov, in the party Secretariat, doublechecked them. When everybody agreed, the matter was placed before the party Presidium for final approval. The Politburo decision, affirmative in this case, was communicated to the Mongols and the Mongols concurred. Thus on January 15, 1966, Brezhnev and Tsedenbal needed only to perform the ceremonial signing of the treaty.

This was the time when both Moscow and Peking were feverishly attempting to make friends and allies among the Asian Communist parties; therefore the signing ceremony served also to demonstrate the unity between the Soviet Union and the People's Republic of Mongolia in the face of Chinese threats to split the world Communist movement. As Tsedenbal stated at the friendship rally that followed the signing: "The Mongolian People's Revolutionary party has been doing and will continue to do everything in its power to contribute jointly with the Soviet Communist party and other fraternal Marxist-Leninist parties toward overcoming the present difficulties in the world Communist movement."[26] And Brezhnev with apparent satisfaction acknowledged his Mongol friend's profession of loyalty.

The fact that the talks did not hit a snag, that the new treaty was concluded without difficulty, and that Brezhnev was able to rally Mongolia behind him in the Sino-Soviet dispute demonstrated that he could deal with the Mongols at least as well as Stalin and could enlist their support even more efficiently than did Khrushchev. In other words, his personal diplomacy was effective.

Like everyone else in the Soviet leadership, Brezhnev remembered well how Stalin had governed the People's Republic of Mongolia. It was the same way he had ruled all other autonomous national oblasts (provinces) in the Soviet Union. He appointed to the Mongol leadership only those who enjoyed his personal confidence. When he wished to communicate a decision to Ulan Bator, he simply telephoned his message or summoned his satrap Choibalsang to Moscow. It was also a routine procedure in the Stalin years to dispatch secret police agents to Mongolia to carry out the bloody purges which for three decades scourged every stratum of society. It was no secret that in the course of Stalin's forced collectivization campaign in Mongolia thousands of lamas, well-to-do peasants, and simple herdsmen were killed; the fellow-traveler Premier Gendung and the commander-in-chief of the Mongol armed forces, Marshal Demid, were among those liquidated by Choibalsang, and many of the revolutionary old guard fell victim to the Mongol show trials, which took place shortly after the great trials staged in Moscow of the 1930s and 40s.[27] All in all, Choibalsang's terror matched and in some respects perhaps even surpassed that of Stalin himself. But in spite of Choibalsang's crimes and abuses of power, Brezhnev would not denounce the past, as Khrushchev had. He would not press an all-out "de-Choibalsangnization" policy, as the Mongol version of de-Stalinization was called. For Brezhnev could easily foresee what Khrushchev could not, namely, that undue denunciation of the unpopular Communist rule in Mongolia, past or present, could only weaken Soviet influence. Thus he endorsed as mildly as possible Tsedenbal's political strategy of criticizing the "cult of personality" of the late Mongol leader while at the same time reminding the people that "his great revolutionary merits" should never be forgotten.[28]

At the time of Brezhnev's visit in Ulan Bator, Tsedenbal was the undisputed head of the staunchly pro-Soviet Mongol regime. Originally trained as an economist at the Institute of Economy and Finance in Moscow, he started out as a professor in the School of Economics in the Mongol capital. In 1939, after several years of teaching, Choibalsang named him to the post of deputy premier and later made him finance minister. Probably he would never have moved further up had the doctors not discovered in 1941 that Choibalsang had cancer. Stalin, looking for a replacement, selected the young Tsedenbal as Choibalsang's successor, probably because of his economic expertise. But thanks to a strong physique, Choibalsang lived eleven more years and retained all his functions and titles (premier, foreign minister, commander-in-chief of the armed forces, marshal of Mongolia), Tsedenbal for his part accepted the role of second violinist with apparent willingness and, along with everybody else in the regime, participated fully in the frenzied "personality cult" of Choibalsang. Among other things, he named a town and a university after the premier and published an official biography of the master. Behind the scenes, however, Tsedenbal moved quickly to enlarge his power. In 1941 he became deputy commander-in-chief and in 1945 deputy premier and chairman of the State Planning Commission. Then in 1952, when the cancer finally caught up with Choibalsang, Tsedenbal took over the premiership with Stalin's blessing. Two years later, following Stalin's death, Tsedenbal, like the other Stalin appointees in the Soviet bloc, had to retreat—at least temporarily.[29] He was forced to hand over the party first secretary post to his deputy, Damba.

Seemingly, the new Damba-Tsedenbal team ruled in harmony. Under the surface, however, a bitter power struggle had begun. It turned out that Tsedenbal had the better connections in Moscow and was able to eliminate Damba from the Politburo. Then in 1962, using the pretext of "de-Choibalsangnization," he dismissed the minister of public security and the army chief-of-staff. In the same year he stripped Tumur Ochir, the ideologue-party historian and Politburo member, of all his functions. Tsedenbal then "revealed" that Tumur Ochir and the second secretary of the Central Committee, L. Tsend, had attempted to overthrow him and his pro-Soviet regime and that the "conspirators" had received Peking's support. Moscow sent congratulatory telegrams; Peking sent protest notes. With Brezhnev taking over in the Kremlin, the anti-Chinese purges in Mongolia did not stop. The first secretary of the South Gobi Province on the Chinese border, B. Nyambuu, and others were subsequently accused of stirring up anti-Soviet nationalist passions and were stripped of their functions. As a followup to this latest purge, the Kremlin's trouble-shooter Shelepin had arrived in the Mongol capital on January 28, 1965, and during a ten-day visit had helped to reinforce support for Tsedenbal, whose position was still thought to be threatened by the remaining pro-Chinese faction of his party. Shelepin had also coordinated security measures and military matters in the midst of the growing number of border incidents and ongoing Chinese military buildup along the Mongol-Chinese border.[30]

The next step of the Kremlin's policy makers was to boost Soviet economic aid for Mongolia's fourth five-year plan (1966-71) to 660 million rubles, an increase of nearly 200 million. In addition, at Soviet request, the East European COMECON countries (the Soviety bloc's "common market") had raised their Mongolian assistance program to 55 million rubles. The Shelepin visit and the economic aid were only the beginning of the Soviet drive to recapture and solidify the strategic position of Mongolia. Brezhnev's tug-of-war with the Chinese had reached a point where he had to move to assure Soviet state interests at all costs. In his political maneuvering he adopted a strategy that had served his predecessors well, Tsarists and Bolsheviks alike. He played up to the autonomist tendencies of the Mongols—who traditionally feared Chinese colonization—in an endeavor to transform the People's Republic of Mongolia into a buffer zone between Russia and China.

From the military standpoint, the new treaty replacing Stalin's mutual assistance treaty of 1936 was of little significance—both treaties permitted the stationing of Russian troops in Mongolian territory. What had become outdated, however, was the political content. The previous treaty was aimed against militarist Japan; the present one had to be an instrument directed against Communist China. Naturally the ten articles of the new treaty provided for cooperation in all fields of national effort—economic, scientific, and technical. Article five contained the usual provisions for assistance in defense matters, for insuring security, independence, and territorial integrity for the two countries. As a new feature, however, the treaty called for mutual assistance on the basis of "socialist internationalism" and set itself the task of "constantly strengthening the defensive might of the socialist community." This formula put the Soviet-Mongol cooperation on a multilateral basis and attached Mongolia informally to the Warsaw Pact Treaty.[31] At the same time this international footing assured Tsedenbal that he could count on the members of the Warsaw

Pact for support if Mongolia found itself under attack from Peking. Under these terms, the Kremlin deployed two of its divisions, backed by heavy logistic and air support, and supplemented them with rocket forces equipped with a wide variety of nuclear weapons in the south and east of Mongolia. By this concentration of power alone, the Soviet armed forces moved within 600 miles of Peking, and the ground-to-ground missiles made the Russians capable of reaching vital areas in west and northwest China in a matter of minutes.

As expected, the Chinese, whose political influence in Mongolia by then was almost eliminated, sharply criticized Brezhnev and assailed the mutual defense treaty. They also attacked the Tsedenbal leadership for serving the interest of the Khrushchev-Brezhnev "revisionists," claimed that Mongol army units were violating Chinese territory, and charged that the Mongols and the Russians were planning an all-out armed aggression against China.[32] For all their harsh rhetoric and grave accusations, however, the Chinese refrained from taking drastic action. Instead, they took precautionary defense measures by deploying more troops along the Sino-Mongol border and stepping up their intelligence activity in Outer Mongolia.

The Chinese pressure had little impact on the Mongol leadership. Tsedenbal continued to follow his pro-Soviet policy line without hesitation. In statement after statement he stressed that Mao Tse-tung's policy toward Mongolia was nothing but a modern version of the old Chinese threat to colonize Mongolia. At times, in a particularly combative spirit, he even promised to carry the fight against the "Mao clique" into China itself. Whether these threats had any substance is a secondary question. What is relevant is that Tsedenbal was well aware of the geographic importance of his own territory in Soviet strategic planning, and he fully realized that the Mongolian buffer zone afforded extremely advantageous sites for Soviet missiles.

On January 17, Brezhnev flew back to the Soviet capital. On board the same special plane when it arrived in Moscow were Secretary Shelepin and his party, who on their way home from the DRV had joined Brezhnev at the Siberian city of Irkutsk. During the flight the two had plenty of time to compare notes. Though one can only guess what they discussed, it seems safe to suppose they were pleased with the results. In Vietnam, Ho Chi Minh had swung to a neutral position in the Sino-Soviet dispute and was ready to send a delegation to the forthcoming Soviet Communist party Congress. Moreover the delivery of the growing number of SAM anti-aircraft missiles, tanks, artillery, and other modern Soviet military hardware made it likely that the DRV leadership would stay on this course.

Considerable gains had also been made in Mongolia, again at China's expense. The mutual assistance treaty reaffirmed legal access of Russian troops to Mongolian territory; it also became an effective politico-military tool to make the Mongol leadership accept the Soviet strategic interest as their own; and, last but not least, it gave the Kremlin a powerful hand to play against China, should the need arise.

In addition, Kosygin's diplomatic triumph on the Indian subcontinent enhanced Soviet prestige, laid the groundwork for future Russian expansion, and weakened Chinese influence in that part of the world.

There is certainly no exact measure to weigh success in international politics. There can be little doubt, however, that the upsurge in Soviet diplomatic and inter-party maneuvering in late 1965 and early 1966 was of lasting significance. It considerably extended Soviet spheres of influence and consequently gave Moscow a distinct advantage over Peking in the battle to reassert leadership in the international Communist movement and to establish Asian supremacy.

CHAPTER VIII

More Peace Feelers and a Peace Hoax

The considerable political and diplomatic gains so methodically pursued by the Soviet Union in Asia in early 1966 were to have far-reaching consequences. Specifically, it seemed to me that the impact of the growing Soviet influence in Hanoi overshadowed that of the Chinese. Moreover, increased Soviet military assistance had a significant bearing on the unfolding events in Vietnam. All this occurred, however, at a time when the steadily escalating war dominated the news spotlight over much of the world and tended to eclipse Soviet maneuvering.

A major development in the war was the expansion of American aerial bombing: in the first six months of 1966 United States Air Force planes broadened their attacks beyond the usual logistic targets in North Vietnam to pound petroleum and oil storage facilities, Russian-made surface-to-air missile sites, and conventional anti-aircraft batteries (including those located in and around Hanoi and Haiphong) in an unrelenting fury. In addition, President Johnson agreed to increase the American troop level in South Vietnam to a record high of

400,000.[1] These actions were intended as clear indications that Washington was indeed determined to do whatever was necessary to protect the Saigon government and to make the war as costly as possible for Ho Chi Minh. Meanwhile, the initial successes of new pacification programs raised hopes that with United States assistance the Saigon government could extend its control to the rural areas.

At the same time the Hanoi leadership also made great efforts to strengthen its power base. But first and foremost, the morale of the exhausted population had to be restored and spreading pacifist sentiments as well as the deviation from the party line stamped out. A "rectification campaign" (as the process of eliminating dissatisfaction with the regime's war policy was called) was launched. Our embassy in Hanoi reported that the People's Security Forces (the counter-espionage agency) arrested and deported "suspicious elements" to remote mines, while the disciplinary organ of the Communist party, the Control Commission, carried out, under the guidelines of the Politburo, a large-scale purge at different levels of the party organization. The campaign started in February 1966 with the publication of Politburo member Le Duc Tho's article, "Let Us Change the Trend and Step up the Party Building Task in Order to Insure Successful Carrying out of the Anti-U. S. Struggle for National Salvation." It lasted all year. Le Duc Tho attacked an unspecified number of party organizations and individuals who did not "exert wholeheartedly every effort to support and aid the revolution in the South and to defeat the U. S. imperialist war of destruction in the North." Tho warned that there was a long struggle ahead, and North Vietnam must be on the alert to foil "all plots and tricks of the enemy." He added:

> Faced with great changes in the situation and with the revolutionary tasks, a small number of comrades have developed erroneous thoughts and views. Concerning the combat task, they have made an incorrect assessment of the balance of power between the enemy and us. . . . Now they entertain subjectivism and pacifism, slacken their vigilance, and fail to get ideologically ready for combat. Now they see only difficulties and do not see opportunities; display pessimism, perplexity, and reluctance to protracted resistance; fail to realize

clearly the deceptive peace negotiation plot of the enemy; and rely on outside aid.

Le Duc Tho labeled the opposition "rightist deviation" and sternly stated that rightist views had been eliminated in the past and "it [is] all the more necessary for us [the party leadership] to hold more firmly to this course of action."[2]

Officials in Washington were puzzled whether or not Le Duc Tho's article reflected division within the Hanoi Politburo. Such division was never reported by the Hungarian Embassy in Hanoi, and the Soviets had never mentioned to us such factionalism. There were no purges in the Politburo following the 37-day bombing pause, and the Hanoi Politburo maintained its extraordinary record of cohesion and consensus afterwards.

As in the past, the tightening of general security not only halted opposition but also resulted in the desired obedience. In addition, with some outside help, it became possible for Hanoi to withstand the growing American military pressure. The outside help amounted to substantially more than before the bombing started and even more than in 1965. It came in the form of increased economic and military aid from the Soviet Union, the East European Communist governments, and China. Economic aid was raised from $150 million (1965) to $225 million, and military assistance programs received an even bigger boost. The total of $270 million supplied by the Soviet bloc and China in 1965 was now almost doubled (to $455 million). The bulk of the aid—$260 million—was provided by the Soviets and East Europeans. The Chinese made up the difference partly by arms delivery, partly by sending Chinese labor battalions to repair damaged railroad tracks, bridges, and roads, mainly in the northern part of the DRV.[3] Revitalized by the massive assistance, Hanoi was now able to concentrate on the war. It improved the road networks on the Ho Chi Minh trail, built extensive alternate routes in the southern part of the DRV, and kept the flow of men and material going south at a virtually unchanged level. Further, despite their heavy battlefield losses, the Communist troop strength in South Vietnam reached 260,000–280,000 men in the first half of 1966.[4]

By July an entirely new situation had developed. Northern regular troops started to cross the Demilitarized Zone directly at the 17th parallel. First the 324 B Division, equipped with brand new Russian and Chinese weapons, passed through the jungle routes of the Zone in small groups, making detection by U. S. reconnaissance almost impossible. The division quickly established a base area with underground trenches and hidden food and ammunition storage facilities. Then in a matter of weeks, the North Vietnamese High Command reinforced the beachhead with the 341 and 325 B Combat Divisions.[5]

This bold move caused general consternation in Moscow and the East European capitals. No one had expected that the Vietnamese would dare to use the DMZ as a military springboard. High party officials in the Kremlin were seriously concerned that the Americans would not tolerate this open invasion, would call up the reserves and launch an all-out attack against North Vietnam. Soviet Defense Ministry experts even predicted that American marines would execute amphibious landings deep in North Vietnamese territory as they did during the Korean War. These same experts also thought the United States might use tactical atomic weapons if the Chinese intervened militarily in the conflict. The gloom deepened when reports reached Moscow (and from there, the East European capitals) that the Chinese had offered to help Hanoi, if necessary, with an army of a half-million men on the condition that the DRV would launch simultaneous general attacks against South Vietnam and Laos. It was a great relief when Ho Chi Minh sidestepped that plan, but the tension remained because Hanoi, despite Russian warnings, continued to send its troops through the Zone.[6]

As it turned out, however, the Kremlin had little cause for such alarm. The Johnson administration had no intention of retaliating by extending the ground war to North Vietnam. It simply accepted the violation of the DMZ as another incident in the rapidly escalating fighting and stoically categorized it as part of General Giap's version of "strategic mobility in Hanoi's protracted war of attrition." Indeed, Washington forebore even to exploit the propaganda aspects of the action, though North Vietnam at the same time severely condemned the American bombing of Hanoi and Haiphong.

While Washington remained calm, American troops in South

Vietnam started Operation Hastings, a large combined-operations sweep against the newly infiltrated North Vietnamese division. In addition, U. S. Marines began amphibious landings—not, as Soviet experts had imagined, in the North but in the South below the DMZ, attempting to push back those Northern troops which had infiltrated along the coastline. Parallel with the fighting, General Westmoreland proposed to President Johnson the organization of a multi-national military organization to bar enemy infiltration through the Zone. He called it the KANZUS Forces from its national components—Korea, Australia, New Zealand, and the United States. Furthermore, he came up with the idea of defoliating the southern portion of the Demilitarized Zone or an area just south of the Zone to prevent further infiltration. Back in Washington the Joint Chiefs of Staff worked on the so-called Jason project—an air supported anti-infiltration barrier that was planned to extend all the way across the country to the Mekong River, blocking not only the DMZ area but also the Laos infiltration routes. But as we know today from the Pentagon Papers, none of these ideas for halting or slowing down the infiltration through the Demilitarized Zone ever became effective.[7]

In this new phase of the war, statesmen and diplomats tried to bring the conflict to an end, or at least tried to discover whether there were any mutually acceptable grounds on which the belligerents could move toward a peaceful solution. In March, Secretary General U Thant proposed a three-stage plan, which, in summary, was 1) an end to the bombing of the North, 2) de-escalation of the fighting, and 3) negotiations. Washington expressed readiness to consider the plan; Hanoi rejected all stages but the first. In April, Japanese special envoy Masaichi Yokoyama toured twenty countries and attempted to organize a committee of nations to bring about a negotiated settlement. The North Vietnamese flatly rebuffed this initiative.

The sinologist and retired Canadian diplomat Chester A. Ronning visited Hanoi twice—in March and in June—as a special envoy of Ottawa. But he too was unable to bring the two sides closer to peace. He found the North Vietnamese leaders convinced they were winning the war and uncompromising in their attitude concerning negotiations. As Ronning reported to

Ottawa, he was simply unable to move the North Vietnamese from their insistence that the U. S. withdraw its forces from South Vietnamese territories and recognize the NLF as sole representative of the South Vietnamese people. The only new proposal made to Ronning was Premier Pham Van Dong's suggestion that the DRV enter in some form of "talk" if the United States declared an unconditional and permanent halt to the bombing of North Vietnam. But Hanoi at the same time was not willing to de-escalate or to pay any price for the cessation of the bombing. The Canadian envoy had no better luck in Washington. The U. S. government was not interested in "talks" but only in formal negotiations, and it would proceed with reduction of hostilities only if a reciprocal arrangement with North Vietnam could be effected: the bombing of North Vietnam would cease if that would bring an end to the infiltration from the North.[8]

Prime Minister Indira Gandhi, President de Gaulle, and Pope Paul also attempted to find ways to end the war; but none of them could get so much as a suggestion that Hanoi would take any reciprocal military action whatever. And finally Adam Rapacki, Alexei Kosygin, and János Péter from the socialist camp came to the forefront to present their plans for a final settlement of the conflict.

The Polish Episode–the "Marigold Affair"

Polish Foreign Minister Adam Rapacki's mediation attempt, the so-called "Marigold Affair," resembled the Péter mediation in some respects, but as a diplomatic ploy it was far more masterfully executed. He made a tempting offer to the Americans to "prove North Vietnam's readiness for negotiation" while in fact he had nothing firm from Hanoi to offer. He then instigated prolonged Polish-U. S. exploratory talks to obtain concessions from Washington that could be presented as an American position to Hanoi. And, finally, he made an effort to work out a package deal favorable to Hanoi for the settlement of the war.

The Polish action started on June 27, about a week after Ronning left Hanoi empty-handed. On Rapacki's instruction, the Polish I.C.C. representative, Janus Lewandowski, contacted Giovanni D'Orlandi, the veteran Italian diplomat and dean of the diplomatic corps in Saigon, to report a "very specific peace offer." Lewandowski told D'Orlandi that he had just returned from a meeting in Hanoi with Ho Chi Minh, Pham Van Dong, and General Giap, who, he said, were disappointed with Ronning's proposal of a U. S. bombing halt in exchange for a DRV infiltration halt. Nevertheless, the Pole observed, there was still some hope for a compromise. The Hanoi leaders would be willing to start negotiations if NLF representatives could take part and if the United States would suspend the bombing. Hanoi would even make a few "concessions." It would not, for instance, ask for immediate reunification; it would not demand the establishment of a "socialist" system in South Vietnam, and, although Hanoi did not want Ky, it did not want to interfere with the South Vietnamese government; Saigon would not have to change its relationships in the field of foreign affairs; and neutralization of South Vietnam would not be asked. Moreover, American troop withdrawal could be arranged according to a "reasonable calendar."

Lewandowski said nothing to indicate he was acting on behalf of either Hanoi or Moscow, but he did suggest that the preliminary discussions should be held between the Soviet and the American governments inasmuch as the North Vietnamese were "tightly controlled" by the Chinese Communists.

The Italian reacted with amazement and then bewilderment. Why, he asked, was his Polish colleague bringing this message to him? Because D'Orlandi was known to be an able debater who could put the case to President Johnson, and because Italy had the sympathy of the United States, was Lewandowski's sycophantic answer.[9]

The Polish message was in American hands within two days. But Rusk, who received the news while on a state visit in Canberra, Australia, had mixed feelings about it. On the one hand, it was encouraging if the NLF was no longer pressing its claim to be the sole representative of the South Vietnamese people. On the other, a "suspension" of bombing could easily incur heavy pressure for an unconditional cessation. In addition, this Polish-Italian channel looked suspiciously devious. Ambassador Lodge felt the offer was too good to be true, and said so. He also expressed doubts about the credibility of the Polish intermediary. D'Orlandi, for his part, was convinced that the Poles were striving to find a solution on Moscow's instruction.

Despite its strong reservations, Washington decided to pursue the lead and instructed Lodge to try to find answers to the procedural questions of where, when, and with what parties Hanoi proposed to negotiate. Washington also wanted to know what action, if any, Hanoi would take in response to a bombing pause.

On July 9, Lodge met secretly with Lewandowski in D'Orlandi's office, but no immediate answers were forthcoming. Just a day before, Gomulka, Brezhnev, and the other leaders of the Warsaw Pact had signed a bombastic declaration at a meeting of the Warsaw Pact Political Consultative Committee in Bucharest condemning the United States for its "barbaric intervention" in Vietnam, ridiculing the American peace proposals, and warning Washington that the Warsaw Pact countries were ready to send volunteers to Vietnam. Thus, not surprisingly, Lewandowski had received new instructions from Rapacki—instructions that did not support the message he had communicated to the Americans. He now bluntly stated that the United States government had no right to bomb North Vietnam and therefore no right to propose conditions for cessation; that in the opinion of his government there could be no accommodation without a halt of the bombing; and that the United States must recognize the Four Points proposal of the DRV if it wanted a peaceful solution. With this, the Polish mediation came to a temporary halt. Rusk and Lodge felt their suspicions had been confirmed. As I learned much later, Rapacki was not happy with this turn of events. His ambassador at the I.C.C., however, felt otherwise. In reality, Lewandowski was not a career diplomat but a former high-ranking officer of the Polish

Intelligence Service, a hardliner, a man consistently hostile to America.

The rest of July and August was rather uneventful for Polish diplomacy as far as Vietnam was concerned. The usual coordinating conference of senior officials of the foreign ministries of the Soviet bloc countries convened in August to discuss strategies for the upcoming U. N. General Assembly session. The Russians urged their allies to do everything they could to achieve another suspension of the bombing. But that was just a general foreign policy guideline of the kind the Soviet Foreign Ministry routinely gave out to the East Europeans. Concrete action-plans, such as Rapacki's Vietnamese mediation, were always discussed on a strictly bilateral basis and kept in strictest confidence. János Péter, for instance, knew nothing about his Polish colleague's dealings despite the fact that in the fall of 1966 he himself was on a "fact-finding tour" in North Vietnam and discussed his findings and plans at great length with Soviet Foreign Minister Gromyko.

By September Gromyko and Rapacki decided to revive the Polish mediation effort. In fact, there was still nothing to mediate. Hanoi still demanded a bombing suspension before "talks" could begin, and Washington still wanted to trade the bombing pause for the cessation of North Vietnamese infiltration. Both Gromyko and Rapacki, however, were eager to take a new reading on American attitudes in the light of the rapid escalation of the war, which was making things difficult for Hanoi.

Again Lewandowski was entrusted to establish contact with Lodge in Saigon, and again D'Orlandi was used as a go-between. The contact was made and talks began. For more than two months they led nowhere. Lewandowski, intent on obtaining the best possible terms for Hanoi, was not interested in establishing Hanoi's bottom-line position or facilitating mutual de-escalation. Even so, some of the remarks he made sounded intriguing to Washington. For instance, he stated that, although he could not work to preserve the present Ky government intact, he "envisioned" a coalition government of "sensible South Vietnamese politicians" with a man or two from the right (the Ky government) and a man or two from the left (the NLF).

He also stated that further debate on the bombing question or de-escalation would be pointless, and instead a package deal—an overall solution of the Vietnam War—should be worked out.

Slowly Washington began to show interest, and by mid-November Lodge, on Rusk's instruction, was able to give the Polish diplomat a full description of the U. S. position regarding an eventual package deal. This position contained all the elements of the secretary's Fourteen Points as well as the statement of the Manila conference that U. S. troops would be withdrawn from Vietnam in six months on condition that the North Vietnamese troops would be withdrawn from the South. In addition, it offered a new de-escalatory formula—the so-called "Phase A-Phase B" face-saving package worked out by the State Department. Under this plan, the United States would suspend the bombing (Phase A). After some adequate time period both sides would undertake mutually agreed de-escalatory measures (Phase B). Thus Hanoi's actions taken in Phase B would appear as a reciprocity to the American steps made in Phase B rather than to the suspension of the bombing.

The Pole listened carefully, took extensive notes, and promised to bring the ambassador's every word to the attention of

*Lewandowski summarized the 10 points to Lodge as follows:
1. The U. S. is interested in a peaceful solution through negotiations.
2. Negotiations should not be interpreted as a way to negotiate surrender by those opposing the U. S. in Vietnam. A political negotiation would be aimed at finding an acceptable solution to all the problems, having in mind that the present status quo in South Vietnam must be changed in order to take into account the interests of the parties presently opposing the policy of the U. S. in South Vietnam.
3. The U. S. does not desire a permanent or a long-term military presence in South Vietnam.
4. The U. S. is willing to discuss all problems with respect to the settlement.
5. The U. S. is willing to accept the participation of "all" in elections and the supervision of these elections by an appropriate international body.
6. The U. S. believes that reunification should be settled by the Vietnamese themselves after peace and proper representative organs are established in South Vietnam.
7. The U. S. is prepared to abide by a neutral South Vietnam.
8. The U. S. is prepared to stop bombing "if this will facilitate such a peaceful solution." In this regard the U. S. is prepared to accept DRV modalities on the cessation and not require the DRV to admit infiltration into South Vietnam.
9. The U. S. will not agree to "reunification under military pressure."
10. The U. S. "will not declare now or in the future its acceptance of North Vietnam's 4 or 5 points."

the authorities in Hanoi. Following the meeting, Lewandowski left for the North Vietnamese capital. He returned to Saigon on November 30, and in a matter of hours was conferring with Lodge in secret session. He told Lodge that in Hanoi he had summarized the American position in 10 points* and presented them to the "most respectable government sources," who in turn authorized him to report as follows to the American government: "If the U. S. is really of the views which I have presented, it would be advisable to confirm them directly by conversation with the North Vietnamese ambassador in Warsaw."[10]

The Lewandowski version of the American position seemed to Lodge at first glance to be in order. Nevertheless, he could not give an immediate answer without Washington's approval. In Washington, the State Department—after close scrutiny—established that Lewandowski, intentionally or by mistake, had partially misrepresented the U. S. position: he had not included the Phase A–Phase B formulation. When asked about this omission, he simply stated that he had presented it orally to Pham Van Dong.[11] Despite these obscurities, Lodge, on instruction from the State Department, conveyed the message to Lewandowski (on December 3) that U. S. Ambassador Gronouski in Warsaw would contact the DRV Embassy on December 6 or soon thereafter. Lodge added that the Ten Points only broadly reflected the U. S. position; thus "several specific points were subject to important differences of interpretation."

At this point Rapacki personally took charge. He summoned Gronouski to his office, expressed deep concern about the clarified U. S. position, and warned that deviations from the interpretation given in Lewandowski's Ten Points might have a negative effect on Hanoi. He also protested the stepped-up bombing of Hanoi which had occurred while the delicate negotiations were in progress. (Among others, the Yen Vien railyard and the Van Dien vehicle depot on the outskirts of Hanoi were hit on December 2nd and 4th.) He rejected Gronouski's explanation that the target lists had been established and the orders given long before, and the orders had been carried out at that time only because of clearing weather over Hanoi.

After crossing swords with Gronouski, Rapacki contacted

Foreign Minister Fanfani in Rome and D'Orlandi in Saigon and in a sternly worded message complained about the United States insisting on its reservations concerning the interpretation of the Ten Points. Moreover, he warned that intensified air bombardment would destroy all possibility of a contact through Warsaw.

On December 9, Rapacki's efforts met with partial success. Gronouski assured him to his satisfaction that he would inform the North Vietnamese at their first meeting that the Lewandowski formulation was consistent with the U. S. views. (In fact, as far as the bombing was concerned, there had been no change in the U. S. position: Washington had no plan to alter the bombing pattern of the Rolling Thunder campaign. Gronouski, therefore, took pains to avoid discussing the U. S. intent regarding either escalation or de-escalation.) Gronouski reminded the Polish foreign minister that the subject of the bombing of North Vietnam had been discussed in Hanoi by Lewandowski, and he (Gronouski) assumed that the U. S. proposal for solution of the problem had been outlined in connection with the Phase A-Phase B de-escalation formula. Thus the current air raids had nothing to do with the diplomatic efforts "to get underway the projected U. S.-North Vietnamese talks."

Rapacki disagreed, contending that stepped-up bombing was a provocation because "the leaders in Hanoi cannot and will not yield under pressure." On December 13, U. S. planes again attacked the Yen Vien railroad yard and the Van Dien vehicle depot. The Soviet news agency *Tass* reported that residential areas and the suburbs of Hanoi were severely damaged and casualties ran high. The Rumanian and Chinese embassy buildings were also hit. The strikes made sensational headlines everywhere. Several Western governments and non-aligned countries expressed "deep regret," and the DRV lodged an official protest to the International Control Commission. In the midst of the uproar Rapacki summoned Gronouski to his office and abruptly informed him that on Hanoi's request the Poles would terminate their mediation for arranging a direct contact between the governments of the DRV and the United States. In a calm, serious, and matter-of-fact voice he said that "the whole responsibility for losing this chance of a peaceful solution to the Vietnam War rested on the United States government."

With that statement, the Polish mediation was almost over. Gronouski rejected Rapacki's accusations and countercharged that the Polish government had backed out of Lewandowski's earlier restatement of the U. S. package deal and then sought to blame the American side. Rapacki then staged a scene, throwing his spectacles on the floor and in an agitated voice insisting the bombing had torpedoed the Polish peace initiative.[12]

Before Christmas the United States called off the bombing of targets within ten nautical miles of Hanoi and proposed direct talks with Hanoi's representatives, again through the Poles. Rapacki, after some hesitation, agreed to forward the message to Hanoi, but the answer was completely negative. The situation had completely changed, he explained to Gronouski. Now the Americans had to stop the bombing over North Vietnam for at least three or four weeks if they wanted the Polish government to undertake another peace mission in Hanoi. But the State Department, extremely doubtful that Warsaw had ever had any commitment from the DRV government to a meeting in the Polish capital, now flatly rejected this condition.

The Soviets, who had so far remained in the background, made a surprise move. The second man in the Soviet Embassy in Washington, Minister Counsellor Alexander Zinchuk, called on William Bundy (on December 22) and notified him that his government was aware of the "Marigold Affair" and supported the Polish role in it. As "background information" he revealed that the bombing was an extremely sensitive issue in Hanoi. The raids against Hanoi had left the North Vietnamese leaders—as well as the Soviets—in doubt about the real intentions of the United States. To many in Moscow it seemed the U. S. government was seeking a military solution. The Soviet diplomat also disclosed that in early December Brezhnev and Kosygin had discussed the whole matter with Le Duc Tho, who stopped in Moscow on his way back to Hanoi from the Hungarian Communist party conference. In the face of the bombing escalation, however, the Soviet leaders could not advise the

Hanoi leadership to go ahead with the Warsaw meeting. To give his *démarche* more weight, Zinchuk reminded Bundy that the Soviet Union had promised in the recent "Warsaw Pact Bucharest Declaration" to send volunteers to Vietnam (if the United States further escalated the war and if Hanoi requested the volunteers). He earnestly hoped such an unpleasant situation would not occur.[13] Zinchuk's message was echoed a week later by Ambassador Dobrynin, when he told the State Department's Russian expert, Ambassador Thompson, that the bombing of Hanoi had destroyed the hopeful "Marigold Affair." Dobrynin added that the Kremlin was not sure whether the peace initiative had been deliberately undercut by the American military or whether the U. S. government was determined to achieve a military victory instead of a peaceful solution.

As the Russians "wondered" about the American intentions, high officials in the State Department wondered about the Russian diplomatic intervention. Why was it necessary for the Kremlin to get involved in the affair after Rapacki had already cancelled the Warsaw contact? Was the Soviet move merely another attempt to exert pressure for a permanent bombing halt? The answer to the puzzle became clear in late January 1967 when Politburo member and chairman of the Supreme Soviet, Nikolai V. Podgorny, told Ambassador Thompson that only a halt of the bombing of the North could result in talks with North Vietnam. His authoritative statement was thereafter reiterated publicly as well as privately by Hanoi many times.

I personally had no information about "Marigold" while it was going on. My contacts with the Polish chargé in Washington, Zdzislaw Szewczik, were infrequent and not as frank as my contacts with the Czechoslovakian and Rumanian ambassadors, which may explain why I heard nothing. It is also entirely possible that Szewczik did not know what Rapacki was doing in Warsaw or Lewandowski in Saigon. In early January, however, the secrecy surrounding the "Marigold Affair" came to an end. The Polish U. N. Mission in New York quietly began to leak the story all around the world organization. Robert Estabrook of the *Washington Post* received a great many details from "unidentified" Polish sources. At the same time Polish Permanent Representative Tomorowicz briefed the other bloc diplomats, and finally I learned the Polish version of the story from our U. N. ambassador, Csatordai. I once broached the matter with Dobrynin, but he simply informed me that nothing had come of it. He offered no elaboration, not even to assert as a cause of failure the "interpretation of the Ten Points" or the U. S. air raids near Hanoi. All he would say was that there seemed to be little possibility of any progress, since Hanoi was insisting on unconditional cessation of the bombing while the United States still firmly insisted on reciprocal action by Hanoi.

Moscow Channel

With the "Marigold Affair" closed, the center of action shifted from Warsaw to Moscow. In early January, for the first time in the course of the war, Soviet Foreign Ministry officials hinted in private conversations to Americans that diplomats of the Democratic Republic of Vietnam in Moscow would be available for preliminary talks if such was the desire of the United States government. About the same time, *New York Times* senior correspondent Harrison E. Salisbury sent word from Hanoi to Rusk through the British consul-general that during a four-hour interview, North Vietnamese Premier Pham Van Dong had strongly indicated to him that U. S.-DRV talks could start once air attacks against the North were halted. Both pieces of information were judged serious enough to warrant a follow-up, and Dean Rusk instructed American Chargé D'Affaires John C. Guthrie in Moscow to get in touch with the North Vietnamese and try to work out a direct and secret channel of communication. To Washington's wonderment, Guthrie achieved in four days what the Polish Foreign Minister Rapacki had promised to arrange in seven months: Minister Counselor Le Trang of North Vietnam expressed readiness to confer with the American. The rest was routine.

At their first meeting, on January 10, Guthrie delivered Rusk's message. He opened by saying that the United States government placed "the highest priority in finding a mutually agreeable, completely secure arrangement for exchanging communications with the government of the Democratic Republic of Vietnam about the possibilities of achieving a peaceful settlement of the Vietnamese dispute." Then, in a business-like manner, he added that his government would do everything possible to work out an agreement with the DRV regarding the time and place of such discussions.[14]

Le Trang seemed nervous and perhaps somewhat irritated at having to meet the enemy in the diplomatic arena and not on the battlefield. He launched into a verbal barrage, charging that the United States was steadily escalating the war and the American peace intitiatives must be considered as nothing but a sinister plot to deceive the people of his country and the world. His outburst expended, however, he slowed down and at the end of the meeting promised to forward Rusk's message to Hanoi. Before Guthrie departed, they agreed to conceal the fact that they had met.

At their second encounter seven days later, after a few technical questions about communication, Le Trang asked for a summation of Washington's plan for settlement of the conflict. This Guthrie could not provide right away; he must wait for State Department instruction. In three days he supplied the answer. Washington proposed a cease-fire or mutual troop withdrawal from South Vietnam. In addition, it suggested placing on the agenda questions relating to South Vietnam's future, including the recognition of the integrity of South and North Vietnam and the problem of unification. When Guthrie handed over this memorandum to Le Trang, he emphasized that Washington would be willing to incorporate on the agenda any topic Hanoi deemed in need of review, including Hanoi's Four Point proposal which contained the problem of the representation of the NLF.

The Vietnamese thanked Guthrie for the message and promised to transmit it to Hanoi without delay and inform him of the result. The atmosphere by now was relaxed. Occasionally the two chatted about the Moscow weather and even exchanged diplomatic pleasantries. Guthrie's newly arrived boss, Ambassador Thompson, in Moscow, and Dean Rusk and William Bundy in Washington followed this development with cautious optimism. Maybe Ho Chi Minh really was willing to sit down to talk, since the raging Cultural Revolution could have diverted Mao Tse-tung's interest in supporting the Hanoi cause. Perhaps the Vietnamese leader now looked upon his own country's future with less certainty than before. Perhaps the Soviets were influencing the North Vietnamese leadership to seek a compromise, or perhaps the bombing of the North and the growing U. S. military pressure had simply forced Hanoi to try to seek a way out.

Alas, Washington strategists who tried to analyze the situation soon learned that Ho Chi Minh had not changed his negotiation stance, whatever the changing pressures. On January 27, Le Trang handed over to Guthrie Hanoi's answer to the American overture. It again accused Washington of intensification of the war, branded the U. S. bombing of North Vietnam a blatant act of aggression, and categorically demanded an unconditional cessation of bombing before even the dates and places of contact between the DRV and the United States could be discussed. In addition the Vietnamese diplomat cited several cases of serious escalations, including the destruction of Ben Suc in South Vietnam and the bombing of densely populated areas of Viet Tri, Thai Nguyen, and Thanh Hoa in the North.

The next day Radio Hanoi broadcast a report of an interview between Foreign Minister Trinh and his trusted friend, the Australian journalist Wilfred G. Burchett. Trinh in essence stated publicly what Le Trang had stated in private: only after unconditional cessation of bombing and all other acts of war against the DRV, he insisted, could the talks begin.[15]

Guthrie quickly called on the Vietnamese chargé and expressed displeasure over the broadcast. He then reminded Le Trang that the four-day Tet holiday was approaching and that both sides had already agreed to suspend the hostilities for its duration. The lull would afford a good opportunity to start mutually agreed de-escalatory measures or to start secret negotiations to settle the whole conflict and work out a formula for a bombing halt. Guthrie's arguments had no effect on Le Trang or his superior, and again the situation was deadlocked. But again, as on previous occasions, a volunteer appeared on the scene with new propositions to "show a way out of the impasse." This time the volunteer was British Prime Minister Harold Wilson.

The Wilson-Kosygin Episode

Wilson was not a newcomer among those who tried to close the Vietnam conflict through a negotiated settlement. Like the others, he had met with little success thus far. His earlier efforts to revive the Geneva Conference had come to naught. He could, however, claim partial credit for halting the preparation in the summer of 1966 of "war crimes" trials of U. S. pilots captured in Vietnam. This he achieved by working through the Russians to persuade Hanoi that such trials could only inflame the "hawks" in America and lead ultimately to further escalation of the war. Perhaps this success prompted him to try further. Or perhaps he perceived mediation as a political necessity once his own Labour party began to criticize his pro-Washington stand on Vietnam. Some of those who knew Wilson well also felt he would gain considerable personal satisfaction from helping to end the war and believed this notion affected his decision. At any rate, Kosygin had scheduled a week-long visit to England in early February, and this visit offered a likely opportunity to carry out his plan.

Whatever his hopes, personal or otherwise, they received little encouragement from President Johnson's special envoy Chester Cooper, who arrived in London just before the Russian's visit to brief the British about recent developments. The American envoy revealed that Washington was in direct contact with Hanoi. He did not say that the contact had been established through Moscow, but he reported that his government had failed to uncover any sign that Hanoi was interested in starting negotiations. (This last revelation was important and contradicted the opinion of many Western observers who had read just the opposite message into the recent public statement of North Vietnamese Foreign Minister Trinh.) Cooper suggested that the British urge the Russians to keep in mind "their short-run opportunities and responsibilities to insure Hanoi against Chinese economic, political, or even military actions in the event Hanoi moved toward negotiation."[16] Apart from this consideration, Cooper observed, Russian interests would be more or less in tandem with Washington's policies because both superpowers could only gain from a reduction of tensions in Asia. Finally, the envoy informed the prime minister that President Johnson planned to send Ho Chi Minh a personal message proposing an early negotiation along the line of the latest American de-escalatory formula, the "Phase A-Phase B" package deal. (This was the same plan that British Foreign Secretary George Brown had presented to the Russians in November, but it was never answered directly or indirectly by either Moscow or Hanoi.)

From the Cooper briefing Wilson picked up the idea of reviving the Phase A-Phase B formula as the most realistic proposition, and at his first meeting with Kosygin on February 7 he brought up the question. He also spoke at some length about the Trinh interview and came to the not-too-obvious conclusion that the two-phase agreement could serve as a basis to start negotiations. On the one hand, it "could guarantee" an unconditional halt of the bombing—a constant demand of Hanoi; on the other, it could satisfy Washington's request for a mutual de-escalation. After laying his cards on the table, Wilson asked Kosygin whether he would be willing to use his good offices in Hanoi to provide Washington with a "firm sign" during the forthcoming Tet holiday cease-fire. If this could be done, Wilson himself would use his influence to get a clear and immediate answer from Washington.[17]

Kosygin at first said very little. To begin with, he hoped to promote trade and scientific exchanges with Great Britain, and he wanted to use this visit to enhance his country's public image. (As a "goodwill gesture" he had even brought his daughter Ludmilla and his grandson Alexei with him.) Secondly, he had not done his homework on Vietnam, and the only high-level Foreign Ministry representative in his delegation was Deputy Foreign Minister Soldatov, an expert in European affairs.

Thirdly, and perhaps most importantly, the North Vietnamese had not asked him to act as an intermediary. All this does not mean he was entirely out of the picture. Just a few days before he left for London, he had met with U. S. Ambassador Thompson in Moscow and talked about Vietnam. In addition, the Hanoi Politburo had kept him posted through party and diplomatic channels, and Chargé Le Trang, a constant visitor at the Department of International Relations of the Soviet Central Committee and the Soviet Foreign Ministry, had provided detailed information concerning his dealings with Guthrie.

For all these reasons the pragmatic Kosygin opted for discretion and simply endorsed Trinh's formula (Hanoi would talk once the bombing had been stopped) as a basis for negotiation. At the same time he quite frankly admitted to Wilson that he had not negotiated with the DRV government on the subject; he could only refer to Trinh's public statement. At this point Foreign Secretary George Brown chimed in, and the discussion became more animated. To Brown's warning about the negative consequences of North Vietnamese infiltration through the Demilitarized Zone, Kosygin retored that the United States was steadily shipping troops to South Vietnam. The first session ended having gotten nowhere—aside from a generally accepted and unspoken understanding that the British would inform the Americans immediately and the Russians would send word to their friends in Hanoi.

In the evening of the same day Wilson and Kosygin spoke again about Vietnam. Kosygin reiterated his belief that the "Trinh formula" would lead to U. S.-Vietnamese negotiations. He emphasized that he had been in contact with Hanoi since the afternoon session and had been assured of DRV readiness to talk. The Soviet premier suggested that Wilson use the "hot line" to inform Washington or send a cable to the White House. The astonished Wilson first hesitated, then suggested sending a joint telegram to Johnson explaining the meaning of the "Trinh formula." Kosygin sidestepped the offer, and the talks came to a temporary halt.

Then, overnight, the situation changed. Wilson learned from Washington that President Johnson was preparing a message to Ho Chi Minh in which he would further elaborate the "Phase

A-Phase B" formula. It now appeared the president was willing not only to stop the bombing of the North but also to halt the augmentation of U. S. forces in the South if Hanoi would agree to stop infiltrating troops into South Vietnam. The rest of the Washington report was not encouraging. There were no signs of North Vietnamese willingness to negotiate or discuss mutual de-escalatory measures. Nevertheless, any Russian counter-proposal to the United States suggestion of mutual military de-escalation would be carefully studied by the president.[18]

On February 7 Wilson duly forwarded the presidential message, but Kosygin was not impressed. The Americans were asking too much in exchange for a cessation of the bombing, he maintained.

There followed a two-day interlude in the talks, during which time Kosygin attended to British-Russian affairs. Then, in the afternoon of February 10, at a private session, Wilson, Brown, and Kosygin returned again to the Vietnam question. They agreed that as soon as possible Wilson would hand over the newly formulated Phase A-Phase B proposal in writing and that the Russian would forward the message to Hanoi via Moscow. The text was quickly drafted by Chester Cooper and two British Foreign Office officials. By late afternoon it was already in Soviet hands. It followed closely the presidential message of February 7 and spelled out the following steps to be taken by the two sides:

A. The United States *will stop* bombing North Vietnam as soon as it is assured that infiltration from North Vietnam to South Vietnam *will stop*. This assurance can be communicated in secret if North Vietnam so wishes.
B. Within a few days (with the period to be agreed between the two sides before the bombing stops) the United States will stop further augmenting its forces in South Vietnam and North Vietnam will stop infiltration and movement of forces into the South.[19]

It was also spelled out that the bombing halt and the cessation of U. S. troop buildup would be immediately evident but that the stoppage of infiltration would be more difficult to confirm. Nevertheless, the U. S. government requested only a secret assurance from Hanoi.

Kosygin was satisfied that the text accurately reflected what Wilson had told him. Wilson was overjoyed that Kosygin was willing to forward his message to Hanoi. Ambassador Bruce hailed the British mediation effort as "the biggest diplomatic coup of this century."[20] But the rejoicing was premature. Unexpectedly, in an urgent message, President Johnson asked for a correction: the United States would order a cessation of bombing of North Vietnam as soon as it was assured that infiltration from North Vietnam to South Vietnam *had stopped*, at which time the United States would also stop augmenting its troop strength in the South.

The last-minute change in the draft caused no alarm in Hanoi. The leaders there were not prepared in any case to consider de-escalatory measures. Nor did the change create turbulence in Moscow. By the time Kosygin's cypher telegram arrived with the new version of the two-phase proposal, Brezhnev was well aware that Johnson had sent a letter to Ho Chi Minh via the North Vietnamese Embassy in Moscow. He was also aware that in that letter Johnson had imposed the same condition for the bombing pause as stated in the corrected draft Wilson had sent to Kosygin.

The "battle of the tenses"—as the Pentagon historians diplomatically called the president's last-minute change of the position—had a different effect in London. The already tense British-American relationship was further strained. Wilson openly questioned Johnson's intentions, consistency, and logic. Brown complained that Johnson had destroyed the U.K.'s credibility as a negotiator with the Soviet Union. Johnson, on the other hand, maintained that Hanoi had used the holiday bombing pause to build up forces in the South and to mass three or more divisions along the Demilitarized Zone. In response to the British charge that he was inconsistent, he pointed out that he originally had asked for an "assured stoppage of infiltration," not for an "assurance" that infiltration "will stop," and thus the charge was unjust. Finally he noted that so far Kosygin had only reiterated Trinh's public statement and had transmitted no message from Hanoi.

Who was right in the stormy dispute (and everybody seemed to be right from his own point of view) quickly became an academic question, for the mediation effort was almost out of steam. The Kosygin visit in Britain drew to a close, and, parallel with it, the Tet cease-fire in Vietnam neared its end. Wilson made a last-gasp effort to persuade Johnson to extend the already extended bombing pause. All he got for his pains was an impossible timetable. The president promised that, if Washington could get an answer from Hanoi in eight hours that the movement of men and materiel from North to South Vietnam would stop, then the bombing would not be resumed.

Not surprisingly, Kosygin viewed Johnson's offer as an ultimatum. "The North Vietnamese," he said, "could not be expected to abandon the South or stop all movement of supplies to the South, for it would imperil the security of a hundred thousand of their fighting men there. . . . The DRV forces would be denied food and ammunition. Such a course would be appropriate only if there were a cease-fire."[21] Furthermore, he expressed concern that while the "hawks" in Washington were increasing their influence the Chinese faction in Hanoi would "get a leg up on the Soviet wing." Of course he was experienced enough to know the situation was hopeless; yet he was willing to transmit the "ultimatum" if it could gain for Hanoi a prolonged suspension of the bombing. He even called Brezhnev by telephone to tell him there would be a "great possibility of achieving the aim [i.e., a further suspension] if the Vietnamese will understand the situation that we have passed to them; they will have to decide. All they need to do is to give a confidential declaration."[22]

As Kosygin expected, the North Vietnamese were definitely not interested. Their stand was altered not a jot by an additional six-hour extension of the bombing pause. Finally, on February 13, when no answer was forthcoming from Hanoi and after Kosygin and his party flew home, the bombing of North Vietnam was resumed. Two days later Ho Chi Minh sent off a sternly worded letter to Johnson: "The U. S. government has unleashed the war of aggression in Vietnam. It must cease this aggression . . . it must first of all stop unconditionally its bombing raids and all other acts of war against the Democratic Republic of Vietnam. . . ." Only then, he concluded, could the DRV and the United States discuss questions concerning the two sides. It was Le Trang in Moscow who handed over the answer to Guthrie with the chilly remark that no further meeting with the American representative in Moscow would be possible.[23]

With this act another mediation effort came to an end and another promise of finding a common basis for negotiation flickered out. Like all the previous mediation efforts, this one produced nothing but friction and bitter memories. The North Vietnamese continued to assert that their position was the only correct one and that the United States government, in advancing "obstinate and perfidious" conditions for the cessation of the bombing, had presented yet another ultimatum. President Johnson asserted precisely the opposite. He felt Ho Chi Minh had presented the ultimatum when he demanded that all bombing and military actions against North Vietnam be halted unconditionally, that the United States withdraw its troops from South Vietnam, and that South Vietnam's future be solved in accordance with the well-known Five Point political program of the National Liberation Front, the political arm of Hanoi.

Prime Minister Wilson was extremely discontented, but not with the leaders in Hanoi who had completely ignored his peace initiative. He was convinced that a mere 48-hour extension of the bombing pause would have led to the start of negotiations. But the "disastrous influence" of a White House aide (he had in mind national security adviser Walt Rostow) had blocked the way. Foreign Secretary George Brown was also highly critical of the American action. In his memoirs he bluntly stated, "The fact of the matter was that Mr. Johnson didn't really like the Prime Minister much, and the hot line from No. 10 that went allegedly directly to the President was inclined to go instead to Mr. Rostow."[24] But unlike Wilson, Brown doubted Kosygin's sincerity. He went so far as to say that the Russians were leading everybody up the garden path, including Her Majesty's government, and he suspected that Moscow was interested mainly in showing the Communist world that its influence in Hanoi was far superior to that of Peking.

At the other end of the line, Premier Kosygin retained his usual stoicism. After his return from London, he remarked philosophically to Ambassador Thompson that mediators usually either complicate problems or pretend they are doing something when in fact they are not. By way of explaining his own role in the Wilson mediation effort, he simply repeated what he had said to Wilson, namely, that he was willing to play the role of middleman because "the Vietnamese had for the first time stated they were ready to negotiate if the bombings were stopped unconditionally; this was the first time they had done so and it was a public statement."[25] Then, as if to remind Thompson where the real problem lay, he stated that Moscow now was not confident that the American proposal had been serious and for that reason he could not at this time venture any further assistance.

As in the past, the East Europeans did not receive much inside information about the Kosygin-Wilson episode. The Soviet party leadership gave Budapest only a short background briefing, and of this only a summary was sent to our embassy in Washington. The summary contained no mention of Kosygin's views in the matter, and the Wilson mediation attempt was characterized as a grotesque attempt to sabotage Hanoi's effort to support the fighting in South Vietnam. In the meantime, I asked Ambassador Dobrynin about the Kosygin-Wilson visit. He answered briefly that as far as he knew the British had presented the American view without criticism, although Kosygin had hoped there would be a substantial difference of opinion between Wilson and Johnson. It was from the Hungarian U. N. Mission chief, Károly Csatordai, that I learned the affair was not all that simple. According to Csatordai's information, high officials in Moscow were seriously concerned that Kosygin's mediation effort would lessen Russia's credibility and influence in Hanoi. Some feared the Chinese would use it as an excuse for sending troops to North Vietnam in order to thwart peace negotiations. Others predicted the Chinese would sensationalize Kosygin's involvement and intensify their anti-Soviet outbursts. Finally, according to Csatordai, the most conservative elements in the Soviet capital feared that the "unfortunate" London affair would seriously damage the Soviet revolutionary posture all over the world.

Apart from these somewhat peripheral insights, I learned

little more about the Kosygin visit to London until March 10, 1967. Two days before then, the head of the intelligence service in our embassy was informed by his Budapest headquarters that a confidential report from London indicated there had been some sort of letter from President Johnson to Ho Chi Minh. The contents of the letter were not known, and the intelligence chief was instructed to find out all he could. He at once mobilized his men and had them buttonhole State Department officials, Western diplomats, newspapermen, and covert contacts for two days, without result. Then he asked me whether I had heard anything about the letter. I had not, but I suggested that perhaps I could find out something from the Russians. I quickly arranged a luncheon with Minister Counsellor Zinchuk. We set out for a Polynesian restaurant on 16th Street, and on the way I asked him whether there had been such a letter. Zinchuk confirmed that there had indeed—a letter from President Johnson and also a reply from Hanoi. The exchange of letters had taken place in Moscow, he said, but it had led to no result, partly because the Johnson offer contained nothing new and partly because the North Vietnamese were too stubborn to use diplomacy as a means to counter or at least to ease the American pressure.

I tried to pry more details out of him, but he repeated that the Johnson letter was not significant; it was merely another variation on the old theme and Hanoi was not about to make any concessions. After the luncheon I met Chalmers Roberts of the *Washington Post* and asked him about the Johnson-Ho correspondence. He was completely in the dark. I also contacted State Department officials; they seemed to know nothing about the whole affair. Finally, I closed my inquiries and reported what I was able to find out from Zinchuk. Ten days later Radio Hanoi published the text of the letters between Ho and Johnson. Our embassy was praised for the accuracy of its report.[26]

For the next few weeks I heard nothing more of Vietnam. On March 30 at the monthly dinner party of the socialist countries' ambassadors, I asked Dobrynin's opinion concerning the correspondence between Johnson and Ho Chi Minh. The ambassador replied that the Americans should have waited longer before resuming their bombing; now the prospect for a negotiated solution was nil. That was all he said, yet I felt it was important. It was not the first time that Dobrynin had spoken to me about a "negotiated solution." I got the strong impression that Dobrynin personally wished some avenue to peace could be found without threatening Soviet interests in Indochina. In other words, while he fully endorsed a policy of containment of China and the elimination of American influence in Southeast Asia, he wished to see the end of the war.

CHAPTER IX

Péter's News Conference

A history of the 1966–67 mediation attempts would be incomplete without an account of Hungary's János Péter's renewed effort to convince Secretary of State Dean Rusk that another bombing pause would "certainly" lead to fruitful Hanoi-Washington negotiations. Péter's move came at a time when all signs indicated that he was the rising star in Hungarian public life. He was given partial credit for the successful extension of the previous year's long bombing pause, which had enabled North Vietnam to resupply and regroup its forces in South Vietnam; and the Russians liked the way he collaborated with them. Besides, Gromyko, Brezhnev, and Kosygin got to know him better while he participated (together with party chief Kádár and Premier Kállai) in the Warsaw Pact Political Consultative Committee in Bucharest in July. Then, at the invitation of the Soviet government, he paid an eight-day official friendship visit to the Soviet Union (July 13–21), toured Soviet Estonia and Byelorussia, visited cooperative farms and a tractor plant, and made a sentimental pilgrimage to the little town of Gorki, where Lenin had spent the last years of his life. But what was even more important, Brezhnev and Kosygin, contrary to

Soviet protocol procedures, received him in the Kremlin. This was so unusual (never before had any Hungarian foreign minister been received alone by Soviet party leaders) that after the visit rumors circulated in Budapest that the Russians were considering Péter for the premiership of Hungary. But it was not a rumor that Kádár, who never liked Péter on account of his clerical background, now grudgingly agreed that the former Calvinist bishop be made a member of his Central Committee at the upcoming Ninth Congress of the Hungarian Socialist Workers' party in December.

Thus was Péter almost at the zenith of his career when he conceived the idea of traveling to Hanoi to "gauge the situation" in Vietnam. In Budapest in July 1966, I had mentioned to Péter that he would surely see Secretary Rusk in New York and that the secretary would undoubtedly be interested in whether he had a good reading of Hanoi's thinking. Péter never told me that my suggestion led him to consider the Hanoi trip, but he must have calculated that he could obtain credibility for his words only if the Americans received sure information that he had talked directly with the leaders of North Vietnam. Naturally, his ambassador in Hanoi, Imre Pehr, informed him of the latest North Vietnamese "interest in talking informally" with the Americans, although the ambassador's report stressed that this was not even a change of position but rather a minor tactical shift with the sole purpose of achieving a bombing pause—a breathing period. According to Pehr, Hanoi still clung to its Four Points as the only basis for a political solution.

Péter cleared his Hanoi travel plan with Secretary Komocsin and the rest of the Politburo without difficulty. In the meantime, the customary coordination between Moscow and Budapest was attended to, and the plan was approved in Moscow. After this, there was nothing left to do but "persuade" the North Vietnamese to invite Péter to Hanoi. For greater emphasis, Komocsin and Péter summoned Hoan Luong, the Vietnamese ambassador in Budapest, to party headquarters and not to the Foreign Ministry. In the course of their conversation they informed the ambassador that during the approaching session of the U. N. General Assembly it was certain Péter would meet Secretary of State Rusk. For this reason, they would like to see in detail the position of the DRV, so that Péter might "appropriately" represent it.

The ambassador, assuming this to be a routine consultation, quickly stated that, although the American military pressure was greater than a year earlier, Hanoi and the NLF were in control of the situation. He added that on the Vietnamese side there was no change in thinking about formal negotiations, even though a cessation of the bombing of North Vietnam would be desirable. At this point Komocsin interrupted the ambassador and told him that the Hungarian party wished to send Péter to Hanoi to discuss the matter directly with Foreign Minister Nguyen Duy Trinh and the other leaders of the DRV. The ambassador, Péter recalled later with laughter, "opened his eyes as wide as a slant-eyed Asian diplomat can" and asked, slightly embarrassed, when Péter was planning to travel. As soon as possible, was the answer. At this statement, Hoan Luong promised to communicate the Hungarian wish to Hanoi.

It took several weeks for the invitation to reach Budapest. Finally, Hoan Luong called on Péter and informed him that the Vietnamese foreign minister, Nguyen Duy Trinh, and others would be glad to expound the DRV's position to the Hungarian colleague.

Péter left for Hanoi just a few weeks before he was scheduled to arrive in New York, making the journey via Moscow and Peking. In Moscow he contacted the Chinese chargé, informed him that, at the invitation of the Vietnamese government, he would travel to Hanoi, and requested the Chinese government to reserve a seat for him on a regularly scheduled Chinese flight from Peking to Hanoi. He deliberately planned his trip via Peking rather than by way of Egypt and India, knowing the Chinese would learn of his trip anyway.

The Chinese first replied that all tickets had been sold months in advance on the Peking-Hanoi flight and, unfortunately, the request of the Hungarian foreign minister could not be granted. In that case, Péter then informed the Chinese, he wished to charter a special plane. The Chinese, grudgingly, provided a seat on a plane from Peking heading south.

I knew nothing of this until Péter arrived in New York for the

General Assembly session on September 24, 1966. He told the Hungarian U. N. representative, Ambassador Csatordai, and me about this journey just after he descended from his plane at Kennedy Airport. The next afternoon we learned more details as we walked in a Brooklyn park. The sky was overcast and the sun broke through the clouds only rarely. Csatordai was listening with respect to the narrative; I was curious, but on the basis of what I had seen in the files during my summer vacation I followed the story to its end rather suspiciously. "What will be the upshot of this latest 'peace offensive'?" I asked myself.

In Peking, Péter began, only the chief of protocol of the Chinese Foreign Ministry was present at the airport to receive him—coldly, but with correct courtesy. He conversed exclusively about the Moscow-Peking air trip, and about the weather; then, referring to the onward trip, he reiterated that with great difficulty his government had been successful in postponing the trip of a Chinese specialist who was to travel to Hanoi.

During a short stopover in the Chinese capital, Péter stayed at the Hungarian Embassy. He was eager to do some sightseeing, he told us—visit the Great Wall or the garden of the Heavenly Palace. But that was impossible, as he happened to be in Peking at the height of the raging Great Proletarian Cultural Revolution. Organized and unorganized teenagers demonstrated in the streets; Red Guards surrounded the Soviet Embassy, shouted anti-Soviet slogans, burned Soviet automobiles, and harassed the Soviet chargé d'affaires. Soviet and East European diplomats and personnel rarely left their embassy compounds, though no Hungarians were harmed. Péter explained that Chinese security forces totally surrounded the Hungarian Embassy. Behind the high walls of the embassy, the Hungarian diplomats felt themselves transported back to the days of the Boxer Rebellion of 1900, when barbarian foreigners were held responsible for all evil things in China. But there was more. Maoists tried to convince the East Europeans, especially the Rumanians, the Poles, and the Hungarians, that the Cultural Revolution was "absolutely necessary" since the Chinese bourgeoisie spread too much "revisionist poison." Translators and other Chinese personnel at the Hungarian Embassy (our diplomatic personnel in Peking were well aware that the

Chinese working in our embassy were agents of the Public Security) were also busy propagating the idea that the "Khrushchev-Brezhnev revisionists" opposed carrying out a "genuine cultural revolution" because they were "restoring capitalism in Russia and in Eastern Europe." Once, continued Péter, Ch'en Yi approached Hungarian Ambassador József Halász and tried to explain the "essence" of the revolution, but our ambassador "rightly" refused to listen to him. All in all, concluded Péter, it looked as if Mao Tse-tung and his group had gone completely insane.

Csatordai most probably did not like what Péter said but did not dare to defend his idol, Mao Tse-tung. I agreed with Péter that the Cultural Revolution was madness and sheer nonsense.

Péter traveled from Peking to Hanoi in a small two-engine IL 14 aircraft, which the Chinese pilot flew at a low altitude to avoid American radar detection. After much tossing and shaking, it landed at Wuchan, then Nanning, where Péter was met by the North Vietnamese consul and his Chinese interpreter. An awkward conversation ensued, with the Vietnamese speaking with extreme caution. He made no inquiries concerning the purpose of the Hungarian foreign minister's trip but kept repeating with politeness how glad he was that Péter was going to visit his country and that he hoped he would enjoy his stay in Hanoi. The interpreter, who spoke English, was translating the conversation and at the same time taking notes on what the Vietnamese consul said and what Péter answered. Not wanting to embarrass the Vietnamese, Péter did not discuss the real purpose of his Hanoi visit. Some mention was made of the situation in Vietnam, and the North Vietnamese consul eloquently voiced for the Hungarian's benefit the "eternal gratitude" of the Vietnamese people for the aid from the friendly Soviet bloc countries, but every other word he spoke referred to the tremendous military, economic, and political assistance coming from the inexhaustible sources of strength of the great Chinese people.

In Hanoi, Péter conferred with North Vietnamese Foreign Minister Nguyen Duy Trinh and Premier Pham Van Dong. He learned there, he told us, that the DRV's military situation had worsened in the past year. Pham Van Dong had not believed that the Americans, within a year, would raise their troop strength in Vietnam to well above 300,000 men. The bombing raids had affected the delivery of military supplies to the South. The North Vietnamese foreign minister no longer spoke of a war lasting 10–15 years, continued Péter, adding that the political situation in the South had become less advantageous for Hanoi than the year before: the government in South Vietnam had stabilized somewhat and elections were held. And the NLF had been unable to exploit the revolt of the Buddhists.

"Does this mean," I asked, "that the DRV has changed its conditions and is willing to sit down at the conference table?"

"That is not the question," replied Péter. "The DRV continues to insist that the Americans must stop the bombing and must withdraw their troops from the South. But I got the impression that the North Vietnamese are no longer so rigid. They still feel that they can resist the military pressure, redress the military situation, and win out in the end. But they are beginning to entertain the thought that, while continuing the struggle, they might if their interests so demand start negotiations."

Péter went on to tell us that Pham Van Dong had spoken of the use the Vietnamese had made of this same tactic in their war with the French, and added that Hungarian Ambassador Imre Pehr was also of the opinion that, perhaps by the end of 1967 or the beginning of 1968, the North Vietnamese would be ready to enter into negotiations of this type.

I did not find this encouraging. "Don't they realize in Hanoi," I asked, "that last year the Americans wanted to negotiate seriously? If North Vietnam does not sit down at the conference table, then the war will further escalate and the solution will become more and more difficult. What are they counting on?"

"On two things," Péter replied. "One is the possibility that American public opinion will become jaded with the war, as French public opinion did. The other is the expectation that American casualties will, within a short time, reach the level of the Korean War, and then the Americans will be compelled to bring the war to an end."

"The Chinese are fighting to the last Vietnamese soldier," I said.

"But Soviet influence is becoming stronger," Péter replied. "Soviet military assistance is beginning to have its effect." He added that in Hanoi no one in party or government circles wanted to talk about the Sino-Soviet controversy. The North Vietnamese tried to remain neutral but when pressed to say something, they considered the whole affair only a "difference of opinion."

Péter then made some general remarks about his Vietnamese experiences. He was much impressed by the determination and unity of the North Vietnamese people and by the quality of the North Vietnamese leadership, particularly Pham Van Dong.

At the end of the account, I could not determine what Péter had really learned in Hanoi, and, as I subsequently discovered, neither could the Politburo in Budapest. János Kádár himself noted, "We will not go far with what Comrade Péter brought from Hanoi. We didn't become a lot wiser because of it."

In contrast with his clandestine behavior a year earlier, Péter now circulated freely at the U. N. He sought out promiment Western diplomats, meeting twice with French Foreign Minister Couve de Murville, who had been Péter's guest in Budapest in July.[1] He discussed current U. N. matters with Foreign Minister Marko Nikezits of Yugoslavia, and dined with the Iranian diplomat Abdul Rahman Pazhvak, who presided over the Twenty-first Session of the General Assembly. He called on Secretary General U Thant and in the "strictest confidence" briefed him about his recent Hanoi trip, hoping that the secretary general would pass the news to the U. S. representative, Ambassador Arthur Goldberg. (Péter privately considered U Thant an American agent.) In addition, he conversed with newspapermen and attended cocktail parties, including one given by Dean Rusk. He openly discussed with Communist diplomats his visit to Hanoi and to make sure the Americans heard about it, gave some details to Hungarian journalists to pass on to their American colleagues. But when I was arranging Péter's meeting with Rusk, he stipulated that I should not mention his trip.

"I promised Trinh," he said, "that I would not tell the Americans that I spoke personally with him." I tried to change his mind. I told him since he was in Hanoi he should tell this to Rusk, but he declined to act on my suggestion.

On October 6, we saw Rusk again. The atmosphere was colder than it had been a year earlier. "Mr. Péter," the secretary said with a pale smile, "now what shall we do with Vietnam?"

"The December 1965 bombing pause," Péter replied, "was a reassuring beginning. The leaders of the DRV looked upon it as a positive movement and also showed a certain readiness to talk. Unfortunately, Hanoi was not truly sure that the U. S. really wanted to negotiate."

This did not square with the correspondence I had seen in Budapest. Rusk was quick to point out that he had "exactly the opposite impression," saying: "Except for the first two weeks, North Vietnam used this time to transport as many reinforcements as possible from North to South. Moreover, in South Vietnam they regrouped their military forces. We had precise indication of this. And then in the last two weeks of the bombing pause they transported three or four times more war materiel on the Ho Chi Minh trail than before."

Péter argued that during the bombing pause the United States had also sent additional troops and supplies to South Vietnam, and the DRV interpreted this as a sign that Washington was insincere. In addition, Hanoi appraised Ambassador Harriman's January 1966 trip around the world as a propaganda attack. Finally, President Johnson's presence at the Honolulu Conference was interpreted as a war council, called to impose a puppet regime on South Vietnam.

"You know very well, Mr. Péter," Rusk broke in, "that during the last bombing pause we were prepared to negotiate with Hanoi in Rangoon or in any other place." And he continued, "Peace could be restored in Vietnam if the ever-increasing infiltration from the North would stop, if the leaders of Hanoi decide to withdraw the regular North Vietnamese units that are fighting in South Vietnam, and if in South Vietnam the South Vietnamese could decide their own fate. Hanoi must realize that what comprises North Vietnam is their territory, but what is in the South is not theirs. The basis of a settlement is the acceptance of the 17th parallel. But since it is apparent that they are not prepared to do so," concluded Rusk, "America has no choice but to fulfill in every respect the responsibilities it has accepted with regard to the South Vietnamese government. The North Vietnamese leaders must count on the consequences of this."

Péter said that on the basis of "deep personal conviction and official authorization" he felt the road to negotiations could still be found. First, however, "The U. S. must stop the bombing. If the U. S. were to cease bombing—if Hanoi could have a clear picture of U. S. intentions during and after negotiations—then the leaders in Hanoi would be ready to talk."

"And what would the other side do?" Rusk asked.

"In such a situation the DRV would stop infiltration," replied Péter categorically.

Rusk looked deep into Péter's eyes but let him continue:

"—Hanoi would agree with the United States on the necessity of holding free elections in South Vietnam.

—The DRV was not interested in taking over South Vietnam but could not accept a hostile regime in Saigon.

—The NLF program certainly allowed for a coalition with a South Vietnamese government.

—Hanoi would want to see South Vietnam's independence guaranteed."

Then he played out his last trump. "The 17th parallel could be the basis for a settlement."

"Everything you have told us, Mr. Péter, falls within our objectives," Rusk replied. "We do not want to conquer North Vietnam, and we don't want to maintain military bases in South Vietnam. But the 17th parallel must be accepted." The secretary's interest was obvious. "What is Peking's opinion?" he asked.

"Peking would also accept a neutralized South Vietnam, if American troops were withdrawn and the American military bases discontinued."

I could hardly credit my ears. Péter had not said a word to me about North Vietnam's willingness to stop the infiltration; he had not mentioned that the 17th parallel could be the basis for a settlement. And the Chinese . . . Péter had told Csatordai and me that he had talked with the Chinese protocol officer at the

Peking airport only in a cold and formal way; this subject had not come up.

Péter pressed his point again: "The basis of the solution could be the 17th parallel."

"Mr. Péter," said Rusk very seriously, "everything you have told us now, we had not heard previously from anyone, despite the fact that we can contact Hanoi via several diplomatic channels. We constantly monitor Hanoi and NLF radio broadcasts, but we learn nothing new from them. For this reason what you have said is unexpected and surprising to us. But you obviously are clear as to what dangers are inherent if what you have told us does not correspond to the truth."

"Naturally I am aware," Péter answered without hesitation, "of the dangers and consequences should I lead the government of the United States astray on this question."

I waited for Péter to mention his trip to Hanoi, but he merely said that he was authorized to tell Rusk that if the United States had any new proposals he was ready to work with them. He affirmed that his remarks were based on definite information from Hanoi and that he spoke with a sense of deep personal and official responsibility.

Rusk did not say a word for a minute or so. Finally, he remarked that everything Péter had said involved numerous new factors and that he would make them the subject of thoughtful study. The meeting closed with an agreement to maintain complete discretion—which meant, among other things, not talking about specifics with newsmen.

After the meeting, Péter was in a good mood. "Everything went well," he said to me, "I almost told him that I was in Hanoi. But there will be opportunities for further meetings with Rusk." His optimism was raised by the news he received from Budapest that Foreign Minister Trinh would attend the Hungarian Party Congress opening on November 28. Péter thought this meant Hanoi wished to get firsthand information from him on the discussions he had held with Rusk.

He rushed immediately to U Thant and told him that he was expecting a visit from Trinh in Budapest in the late days of November. Again he hoped that U Thant would pass the news to the State Department, setting the stage for another discussion with Rusk. Unfortunately for Péter, however, the tactic of using U Thant as a message carrier to the Americans did not work. U Thant, who presumably did not consider the "message" urgent, did not give the Americans the information until January of the next year by which time Péter's credentials as mediator were absolutely worthless.[2]

"Perhaps now Pham Van Dong's tactics can be applied—at the same time negotiations can be held and guerrilla war continued," said Péter to me after his meeting with U Thant. "But unfortunately the Americans are now much more rigid than a year ago, and it is not likely that a new bombing pause can be achieved without some concession from North Vietnam."

"Is it conceivable," I pressed him, "that either the DRV or China would accept the 17th parallel as a basis for settling the Vietnamese conflict?" Péter replied, with nervous impatience, that only Ho Chi Minh could answer that, and obviously only toward the end of long negotiations.

On October 18, Péter delivered his annual speech to the U. N. General Assembly. As always, he showed the text to the members of his delegation. "As you can see," he explained, "I am urging the cessation of bombing as most important. In addition, I am going to make it clear that the withdrawal of the American troops from South Vietnam and the dismantling of American military bases are prerequisites for a final Vietnam settlement."

Péter's speech aroused no particular interest. However, in the meantime he had scheduled a press conference for October 20 with the United Nations Correspondents Association. This created some stir in advance, since in previous years he had avoided newsmen.

The day before the press conference, Péter called me to his room in the Croydon Hotel and circuitously explained that I should not take part in the following day's press conference. He pointed out that it would be held in the U. N. building and would deal "strictly with U. N. matters"; he did not want to leave so much as an appearance that any reference had been made at the press conference to the matters discussed at the meeting between Secretary Rusk and himself. If I were there, he said, "Washington would misunderstand."

I did not understand at first what Péter meant by "appearance," since I was a member of the Hungarian U. N. delegation in the capacity of "special advisor." Besides, what would Washington misunderstand? The only thing I understood was that for some reason Péter did not want me to be present. I looked at Péter wonderingly, somewhat taken aback. I had a bad premonition about the whole press conference. I even said that I was afraid that the newsmen would ask too many sensitive questions, since they knew that Péter had been in Hanoi not long ago.

"They're not going to get much out of what I say. That's certain," replied Péter.

As I waited the next afternoon at the Hungarian U. N. Mission for Péter and Csatordai to return from the press conference, Csaba Kiss of the official news agency and Pál Ipper of the Hungarian radio and TV burst in with joyful looks on their faces.

"Why the excitement?" I asked. "What did Péter say?"

"A sensation!" they answered in unison.

Péter's answers to questions had constituted a virtual word-for-word replay of almost everything he had told Rusk in confidence: Hungary was perhaps the "best informed" country concerning the position of the DRV and the NLF; Hanoi would not insist that the NLF should be considered the sole representative of the people of South Vietnam; the DRV would ask only for a proportional representation of the NLF in the new Saigon government, which in Péter's opinion should be a nonaligned coalition government. He acknowledged the presence of the North Vietnamese troops in the South—a fact Hanoi constantly and categorically denied—but added that it was very difficult to establish who, in those military units which came from North Vietnam, were northerners and who were southerners. Hanoi would accept the 17th parallel as a reality and would not demand the immediate reunification of North and South Vietnam under its leadership. Would Peking accept the 17th parallel? "I would hope so," Péter replied. He emphasized that his government had recently conducted very important exchanges of views with Hanoi. He did not say that he had been there, but nearly everyone in the room knew that.

Péter had enjoined the newsmen not to quote him by name but had agreed that he could be identified as an East European or Hungarian "source." In a way, this made it worse, since the device was both transparent and underhanded. Appalled, I asked if Péter had really said these things. Csaba Kiss gave me a copy of his cabled report, and as I read it my gloom deepened.

"Why are you taking this so seriously?" Kiss wanted to know. "Perhaps something is wrong?"

"I think there is a great deal wrong," I replied.

Meanwhile Péter and Csatordai had arrived and had gone into Csatordai's office for coffee. I went in waving Csaba Kiss's dispatch and asked why Péter had said the same things to the newsmen that he had said to Rusk.

Péter glanced at me uncertainly, then permitted himself a sarcastic smile and noted quietly that he who risks nothing in politics can win nothing. "The matter doesn't have to be viewed so tragically," he said. "This will cause a disturbance in the conference now going on in Manila." (Johnson and Rusk were then in Manila for a summit meeting with America's Asian allies.)

I remembered last year's big lie—and now this! Something broke inside me; I was disgusted with this dirty game, but said nothing.

Péter returned to Budapest. There certainly was a "disturbance" in Manila when Rusk learned of a story in the Paris newspaper *Le Monde* which contained a full and accurate account of the "press conference." Péter's name was not mentioned, but there could be no question that he was the "source."[3]

Ambassador Llewellyn Thompson called me to the State Department and politely but firmly expressed wonderment that Péter had chosen to make public the substance of what he had discussed with Rusk. He added that only five or six top officials in the department had known about these conversations. He wanted an explanation. I could only promise to transmit the question to Budapest.

A few days later I passed Péter's reply to Thompson: the Hungarian foreign minister had not made any statement to newsmen which could have related to his conversation with Rusk. On his part, Péter recommended "maintenance of complete discretion."

The ambassador raised his brows, then asked, "Is that all?"

"Yes," I replied. "My instructions were to communicate this to you." The meeting lasted two or three minutes, but to me it seemed very long. When I left Thompson's office, I felt as if a great iron door had slammed behind me.

Rusk and Thompson were upset, and so were the North Vietnamese, who had also read the *Le Monde* article. North Vietnam's foreign minister did not attend the Hungarian Party Congress. Hanoi sent three other high officials: Le Duc Tho, secretary of the Central Committee and a powerful member of Hanoi's Politburo; Ung Van Khiem, interior minister; and Nguyen Song Tung of the Central Committee's Foreign Relations Department. Upon their arrival in Budapest, Le Duc Tho made a terrible scene, demanding that Péter disown what he had said to the newsmen. Péter refused to do this, and a serious breach developed between the North Vietnamese and the Hungarians. In New York Csatordai tried to help Péter by sending a series of cables to Budapest blaming "imperialist hireling Western journalists" who misquoted Péter. But the North Vietnamese were not impressed. Le Duc Tho made it clear that there had been enough nonsense: in the future the Hungarian foreign minister should undertake no mediating activity whatsoever in the interest of the DRV.

To smooth the dispute, János Kádár made a tough speech accusing the American government of committing "the international crime of genocide"; a special Party Congress statement was published associating Hungary with Hanoi and the NLF on the Four Points and the Five Points. The North Vietnamese went home somewhat mollified.

Following his encounter with the Vietnamese, Péter wanted to let the Americans know that the prospects of an early-negotiated settlement of the war were bleak. He instructed Csatordai to tell U Thant that contrary to earlier notifications not Foreign Minister Trinh but Politburo member Le Duc Tho of the Vietnamese Workers' party would come to the Hungarian Party Congress; and Le Duc Tho took a much harder line about the settlement of the Vietnamese conflict than Péter believed would have been taken by North Vietnam's foreign minister. Moreover, Le Duc Tho hinted that it was by no means certain that the NLF would support any peace proposal which might be acceptable to Hanoi. As Péter expected, U Thant passed on what he heard from the Hungarian to Ambassador Goldberg on January 3, 1967.

Why Péter was again playing "high diplomacy" I do not know. But his game did not influence Washington in one way or the other.

While these developments transpired, I tried to understand why Péter had chosen to act as he had. The North Vietnamese had not asked him to mediate. The Chinese were certainly not behind him. And, although Péter willingly served the interest of Soviet foreign policy, cleared all his actions with Andrei Gromyko and briefed him after his meeting with Rusk, I still wonder how much of this he had told the Soviet foreign minister. Ambassador Dobrynin seemed unpleasantly surprised when I got around to telling him privately what Péter had been up to. His deputy, Alexander Zinchuk, felt the whole episode had ended Péter's usefulness in the Vietnam picture.

Probably Péter's personal conceit furnishes us with a large part of the answer to the riddle of his behavior. Dean Rusk, who is well acquainted with the history of central Europe, had asked in a friendly way at our meeting in 1965 if Péter were attempting to revive the Hungarian diplomacy of the 18th century, when a prince of Transylvania named Ferenc Rákoczi won the respect of both the Turks and the French for his wiliness. In his dreams of glory Péter must have seen himself as another Metternich or Talleyrand, or even a winner of the Nobel Peace Prize. But he did not have the good diplomat's instinctive sense of caution. It is inconceivable that a sophisticated diplomat would ever exceed his authority so grotesquely in a matter affecting peace and war in the nuclear age. Péter's personal credit was ruined with all parties. So was Hungary's.

And so was mine. At this point Vietnam became willy-nilly a personal affair. Certainly it had brought great hopes and uplifting moments when I believed I was working for peace. It had caused despair, torment, and immeasurable disappointment when I found that I had become an involuntary actor in Péter's ploy. The awareness that the "Hungarian action" had only served to create confusion in Washington and consequently blocked the way to a peaceful solution was a constant, crushing weight on me.

A Personal Decision

In the Spring of 1967 events crowded hard upon each other with threats of dangerous confrontations between the major world powers. Many signs indicated, for instance, that the Middle East powder keg was about to explode into a full-fledged war between the Israelis and the Arabs. For me it was hard to predict how the pro-Israeli Americans and the pro-Arab Russians could remain neutral, and it was equally difficult to foresee how Hungary with its soldiers fully integrated in the Warsaw Pact could stay out of the conflict.

The news of the steadily escalating war in Vietnam was also disquieting. The DRV military high command was sending more and more troops and materiel to South Vietnam; five divisions were concentrated along the Demilitarized Zone. In reply to the troop movement, the Americans directed heavy artillery fire against targets north of the DMZ and U. S. Marines entered the Zone for the first time in pursuit of the North Vietnamese regulars. Meanwhile, the door to negotiations was firmly closed.

On April 26, I had a brief conversation with Secretary of State Dean Rusk at a White House reception. Rusk, recalling my go-between role in previous peace-feelers, asked me whether his colleague Foreign Minister Péter had any new proposal for settling the Vietnam conflict. To my best knowledge he had none, and I said so. With a faint smile Rusk replied that he was always ready to listen. When I reported the secretary's remark to Budapest, Péter nervously ordered me to forego any Vietnam discussion for the time being.

The tension was high between East and West on other issues as well. The Russians intensified their propaganda campaign against NATO and the West German "neo-Nazi, militarist, and revanchist" elements. The main attack was directed against the new West German Chancellor Kiesinger, who, in contrast to Foreign Minister Hallstein's policy, proposed the establishment of relations with the East European countries.* The Kremlin propaganda claimed that Kiesinger's new *Ostpolitik* was nothing but a cleverly formulated continuation of the old revanchist West German policy, a plot against peace and a dangerous attempt to destroy the unity of the Soviet Union and its East European allies. Behind the propaganda uproar lay the bare fact that the new *Ostpolitik* had started to weaken Soviet influence in Eastern Europe. Among others, the maverick president of Rumania, Ceaucescu, had accepted the West German offer and despite Russian objection established diplomatic relations with Bonn in early February.

For economic reasons the Kiesinger proposal was a matter of prime interest for the Hungarians, too, since West Germany was Hungary's foremost foreign trade partner in the West and the lack of diplomatic ties created constant difficulties. Thus, not surprisingly, after a three-day intensive discussion between West German State Secretary for Foreign Affairs Ralf Lahr, Hungarian Foreign Minister Péter, and Foreign Trade Minister József Biro in Budapest, a brief communiqué on January 26 stated that views had been exchanged on the possibility of establishing diplomatic relations in the near future.

Soon after Lahr returned to Bonn, we at the embassy in Washington learned from the Foreign Ministry that a Hungarian embassy staff was all packed up and ready to go to Bonn. I was particularly pleased by the news. For several months I had been in contact with the minister of the West German Embassy in Washington, Herbert A. von Stackelberg, and had exchanged views about the possibilities of improving our countries' relations. Those were, of course, exploratory talks I had conducted, on Budapest's instruction, and it was my understanding that Stackelberg had informed his headquarters about our talks as well. For my part I pointed out that Hungary had a

*The so-called Hallstein doctrine, in effect until the end of 1966, made diplomatic relations with the Bonn government conditional on non-recognition of East Germany.

special economic interest in achieving a permanent arrangement with the Bundesrepublik; I did not want to play games with him and regularly called his attention to the interdependence of the Warsaw Pact countries in the field of foreign policy. I made clear to him that a basic requirement was Bonn's recognition of the Oder-Neisse borderline and the demarcation line between East and West Germany. On his part Stackelberg offered assurances that the Federal Republic of Germany was ready to accept the Oder-Neisse line and was prepared to discuss the status of East Germany within the framework of an overall accommodation.

This was how the matter stood, and I expected an announcement about the establishment of formal relation after Péter's visit to Bonn not later than late February or early March. But I was wrong. The second meeting between the West Germans and Hungarians never took place. First, the East German Walter Ulbricht raised strong objections to the possible Hungarian move; then the Polish and Czechoslovak governments did everything possible to torpedo the Hungarian-German rapproachement. Finally, the Soviets informed the Hungarian Politburo that until West Germany was ready to recognize the East German government and the Oder-Neisse line, the establishment of diplomatic relations with West Germany would be premature.

I again met Stackelberg and his ambassador, Heinrich Knappstein, at the West German Embassy on April 20. Both reassured me that the Kiesinger government already accepted the disputed Oder-Neisse line and would be willing to settle all outstanding questions with East Germany. Knappstein went one step further to point out that West Germany had renounced forever the possession and the use of atomic weapons, since his government knew very well that the mere possession of them would represent a *casus belli* for the Soviet Union. When I asked him whether he would authorize me to repeat his statement to the Russians, he gladly agreed. Next day I told Counsellor Yury M. Vorontsov, the NATO and disarmament expert of the Soviet Embassy, exactly what Knappstein had said. He found my account interesting and with great seriousness remarked that Knappstein was completely right, the Soviet Union would not tolerate atomic weapons in German hands. Also, I reported Knappstein's remark to Budapest but I received no answer.

I was annoyed and I still can remember how this whole affair increased my already deep disillusionment. Certainly I had been long enough in the service to know that all major foreign policy guidance for the East Europeans was provided by the Soviets, and for this very reason Hungary really had no foreign policy line of its own. Yet in this case I could not understand the Kremlin's behavior, since the West Germans were ready to make all the concessions asked of them. Moreover, the Soviet Union already had diplomatic relations with West Germany. And Rumania? Why could Ceaucescu make a decision on his own while the Hungarian party leadership had to reverse a decision and act against Hungary's best interest? I asked myself this question a thousand times.

There was not too much time for me to meditate. A dangerous power struggle surfaced inside the ancient walls of the Kremlin, a struggle that, it seemed, might conceivably precipitate the most dangerous confrontation of the superpowers yet. I can remember Zinchuk's farewell party at the Soviet Embassy on March 31 as if it happened yesterday. Ambassador Dobrynin, the host of the reception, was speechless and could hardly conceal his nervousness. He stayed for a while with the guests, then disappeared through a side door which led to his office. Every time he came back, he had a worried look. I did not know what to think. Perhaps something important was in the making. I recalled that about four years earlier Dobrynin had disappeared from his military attaché's reception the same way he did now, through this side door. At that time we were in the midst of the Cuban missile crisis, and the ambassador had passed urgent messages to Robert Kennedy on the third floor of the Soviet Embassy building. Was there again a crisis in the making? I could not tell, but I could feel the tension in the atmosphere.

On April 4 I saw Dobrynin for a moment at the reception given in honor of Turkish President Izmet Inonu. On the same day the ambassador attended the Hungarian National Holiday reception at our embassy. He still looked restive, and his moroseness grew when the president of the B'nai B'rith Society, Lebel Katz, put pressure on him to facilitate the emigration of Russian Jews to Israel. Dobrynin, who usually was quite flexible on this question, now turned a cold shoulder to Katz. Afterward, he chatted with State Department officials for a while, then left. I think this time the good Hungarian wines he liked so much did not cheer him up.

Two weeks later I learned that my presumption of a developing crisis was not without foundation. In the first part of April I toured the West Coast, giving a lecture at the World Affairs Council at Tacoma and visiting the Boeing Company's plant in Seattle. My next stop was in San Francisco, where Harry Bridges of the West Coast Longshoremen's Union asked me a thousand and one questions about trade unions in Communist Eastern Europe. I had a hard time explaining to him that trade unions in socialist countries were not primarily representatives of the workers' economic interests but were rather the "transmission belt that carried party policy to the masses," and that strikes were punishable by long prison terms because they "undermine the security" of the socialist state. At that time, in my official capacity, I could not tell him that I shared his view that the ultimate weapon of the worker in any society is the right to strike. I also visited the *Los Angeles Times,* where I spent a long afternoon with the board of foreign editors discussing East-West relations, the Johnson-Brzezinski "bridge-building" policy between East and West, and the new economic reforms in Hungary.

When I arrived at Dulles airport in Washington, Secretary Józan informed me that during my absence Soviet Ambassador Dobrynin had left Washington and would not be returning.

"Exactly how do you know this?" I asked him.

"The Soviet military attaché told our military attaché the other day."

"Why?" was my alarmed question.

"Because his policy toward the United States was too soft," was the simple reply. "I have already informed Budapest of this fact."

We drove from the airport to the embassy, where I immediately asked Colonel Csapo, the Hungarian military attaché, to see me. He entered my office with a disturbed look on his face and in a low voice started talking.

"Two days ago the Soviet military attaché, Major General [Valentin L.] Meshcheryakov, visited me here at the Embassy. As usual, we started drinking coffee and brandy. After the fourth round, my Soviet colleague told me something which I still cannot comprehend. He told me that Ambassador Dobrynin was recalled abruptly and that he will never come back to Washington."

"Yes, I heard that," I said, "but why?"

"Wait," the Colonel said. "As you know, the Soviet Minister of Defense Marshal Malinovsky died of cancer in Moscow at the end of March, and, according to the Soviet military attaché, the new defense minister will be Ustinov. He, together with Politburo member Shelepin and others, has had enough of what he calls 'this double-faced foreign policy.' They believe it is inexcusable to be mild with the U. S., to build bridges between America and the Soviet bloc countries on the one hand and to help the Vietnamese only in a limited way on the other."

Here Csapo stopped for a moment or two, then went on, saying that his Russian friend had told him there would be a complete shift in Soviet policy toward Washington, that no longer would there be a need for a double-dealing diplomat such as Dobrynin, who was too soft with the Americans and whose advice to Moscow should be disregarded. But that was not all. The Russian revealed that under the "new policy" Moscow would intensify its aid to Hanoi, Soviet pilots would be sent to North Vietnam, and anti-aircraft missiles in that country would be operated by Russian personnel. He stated somewhat portentously that the sky over Vietnam would soon be closed to the American raiders, and the whole character of the war in Southeast Asia would change. But what was more important, he expressed the opinion that these things would come about as soon as Ustinov became defense minister and Shelepin achieved all-out control in the party Politburo.

"Is that all?" I asked.

"No," Csapo whispered, and here his nervousness increased.

The Soviet attaché had explained to him that plans were ready in the Soviet Defense Ministry for a bigger, more decisive move. The Soviet armed forces would carry out a thundering attack in Western Europe, occupying first Berlin then West Germany, then the rest of Western Europe. According to Meshcheryakov, the Russian armed forces were so powerful and mobile that when the Western world woke up it would be too late—the Red Army would already be at the English Channel. The United States and its NATO allies would not have enough power to resist with conventional weapons and would not dare to use the atomic bomb.

"Are you serious," I asked the colonel, "or was your friend drunk?"

"I am serious," said the Hungarian colonel, "and the Russian was not drunk at all. He was quite confident about the outcome."

I was at first amazed, then frightened. Never before during my five years at the Hungarian Legation in Washington had a Soviet official conducted such a conversation with a Hungarian colleague. I was deep in thought when I heard the voice of Colonel Csapo again.

"What shall I do?" he asked me. "Shall I send a report about the conversation to Budapest?"

"You are talking nonsense," I told him. "I know for sure that you have already sent it."

"I did not think that you knew me so well," he said. "It is true, I have already sent a detailed report to Budapest."

My grim conversation with the Hungarian military attaché ended at that point. I saw two possibilities. First, the whole story might be nothing more than an expression of personal rivalry between the Soviet military attaché and Dobrynin. Secondly, the Soviet general reflected the view of a restricted group of the Soviet military establishment, and he added big names—such as Shelepin—to his story to make his point. But I also remembered, while Csapo was talking, that Shelepin, together with Ustinov, had visited Hanoi in early 1966 and promised substantial economic and military aid to Ho Chi Minh. I recalled that on his way back to Moscow he had stopped in Peking, and, according to wild rumors, the Chinese had tried to win him over to their side with promises of full cooperation with the Soviet Union if Shelepin took over from Brezhnev.

During the next few days I tried to inquire around and find out more. It was of course true that Dobrynin had left Washington on April 13. Soviet Chargé Yuri N. Chernyakov confirmed to me that Dobrynin had been unexpectedly called back to Moscow for consultation. But Chernyakov was either unwilling or unable to tell me anything more. Then I learned from Czechoslovak Ambassador Duda that his military attaché had received the same "background information" from the Soviet attaché as the Hungarian had.

There was no reaction or comment from Budapest on Csapo's report. But subsequent events strongly suggested to me that Major General Meshcheryakov was not talking completely without rhyme or reason. A factional struggle for leadership was indeed underway. First the Soviet news agency *Tass* reported that on April 11 Marshal Andrei A. Grechko, a 63-year-old professional soldier and longtime friend and supporter of party chief Brezhnev, had been named minister of defense—not Ustinov. Then on May 19, it became public that the head of the Soviet secret police, Vladimir V. Semichastny, a close subordinate of Shelepin, had been replaced by Yuri V. Andropov, a protegé of Brezhnev. Less than a month later another Shelepin man, the powerful secretary of the Moscow City Party Committee, Nikolai Yegorychev, was fired. Finally, on July 11, Shelepin himself lost his position in the inner circle of the supreme decision-making body, the Secretariat of the Central Committee. He was downgraded to a second-rate administrative post, the chairmanship of the All-Union Central Council of Trade Unions. Ustinov's role remained a mystery. Known for his ability to survive, he possibly changed sides in time. On the other hand, one can surmise that he was the one who warned Brezhnev of Shelepin's sinister plot. In any event, Ustinov became an ardent supporter of Brezhnev.[4] Ambassador Dobrynin returned to Washington on June 15; Major General Meshcheryakov's prophecy failed. The Kremlin "hawks" had lost to the realists.

I had lived through the Stalinist terror of the early 1950s and was filled with apprehension that now neo-Stalinist hardliners could very well take over in the Kremlin and in Eastern Europe. I did not want any part of it. I decided not to wait for the outcome of the power struggle. I felt I simply could not delay my personal decision any longer. I crossed the Rubicon.

Late in the afternoon, on May 16, I called Secretary of State Dean Rusk and asked to see him on an urgent private matter. A few hours later we met. I was extremely agitated, wanting to tell at once everything that rankled in my mind. With a voice shaken by emotion I told him that I had been through a long soul-searching and finally had concluded that I had to quit the Hungarian foreign service. Then I said that Foreign Minister Péter had badly misled him and the United States government by stating that Hanoi would agree to peace talks if the United States would halt the bombing of North Vietnam for a few weeks. To begin with, I said, I had found out during the previous summer that Péter had no authority whatsoever to speak for Hanoi. Moreover, the messages I was passing to the secretary from Péter were false, including his proposition for direct talks between the representatives of the United States and North Vietnam during the 37-day bombing pause. Péter's sole purpose was to postpone the resumption of the American bombing. Hanoi had little concern for a negotiated settlement; therefore, Péter knew that direct talks would not take place. I went on, saying that the Hungarian foreign minister had deceived the secretary again in the fall of 1966 when he claimed that Hanoi was interested in some kind of Korea-like solution. Finally, I added that my personal involvement in Péter's machinations had become a serious personal concern and I felt myself trapped in an untenable position serving a policy with which I completely disagreed.

Rusk, who listened all the time attentively, quietly answered that he understood perfectly well that I had been used and added that I should not worry unduly since he himself had always had some reservations about the reality of what Péter had been saying and doing.

Slowly regaining my composure, I began to pour out all the resentment accumulated in me in the course of years. I started by saying that as a steadfast advocate of closer Hungarian-American ties, I did everything I could to bring back to normal the strained relations between our two countries. I had spared no effort to establish cultural exchange programs and to expand trade and tourism between the two countries. Understandably I was particularly bitter that officials in Budapest, closely following the Soviet line, had suddenly changed policy and declared that until the United States government stopped its "aggression" in Vietnam there could be no broader East-West exchange. I also related how I was told that in reality the Johnson "bridge-building" policy was merely a renewed attempt for loosening up the basis of the "socialist society" and was aimed at detaching Hungary from the Soviet Union. For obvious reasons, I said to Rusk, I had to disassociate myself from this policy of hatred. Yet I was still worried that my decision might create problems for the United States, and I asked the secretary to treat my defection in as low a key as possible to prevent it from becoming a major thorn in East-West and U. S.-Hungarian relations.

Rusk agreed with me. Here I waited for a minute or so, then asked whether my family and I could stay permanently in the United States. The secretary promised to speak with his colleagues and give me the answer as soon as possible.

Less than three hours later an aide of Rusk informed me that we were welcome in America and adequate safeguards for our security would be provided. The next day I went into seclusion and sent a simple one-paragraph letter to Péter, stating that I was resigning for personal reasons.

On May 17, 1967, State Department spokesman Robert J. McCloskey made a brief announcement in connection with my decision. He stated that I wished to become a permanent resident of the United States and would be granted asylum in accordance with the "American tradition of extending refuge to those who seek it."

Following the State Department announcement, I issued a statement which said in part:

> I have always tried to work for peace and better understanding in this troubled world. However, in recent months I came to realize that it was impossible for me to act in good conscience and continue to be the representative of the Hungarian Government. Therefore, I have decided to retire from all forms of public life. The reasons for this decision are very personal ones which I do not wish to explain further.

For me the diplomatic battle over Vietnam ended here.

EPILOGUE

When I left Washington and took up residency on the West Coast in 1967, Vietnam stuck to me like my own shadow. I followed even the smallest details of the war and filed away all available information concerning the diplomatic maneuvers, including the protracted peace negotiations. Among my chief concerns was to discern a logic behind the actions and to understand the puzzling behavior of the participants in the drama.

By 1967, the Vietnam War was far from over. It grew worse in the years that followed. The bombing intensified as American planes hit new targets in the North. The ground war in the South heightened as both sides increased their forces and expanded their range of action. In Washington, General Westmoreland told President Johnson and the Congressional armed forces committees that the war was being won militarily and that in the foreseeable future U. S. troops could be withdrawn from the battlefield. In Hanoi, the Lao Dong party Central Committee adopted Resolution 13, calling for a decisive victory in South Vietnam in the shortest time possible.

While the fighting escalated, it seemed to me that the doors to negotiation remained firmly closed. President Johnson, unwilling to stop the bombing merely for talks, was interested only in reciprocal acts of military restraint. Ho Chi Minh clung steadfastly to Foreign Minister Trinh's formula that the DRV would talk with the U. S. only if the bombing of the North were halted unconditionally and for good. In the middle of this deadlocked situation, Peking categorically opposed any negotiations. Moscow, on the other hand, meticulously followed the line fixed by Trinh.

In June of 1967, at the Glassboro summit meeting between President Johnson and Chairman Kosygin, the Soviet statesman repeated Hanoi's old stand that talks could take place between the North Vietnamese and the Americans only after a suspension of the bombing. When Johnson offered a bombing pause and asked for the stoppage of North Vietnamese infiltration through the DMZ, Kosygin *pro forma* agreed to forward the proposal to Hanoi but was unwilling to discuss the matter any further.

Three months later President Johnson announced a new proposal, the San Antonio Formula, in which the president appeared to make a major concession by expressing readiness to halt the bombing if it would lead "promptly to productive discussion." He no longer insisted on a mutual de-escalation, but rather assumed that while discussions were underway the DRV would not take military advantage of the bombing pause.

This proposal was rejected by Hanoi and branded as an ultimatum to the Vietnamese people. Again the Soviets supported the North Vietnamese position. The Soviet press castigated the United States for "piratical acts of bombing" in the DRV and in private Ambassador Dobrynin and other Soviet diplomats insisted the conditions affixed to the San Antonio Formula were unacceptable. Dobrynin stressed that both his government and the DRV believed the San Antonio Formula, taken in the context of the other statements by the United States, was aimed at forcing North Vietnam to "agree in advance to some sort of de-escalation of operations if the U. S. were to stop the bombing."[1]

Years later, I learned from Ambassador Harriman that he turned to the Rumanians as a possible channel for further clarification of the American position set forth in the San Antonio Formula. He felt their neutral position in the Sino-Soviet controversy made them suitable mediators to the North Vietnamese.[2] At Harriman's request, Rumanian Deputy Foreign Minister George Macovescu spoke twice with Foreign Minister Trinh in Hanoi and made one trip to Washington. However, his shuttle diplomacy, though it was an honest effort, did nothing to change Hanoi's attitude toward negotiation. And the fact that the United States was halting the bombing in and around Hanoi during the Rumanian visit was not considered by the North Vietnamese as a gesture of good will either.[3]

From the Tet Offensive to Paris Peace Negotiations

Macovescu left Hanoi after his second meeting with Trinh on January 30, 1968. The following day the Viet Cong and North Vietnamese Army units launched the massive Tet Offensive, attacking virtually every major city in the South and overrunning a number of provincial and district capitals. Specially trained Viet Cong commandos raided radio stations, government buildings, and even the homes of South Vietnamese officials and army commanders. In Saigon, in separate attacks, guerrillas broke through the walls of the new American Embassy and invaded the Independence Palace before being repulsed. Viet Cong troops also captured part of the South Vietnamese Army's General Staff and the Armored Command Headquarters. In an attempt to detach the three northern provinces of South Vietnam, Communist forces moved on a line from the Highlands to the coastal area of Binh Dinh Province, and lastly Northern regulars and Viet Cong surrounded Khe Sanh, the strategically important U. S. Marine stronghold.

Some of the South Vietnamese government troops and militia fought with determination in the midst of the general confusion. Others, demoralized, put up feeble resistance. Finally, the quick, massive intervention by U. S. forces in Saigon, Hue, Ben Tre, and elsewhere saved the situation. However, this intervention came too late to prevent Hanoi from freeing thousands of political prisoners and executing hundreds of civilians in the service of the South Vietnamese government. After two weeks of heavy fighting, the Viet Cong were forced out of all the major cities except Hue, where the ancient Imperial Citadel remained occupied for almost a month. But the Communist drive was not over. A concentrated large-scale rocket and mortar attack against key military installations and urban targets was launched, resulting in high casualties, especially among civilians. And while the suddenness and frequency of these local suicide attacks kept the U. S. and South Vietnamese troops on the defensive, the Viet Cong gained time to extend its authority over territories in the countryside formerly controlled by Saigon. By the end of February, the Tet Offensive had run out of steam, leaving an estimated 1,000 Americans, 2,000 Vietnamese, and nearly 30,000–40,000 Communists dead or captured and pouring 600,000 refugees into allied territory.[4]

Shocked by these dramatic events, the Washington administration could not understand what had gone wrong. Prior to the onslaught both the CIA and the DIA had issued warnings that Hanoi was carefully planning a new offensive. Aerial photos had shown a large-scale movement of men and supplies along the Ho Chi Minh Trail. Combined Soviet and Chinese military and economic aid was known to have reached almost one billion dollars annually. China had provided logistic support, small arms, food, and other supplies for the "fighting South"; the Soviet Union was the source for the sophisticated weapons, including MIG 21 fighters, new types of long range rockets for urban attacks, heavy artillery, T34 medium and PT-76 reconnaisance tanks for conventional warfare.[5] Yet no high level American officials expected a military offensive of such magnitude, and, most important, none foresaw that the Tet Offensive would turn American public opinion against the war as markedly as it did.

But as I see it in retrospect, there were heavy debit entries on Hanoi's ledger also. At the beginning of the offensive, history seemed to repeat itself. Ho Chi Minh and his generals apparently decided to stake everything on one cart, as they have done in 1954 (*see* Chapter I). Communist propaganda called for an irrepressible uprising of millions of people and depicted North Vietnamese Defense Minister Giap as a master strategist who dared guarantee that Khe Sanh would become another Dien Bien Phu. Militarily, however, the Tet Offensive turned out to be a near disaster. Both the regulars and the Viet Cong forces suffered extremely high casualties. Clashes between Northerners and Southerners reportedly flared up, with a number of Viet Cong units apparently holding the Hanoi leadership responsible for the particularly heavy losses incurred during suicide raids. And Khe Sanh did not become a second Dien Bien Phu. Outnumbered U. S. Marines defeated the besieging North Vietnamese with coordinated use of artillery and airpower. Urban dwellers did not side with the guerrillas. Thus, the expected popular uprising did not occur, and all the efforts to overthrow the Saigon government failed. Yet the political consequences of the Tet Offensive both in South Vietnam and in the United States were fundamental and enduring.

On the diplomatic front, the Tet Offensive at first seemed merely to reaffirm the previously held belief that a negotiated settlement was beyond reach. The North Vietnamese, at the zenith of their psychological victory, continued to repudiate the San Antonio Formula. The Americans, on the other hand, considered the Tet Offensive a clear indication of Hanoi's lack of interest in negotiating a settlement. But once fighting subsided enough for both sides to realize how costly it would be to try to achieve political aims solely through military means, interest in the ancient art of diplomatic bargaining came to the fore. President Johnson took the first step in this direction by announcing on March 31, 1968, an order to end all aerial and naval bombardment over three-fourths of North Vietnam and calling on Ho Chi Minh to join him at the negotiating table. Johnson's unilateral action plus his decision not to seek reelection was viewed by many in Washington as only a limited change in existing U. S. policy and in any case too limited to induce Hanoi to negotiate. Misgivings were dispelled, however, when three days later Ho Chi Minh answered: The DRV government was ready for preliminary talks. Interestingly enough, Ho's message came not through some sophisticated mediation channel but rather by means of a simple, direct Hanoi broadcast:

> . . . the DRV government declares its readiness to send its representatives to make contact with the U. S. representatives to decide with the U. S. side the unconditional cessation of bombing and all other acts against the DRV so that talks could begin.[6]

After several weeks of horsetrading the parties agreed on Paris as the meeting site. But now new difficulties arose. A long discussion began over the selection of representatives. Hanoi rejected the idea of negotiating with Thieu and the Saigon government; Washington refused to recognize the National Liberation Front as the sole representative of South Vietnam. The result was that Ambassador Harriman and his negotiating partner Cyrus R. Vance spent considerable time and energy hammering out a compromise. Finally, the North Vietnamese agreed to comply with the so-called "Your Side/Our Side Formula," by which the NLF would participate on the side of North Vietnam and the South Vietnamese representatives would join the United States during the negotiations. (The United States was to call the talks "two-sided," the DRV "four-sided," with neither questioning the other's interpretation.)

It was the question of the bombing pause, however, that gave rise to the most controversy during the initial days of negotiation, with the Americans reiterating basic points asked so often in the past: What would the other side do once the bombing ceased? Would Hanoi respect the DMZ? Would it refrain from attacking vulnerable South Vietnamese cities? In short, how did the DRV government envision a "reduction" in the level of fighting? The North Vietnamese negotiating team of Ambassador Xuam Duy and powerful Politburo member Le Duc Tho answered in a sharp negative: There could be no reciprocity in exchange for a total and unconditional bombing cessation.

As this dispute continued the Soviets joined their Vietnamese allies in pressing Washington for a bombing halt. Radio Moscow charged the United States with "finding pretext to shun public opinion" and not yet wanting "to completely and unconditionally suspend the bombing and other war activities against North Vietnam." In support of this accusation, party chief Brezhnev warned that if the United States "tries to disrupt the talks, this will once again expose before the whole world the aggressive essence of its policy and will lead to new, more serious defeats for the United States on the battlefield."[7] Behind the scenes, Prime Minister Kosygin tried to convince the Americans that a halt in the bombing was the only way to remove the deadlock in Paris. In a personal letter to President Johnson, Kosygin argued that a complete stoppage of the bombing would neither hurt American prestige nor jeopardize U. S. security. As expected, President Johnson disregarded his suggestion. Nevertheless, Defense Secretary Clark Clifford, Ambassador Harriman, and other high officials of the American administration advised Johnson to stop the bombing altogether.

As Ambassador Harriman told me, the Soviets were also involved in patching up differences between the negotiators later in October of 1968. Minister Counsellor Valentine Oberenko, the number two man at the Soviet Embassy in Paris, was a frequent visitor to the Harriman mission. He told the Americans it would be impossible to get a promise from Hanoi of a reduction in the level of fighting while bombs were falling on the territory of the DRV; once the bombing ended, however, the North Vietnamese would know what to do. He managed to persuade the North Vietnamese that it was equally impossible to require a declaration from the Americans that such a bombing halt would be an "unconditional one." Finally, when the Saigon delegation objected to the seating arrangement at the conference, Oberenko was helpful in working out the intricate question of the shape of the table to the satisfaction of all.

Soviet Ambassador Dobrynin was also busy, forwarding messages between the White House and the Kremlin from his Washington post. On October 27 he received a memorandum from Secretary of State Dean Rusk containing a restatement of the American requirement for a bombing pause. After only twenty-four hours he reported Moscow's reassurance that the Soviets were certain the DRV government was "doing everything possible to put an end to the war in Vietnam and to reach a peaceful settlement."[8]

In marked contrast to the active role played by the Soviets at the Paris talks, the Chinese Communists continued to proclaim the principal of the protracted people's war and emphasized that negotiation was not the correct course for Hanoi to follow. This apparent Chinese condemnation of Hanoi's diplomatic actions was demonstrated forcefully in a message signed by Mao Tse-tung on the occasion of the eighth anniversary of the founding of the NLFSV. He warned the Front that "only by persisting in a people's war" would it be able "to drive the U. S. aggressor out of the soil of Vietnam and win final victory." The message also attacked the "Soviet revisionist renegade clique" for "stepping up its dirty political deal with the U. S. imperialism [to] help put out the flames of the Vietnamese people's revolution."[9]

But neither the North Vietnamese nor the Soviets were affected by the harsh criticism from Peking. Hanoi remained the master of its own decision and withstood Chinese attempts to dictate when to fight and with whom to negotiate. Moscow followed its old line of collaboration with Hanoi by extending political assistance to achieve a complete halt of the bombing. It continued to support the North Vietnamese leaders' view that successful continuation of the war required a "negotiate and fight" policy, considering diplomatic negotiation as only another means of achieving final victory. At the same time, Moscow accused the Maoist leadership of doing everything in its power to prolong the war in Vietnam, thus putting the Soviet Union and the United States on a military collision course while keeping itself clear.

Global Diplomacy and the Vietnamese War

On October 31, 1968, the United States halted aerial and naval bombardment over all North Vietnamese territory. Soon thereafter, Washington and Saigon on the one hand and Hanoi and the NLF on the other reached an agreement to begin the "four-party" negotiations in Paris. At the last minute, however, representatives from South Vietnam refused to participate. Later it was reported that those supporting the Republican candidate for the American presidency, Richard Nixon, had advised Thieu to stall until after the November election. Evidently Thieu was briefed in such a way as to expect a better deal from Nixon than from his opponent, Vice President Hubert H. Humphrey.[10] Thieu gladly complied, and finally, in January 1969 after Nixon's victory, the "four parties" were able to be seated together at the Hotel Majestic in Paris to begin talks.

The road was now open for substantive negotiations, yet neither side was ready—or even willing—to move ahead. The Nixon administration concentrated on Vietnamization of the war, hoping gradually to turn the burden of battle over to the South Vietnamese forces. The Saigon government was preoccupied with making its political machinery stable by silencing any and all opposition. Hanoi, emphasizing the strategy of "fighting while talking," made an effort to pile up as big a store of Chinese and Russian supplies as possible for future military operations. In a surprise move in June 1969, the NLF announced the formation of a "Provisional Revolutionary Government of the Republic of Vietnam" and won diplomatic recognition from Moscow, Peking, Eastern Europe, and a number of nonaligned nations.

In South Vietnam the fighting continued, with the North Vietnamese launching an offensive in late February 1969, which did not taper off until mid-June. The Viet Cong poured heavy rocket barrages into major cities, stepping up its "punitive campaign" by kidnapping and murdering military and district leaders by the thousands. In a countermove U. S. air power supported the South Vietnamese combat missions and carried out sporadic "protective reaction strikes" over the North. Finally, in spring 1970, in a common venture, American and South Vietnamese troops crossed the border into Cambodia to destroy North Vietnamese "sanctuaries."

Meanwhile in Paris, the Communist negotiators demanded the unconditional withdrawal of all U. S. and allied troops from South Vietnam and the liquidation of the entire structure of the "puppet Thieu administration." In turn, Thieu called for a policy of "national reconciliation" but ruled out any type of coalition with the NLF. The Americans, intent on finding ways to bring about a political settlement, proposed a cease-fire "in place" throughout Indochina. This was to be effected in connection with a total withdrawal of all non-South Vietnamese troops—both American and North Vietnamese—on an agreed timetable. Furthermore, the United States asked for an immediate and unconditional release of all American prisoners of war and suggested the calling of an "Indochina Peace Conference" for Laos, Cambodia, and Vietnam.

While the "four-party" negotiations dragged on with no signs of progress, Henry Kissinger, then special assistant for National Security Affairs, entered into private negotiations in Paris with Hanoi's powerful Politburo member Le Duc Tho. Kissinger rightly sensed that public opinion in the United States was more than ever determined to bring American involvement in the Vietnam war to an end. Consequently, during his encounters with his Vietnamese counterpart, Kissinger made one concession after another to facilitate the extrication of America from the conflict. He offered a deadline for U. S. troop evacuation in return for a cease-fire agreement and the freedom of all American POW's. He promised that all troops would be withdrawn within twelve months after the signing of this agreement, a deadline later reduced to six, and finally three months. Le Duc Tho remained unmoved, however, maintaining his rigidity even when the number of American soldiers in South Vietnam was reduced from 540,000 to 170,000 by December 1, 1971. He was interested only in their total evacuation and in the ouster of the Thieu government.

I suspect it must have been quite frustrating for Kissinger to report to President Nixon at the end of 1971 that he was no closer to a settlement than when he had begun the secret negotiations in August 1969. Yet he still hoped to break the deadlock by putting the conflict into a broader perspective, emphasizing its significance in light of world power relations between the United States, the Soviet Union, and China. He opened a dialogue with China on the one hand and tried to establish a new relationship with the USSR on the other. It was to his good fortune in this regard that his efforts coincided with the Twenty-fourth CPSU Congress, where Soviet party chief

Brezhnev launched his "peace program," a variant of the old Leninist blueprint of action based on the correlation of forces between different social systems. This thrust reflected the strength of Soviet interests in reaching favorable terms with the United States on the limitation of offensive and defensive strategic arms systems. It was also aimed at enabling the Soviet economy to bring itself up to par with the rest of the industrialized world. A temporary tactical adjustment of foreign policy from a heated "anti-imperialist struggle" to a businesslike "peaceful coexistence" could do wonders for both causes. It did not mean, however, that Russia intended to give up its support of the "national liberation movements" in Vietnam and elsewhere.

A change in the course of foreign policy was also evident in China, where Chairman Mao Tse-tung and his prime minister, Chou En-lai, had come to the conclusion that China's self-imposed diplomatic isolation was only playing them into the hands of their Russian enemies. They now decided that a restoration of relations with the outside world was absolutely necessary, and, accordingly, Chinese ambassadors were sent to a total of forty-five countries where China's interests until then had been represented by chargés d'affaires ad interim. Moreover, the Chinese began efforts at weakening Soviet influence in Africa, the Indian subcontinent, and the Balkan peninsula. Evidently, the Peking leaders also concluded that a normalized relationship with the United States would serve as a useful factor in the highly volatile Sino-Soviet power equation.

For the Americans, arranging talks with the Russians on problems of mutual interest was not difficult. There had been meetings between all the American presidents and Soviet party chiefs since World War II; therefore, planning the Nixon-Brezhnev summit was relatively easy. On the other side of the two-fold plan, however, entering into negotiations with the Chinese posed quite a complex problem. For one thing, any efforts to seek out a normalization of relations with China would certainly require that the United States abandon its long-standing opposition to the admission of the People's Republic of China to the United Nations. For another, the Chinese (especially after their long years of isolation) were generally regarded as inscrutable and unpredictable. And as an added complication, the Chinese showed no haste in replying to the diplomatic feelers sent out by Nixon. Finally, they agreed in principle to a summit meeting, and the remaining roadblocks were eliminated by Kissinger, the American trouble-shooter, and Premier Chou En-lai, the architect of the new Chinese foreign policy. In February 1972, President Nixon traveled to the Chinese mainland. Three months later he sat with Brezhnev in the Kremlin.

Apparently, the new American "global strategy" was working. Or was it? A semiofficial diplomatic line of communication had been opened up between Washington and Peking. The antiballistic missile systems of Russia and the United States had been limited, and a strategic arms ceiling had been specified. Yet the original aim of the "grand design"—to resolve the Vietnamese conflict—had not been achieved. Communiqués issued at the end of the summit meetings showed no change in Chinese and Russian attitudes about Vietnam. Both powers still stressed "unflinching" solidarity with the "just struggle" of the peoples of Vietnam, Laos, and Cambodia "for their freedom, independence, and social progress." Both powers firmly supported the negotiating positions and proposals of the DRV and the Provisional Revolutionary Government of the Republic of South Vietnam. And each demanded the unequivocal withdrawal of the United States troops from South Vietnam. In addition, even while negotiating with Washington, Peking and Moscow increased their military and economic assistance to North Vietnam to an unprecedented high by the end of 1972.[11] In short, Kissinger simply could not cash in on the differences between China and the Soviet Union, and thus the newly established global diplomacy induced neither the Russians nor the Chinese to pressure Hanoi into ending the war in Vietnam.

The Final Settlement

For both the North and the South, the time between spring of 1972 and early 1973 was the cruelest phase of the war. On March 30, 1972, twelve North Vietnamese army divisions crossed the DMZ for the purpose of "liberating" at least two-thirds of the South. These soldiers were equipped with sophisticated Russian-made weapons, including the most modern T-54 tanks. In a frontal attack the Northern troops pierced the lines of Southern defense easily, capturing Quang Tri and encircling Hue. Another Northern army corps advanced from Cambodia to engage in a fierce battle at An Loc. Heavy fighting occurred in the Central Highlands and, to many observers, it seemed as if the Thieu government would collapse in only a short time. Despite the initial confusion and some severe setbacks, the Saigon army, with American tactical air support, was able to gain ground.

On April 10, President Nixon, indirectly criticizing the Soviet Union's support of the Northern offensive, stated with vigor that "every great power must follow the principle that it should not encourage directly or indirectly any other nation to use force or armed aggression against one of its neighbors."[12] His warning remained unheeded, and six days later he ordered his B-52 bombers and tactical aircraft to strike military targets in North Vietnam, specifically rail lines and all major communications facilities, and the mining of major North Vietnamese ports. Finally, by August, the Northern offensive was halted, with both sides reporting extremely high casualties—military and civilian. Cities like Quang Tri and Hue lay in ruins, as hundreds of thousands of refugees fled the embattled areas. The Viet Cong executed scores of so-called "spies and traitors of the Saigon regime" in the areas which had been "liberated" by Northern forces. The escalated American bombing brought massive destruction to population centers around Hanoi and Haiphong and partly damaged the Red River Delta dike system, threatening a major part of the North with flooding. By the end of the summer Hanoi controlled many pockets of territory in a leopard skin pattern across the South containing about ten percent of the total land area and approximately two percent of the population. Saigon managed to regain some of the heavily populated areas like Quang Tri, but even with American aid it lacked the strength to force the North Vietnamese troops and the Viet Cong from the countryside.

As the battles raged, Kissinger took his own initiatives. On April 20, he rushed to Moscow to inform Brezhnev that the Nixon administration was no longer insisting on the evacuation of the over 100,000 Northern troops in the South. In making this major concession, he evidently hoped to gain Soviet assistance in stopping Hanoi's offensive. He did not. The Soviets took an extremely hard line, blaming the United States for the failure of the Paris negotiations. Brezhnev even condemned the bombing escalations on the part of the United States, maintaining that the Hanoi invasion was merely "a just struggle of the people of Vietnam." After lengthy discussions, however, Brezhnev grudgingly agreed to transmit the American concession to Hanoi. A month later, at the Nixon-Brezhnev summit, Kissinger used this Moscow channel to forward two more concessions. First, he promised that a cessation of the bombing in the North could come earlier than the liberation of American prisoners of war (this was completely contrary to the administration's public stance on the matter). In addition, he was ready to accept the formation of a coalition government, proposing as a first step a tripartite election committee with the participation of the neutralists, the NLF, and representatives of the Saigon government. These concessions, however, did nothing to alter Russian rigidity. Brezhnev continued to warn Nixon that the newly established U. S.-Soviet "détente" would be destroyed by a resumption of American bombing and mining in North Vietnam.

As I learned much later from Jacob D. Beam, then U. S. ambassador to Russia, Kissinger's trip to Moscow was made primarily to discuss Vietnam, which was normally outside Beam's sphere of interest—the State Department was not being kept fully informed on this matter. On the evening of Kissinger's departure, the ambassador went to visit him at his guesthouse, near Brezhnev's living quarters, the Dom Prymov. There Beam was briefed by the American secretary of state about SALT and preparations for the upcoming summit. Regarding Vietnam, Kissinger told Beam that the Soviets had been terribly tough but had agreed to transmit a message to Hanoi which, Kissinger thought, would bring about a favorable change in the course of the war. It was during this briefing that both Beam and Kissinger were almost shot accidentally by an over-zealous Russian guard at the complex. Beam recalled the incident which abruptly broke their conversation: "Kissinger took me out into the garden among the shrubbery to talk to me when I heard the click of a safety catch being released on a rifle. I told the Secretary to stand very still and shouted out in Russian that we were Americans."[13]

Moscow forwarded Kissinger's offer of the secret concessions to Hanoi, but as in the past, the North Vietnamese were slow in replying. Finally, in June 1972, at the conclusion of his three-day state visit to the North Vietnamese capital, Soviet President Podgorny indicated that Hanoi was about to resume the Paris peace negotiations. By then it had become apparent to everyone that a stalemate had developed on the battlefield; Hanoi was forced to negotiate seriously. A month after Podgorny's visit, the Hanoi Politburo sent its chief negotiator, Le Duc Tho, back to Paris. Two secret sessions were held between Le Duc Tho and Kissinger in August, three in September. In October, Le Duc Tho put a Nine Point proposal on the conference table, which led to a breakthrough: most importantly he dropped his demand for a coalition government and for Thieu's removal. On his part Kissinger agreed to the presence of 150,000 North Vietnamese troops in the South. Soon a draft agreement was reached which included: a cease-fire in place in South Vietnam; a provision for the total withdrawal of U. S. troops within sixty days; the release of all American POW's within sixty days of the signing of the cease-fire agreement; the creation of a Council of National Reconciliation and Concord to assist in upholding the cease-fire and supervising the future election. The draft agreement provided also for the establishment of a four-sided commission to guarantee the terms of the final agreement.[14]

Kissinger's deputy, Ambassador William H. Sullivan, was also busy hammering out an understanding with his North Vietnamese counterpart, Vice Foreign Minister Nguyen Co Thach, about the composition of an International Commission of Control and Supervision for the agreement. As I learned later from the ambassador, essentially the problems involved in this hasty negotiation lay in the fact that the United States aimed to have an effective Control Commission which would genuinely enforce the cease-fire and police an honest execution of the future agreement. The North Vietnamese, on the other hand, clearly wanted to have a totally ineffective supervision of the agreement. Sullivan started out by proposing an all-Asian commission, composed of representatives of various states in the region which would have interest in preserving peace in Indochina but which would generally be considered "neutral." This was flatly rejected by the North Vietnamese. Then the American shifted to an Asian commission with two members selected by the U. S. government, two by the DRV, and with a neutral chairman to be designated. When Sullivan indicated that the U. S. candidates would be Japan and Indonesia, the Hanoi delegation expressed exceptionally strong aversion to the Japanese membership. Eventually the negotiations reached a compromise on the structure of the commission which made possible individual commission members or a combination of individual members to submit reports without the necessity of total unanimity by the commission. Thus defined, the internal political balance of the group became less important and a strong neutral chairman became less significant. Having arrived at that understanding, Washington proposed Canada and Indonesia to serve on the International Commission of Control and Supervision; Hanoi named Hungary and Poland. Neither side raised objection. The American assumed that Hanoi believed the Hungarians and the Poles could be reliably counted upon to follow Soviet directions and that the Soviets would in turn do nothing to frustrate or embarrass North Vietnamese intentions. And, of course, this assumption proved to be entirely correct.

This preliminary agreement in principle did not lead to an early settlement, however. Much to Kissinger's dismay, President Thieu opposed the presence of Northern troops in the South and objected to the creation of the Council of Reconciliation as a "coalition government in disguise." To make matters even worse, the North Vietnamese tried to squeeze last-minute concessions from the Americans. Pressured from both directions, Kissinger began to toughen his own negotiating stance. His rigidity became especially apparent after intelligence reports warned Washington that Communist forces were preparing an all out attack in South Vietnam at the eve of the cease-fire. On December 13, 1972, the talks abruptly broke down. Five days later President Nixon ordered heavy bombing of the Hanoi-Haiphong area and laying of new mines in the ports north of the 20th parallel. As a justification, White House Press Secretary Ronald Zeigler underlined that the United States government will not "allow the peace talks to be used as a cover for another North Vietnamese offensive." On December 30 the use of military power for political purpose was stopped, and the White House announced that Kissinger would be returning to Paris. In the meantime General Alexander Haig, White House chief of staff, rushed to Saigon, carrying President Nixon's written guarantee that "if Hanoi fails to abide by the terms of the agreement, it is my intention to take swift and severe retaliatory actions."[15] In spite of the presidential assurance the general had a hard time persuading Thieu not to throw any more obstacles in the way of a settlement, and only after long hours of argument did the South Vietnamese leader back off from his rigid position.

On January 8, Kissinger and Le Duc Tho resumed talks. The two spent a week in direct negotiation. Among other matters, there was discussion of a massive U. S. aid program to Vietnam, Kissinger agreeing to a sum of 3.25 billion dollars to assist in the rebuilding of the bomb-ravaged North. But he made it clear to Le Duc Tho that such assistance would be subject to approval by the United States Congress and the carrying out of all provisions of the agreement.[16] Meanwhile the lion's share of work was taken up by Ambassador Sullivan and the deputy legal adviser of the State Department, George H. Aldrich. They met daily with North Vietnamese Deputy Foreign Minister Thach and resolved the few ambiguities in the wording of the agreement. They also drafted the protocol on the cease-fire and the Joint Military Commission; they feverishly negotiated protocols on the prisoners and detainees, the International Commission of Control and Supervision, and mine clearing in

North Vietnam. Sullivan and Thach concluded their meetings on January 22, 1973. The next day Kissinger and Le Duc Tho put their initials on the final settlement.

On January 27, "An Agreement on Ending the War and Restoring the Peace in Vietnam," as it was formally titled, was signed by the foreign ministers of the United States, the Republic of Vietnam, the Democratic Republic of Vietnam, and the Provisional Revolutionary Government of the Republic of South Vietnam, to be endorsed a month later at a conference in Paris by Great Britain, France, the Soviet Union, China, the members of the International Commission of Control and Supervision, and the secretary-general of the United Nations. To many observers, the agreement was for all practical purposes an act of surrender to Hanoi, since the North Vietnamese divisions were permitted to remain in South Vietnam. Close friends of Harriman claimed that the ambassador and Cyrus Vance could have concluded a much better treaty in 1968. Others thought the final settlement was not so different from the terms originally announced by North Vietnamese Premier Pham Van Dong in his famous "four point position" of April 1965.[17] Some even hoped, for a short time, that the wounds of war might be healed and—step by step—life might return to normal. But those who entertained the idea that this agreement would bring an era of reconciliation among the Vietnamese peoples were wrong. After sixty days the Americans had withdrawn their troops, dismantled their bases, and seen their POW's returned home. From then on, the cease-fire was constantly violated. Hanoi was no longer interested in living up to the remaining provisions of the agreement. And Saigon, too, did little to keep up its part of the bargain.

In late 1973 Hanoi charged the Saigon government with 270,000 violations, while Saigon held Hanoi and the Viet Cong accountable for 28,000. The North Vietnamese continued their influx of troops and war materials into the South but refused to allow the ICCS to establish observation posts. Even on the Commission itself, Communist Poland and Hungary favored the interests of Hanoi and the PRG by insisting on the investigation of only Saigon's violations. The Indonesians kept clear of confrontation with anyone. The Canadians at first tried to ensure fair treatment to all parties involved; but their efforts came to nothing, and the Canadian contingent withdrew from the ICCS. Their place was taken by Iranian observers and the matter rested there. Areas of control were not marked off. The "liberated" Communist-held territories were fortified by the arrival of fresh troops, newly installed heavy artillery batteries, and SAM missiles. The old Ho Chi Minh trail, which had gained such fame as a avenue of infiltration, was transformed into an all-year, two-lane super-highway, complete with pipelines, filling stations, and depots. A hastily constructed network of airstrips and airfields further improved lines of communication between Hanoi and the PRG. Consolidation of the Communist positions often involved some land-grabbing operations, which in turn triggered harsh counterattacks from Southern troops. Soon, once again, major battles erupted in many parts of South Vietnam.

As the fighting resumed, representatives of the PRG and Saigon held innumerable meetings at La Calle Saint Cloud, near Paris, without even nearing a mutual understanding on any of the political provisions of the Paris agreement. Thieu's ambassador proposed a timetable for elections and the creation of a national body to direct them. Each such proposal contained a carefully inserted clause demanding the withdrawal of the North Vietnamese forces from the South. Naturally the PRG rejected each one, and the attendant negotiations were futile. A final exchange of Vietnamese prisoners was completed in Saigon on March 7, 1974, and after that date no progress was made on any of the other pressing military questions. Sessions of the two-party Military Commission degenerated into senseless exchanges of heated arguments. Systematically the PRG blocked all American efforts to recover the bodies of U. S. servicemen lost in action. Unilaterally, it charged the Iranian and Indonesian delegations of the ICCS with investigating only Communist cease-fire violations and abruptly suspended paying its share of the Commission's expenses. October brought the issuance of a major policy statement from the PRG in which, for the first time since the cease-fire agreement, it called for the overthrow of the Thieu government.

In the midst of these events, the Hanoi Politburo earnestly

began plans for a general offensive. As North Vietnamese Armed Forces chief of staff, General Van Thien Dung, pointed out in his memoirs, the DRV's political and military leaders were cheered by reports reaching the North Vietnamese capital. Perhaps most encouraging of all was the news that the United States Congress had cut military appropriations substantially, with the result that "Nguyen Van Thieu was forced to fight a poor man's war."[18] Equally important was the decline once more of South Vietnamese troop morale, with deserters numbering 20,000 per month. A movement of urban, non-Communist opposition to Thieu was steadily gaining momentum, only adding to the problems already existing. Also, Hanoi presumed that the Watergate affair, the economic recession, and the energy crisis were factors undermining American determination to rescue Saigon in case of a Northern attack. Fully concurring in this assessment were the Soviet leaders, who in the fall of 1974 reported a progressive erosion of American desire to continue aid to South Vietnam and urged Hanoi to "exert maximum pressure on Saigon before the latter could purchase arms from sources other than the United States."[19] Such Soviet counsel was coupled with increased arms shipments in great quantity, including heat-seeking Strela guided missiles, a deadly threat to South Vietnamese air power. The visit to Hanoi in December of General Victor G. Kulikov, Soviet armed forces chief of staff, was further evidence that the Russians now were "silent partners" in the upcoming offensive with the Kremlin's best military mind on hand for last-minute consultation.

By the time Kulikov and Giap concluded their meetings, North Vietnamese forces were on the move. They overran six district capitals in the Delta and attacked Phuoc Long province, seventy-five miles north of Saigon. In less than two weeks of fighting, the province, along with its picturesque capital of Phuoc Binh, fell. In the next two months North Vietnamese troops under General Dung's command advanced simultaneously in the directions of Saigon, Pleiku, and Kontum. Thieu interpreted this move as a sign that the Northerners would strike against Saigon, while his generals believed it meant they would strike in the Highlands. Instead, the invading army used the splitting tactics employed by the Soviets in World War II. They launched a surprise attack halfway between Saigon and Pleiku against the Montagnard capital Ban Me Thuot. South Vietnamese intelligence failed flatly; the defenders were literally sleeping when the onslaught began. The Montagnards, who were supposed to form a defensive line around the city, sided with the North Vietnamese and let the attackers through. To add to the confusion, the South Vietnamese Air Force destroyed its own troop headquarters. Communication with Saigon was cut off. On March 31, 1975, after only a three-day battle, the city fell into the hands of the Communists.

Then, like a huge steel wedge, Dung's armored tanks pushed eastward toward the coastal city of Tuy Hoa. His three divisions roadblocked two slowly advancing South Vietnamese regiments belatedly trying to reach Ban Me Thuot. Other North Vietnamese forces pressured the highland capitals of Kontum and Pleiku. At that point, Thieu, as commander-in-chief, made the fateful decision to order the immediate evacuation of the entire Highlands. This strategic withdrawal (as the retreat was called) in the face of superior North Vietnamese divisions quickly degenerated into chaotic, headlong flight. Kontum and Pleiku fell in a matter of days. Quang Tri was overrun; Hue was simply abandoned. Resistance at Da Nang melted away. The whole string of coastal provinces fell as easy prey into Hanoi's hands.

By the end of March, six of thirteen Southern divisions vanished from sight, and the once promising air force became nonexistent. An estimated 800 million dollars worth of military supplies and equipment was lost. Half a million refugees fled southward. Terror, looting, and panic broke out on an unprecedented scale. In the middle of all this turmoil, the armies of the North rolled onward faster than those who fled. The Viet Cong forces began a drive in the Mekong Delta, south of Saigon. Simultaneously, Dung's elite troops struck north at Xuan Loc, the last stronghold in the capital's defense.[20]

With the rapidly deteriorating situation, the Ford administration made a last-minute effort to save Saigon. On April 10, the president addressed a joint session of Congress, recommending 722 million dollars worth of military assistance for South Vietnam. He argued that if his aid could be immediately granted, the Thieu government still had a chance to hold on to the shortened military front line. After some hearings and agonizing arguments, Congress turned down the request. While the debates were on, Secretary of State Kissinger came forth with a statement before the American Society of Newspaper Editors that the Soviet Union and China had helped North Vietnam to make a mockery of the 1973 Peace agreement. He warned that the two Communist powers must bear responsibility for their actions. "Relaxation of tensions," he maintained, "cannot be practiced selectively." His remarks went almost unnoticed. Then Philip C. Habib, assistant secretary for East Asian and Pacific Affairs, forwarded diplomatic notes to the guarantors of the Paris Peace Agreement—the Soviet Union, the People's Republic of China, and the other governments represented at the International Conference on Vietnam—reminding them that the Hanoi government "accepted a solemn obligation to end the fighting in Vietnam and shift the conflict there from the battlefield to the negotiating table." Yet North Vietnam had now undertaken a massive all-out offensive against South Vietnam in complete contempt of the Paris agreement, Habib continued, and the Northern aggression had caused a human flight of historic proportions and an "untold misery [to be] inflicted on the land which had already seen more than its share. . . ." He closed his diplomatic statement with a dramatic call upon the Soviet Union, China, Great Britain, and France, along with the members of the ICCS and the secretary-general of the United Nations, to meet their obligations by using their influence to stop Hanoi's military operations and enforce the Paris agreement. The Russians promptly retorted that first and foremost all parties must implement the Paris agreement in all particulars. The other powers also seemed uninterested or were unable to intervene. Needless to say, Habib's appeal went unheeded.[21]

During these last weeks, with the days of the South Vietnamese government clearly numbered, France and Hungary still tried to convince the Americans that a last-minute political solution was a real possibility. The French assured the United States that "Hanoi does not want to see the United States more humilitated than it is already [sic]."[22] Major General Antal Tölgyes, the commanding officer of the Hungarian military contingent at the ICCS, and his chief of staff, Colonel János Tóth, were also active in this make-believe diplomacy. They met several times in Saigon with Thomas Polgár, a Hungarian-born CIA station chief, to urge the notion that Hanoi was interested in a political settlement. As late as April 19, Colonel Tóth still insisted that "the other side" would be willing to negotiate a "dignified" settlement. Naturally, such a settlement would have to be based on the realities of the situation and could not be a disguise to perpetuate the Thieu regime. Therefore, said Tóth, "the other side" specified three prerequisites to "meaningful negotiations." First, Thieu must be removed; second, the negotiations for a cease-fire must be conducted by the successor government in accordance with the previously published policy positions of the PGR; and, third, the United States must restrict its activities and presence in South Vietnam to traditional embassy functions. Tóth added that action to meet these requirements would have to take place within a matter of days, not weeks. He emphasized again and again the absolute necessity for speed if there were to be any negotiations. The Hungarians also contacted the *New Yorker's* Saigon correspondent, Robert Shaplen, and told him too that negotiations might be possible. But the prerequisites for the initiation of talks could not be complied with by either the South Vietnamese or the American governments. And it was too late for any kind of negotiation, anyway. The decision had already been made by Hanoi a long time ago to "go for broke" militarily.

Meanwhile, the demoralized Southern capital drifted toward total collapse. President Thieu was blamed (and rightly so) for the loss of over ninety percent of the country to the Communists. Air Vice Marshal Nguyen Cao Ky and General Cao Van Vien, the head of the Joint General Staff, were ready to assume military command. Premier Tran Thien Khiem and other members of the cabinet resigned. The South Vietnamese Senate passed a resolution calling for "a new leadership" to end the war and charged the president with abuse of power, corruption, and social injustice. But Thieu held on tenaciously and in an irrational move ordered the arrest of some of his political opponents. On April 20, during a private audience, U. S.

Ambassador to Saigon Graham A. Martin informed Thieu that neither his supporters nor his enemies believed he could lead the South out of its crisis and that "if he did not move soon, his generals would ask him to go"[23] The following night of April 21, Thieu resigned. For all practical purposes his resignation did not solve anything. It came too late, and because of the rapidly deteriorating military situation it meant little. His replacement by his equally hardliner vice president, Tran Van Huong, was naturally not viewed by Hanoi as a conciliatory gesture.

Finally power passed to retired General Duong Van "Big" Minh, a neutralist. Minh promptly offered a cease-fire to the Communists, and, complying with their previous demand, ordered all Americans out of South Vietnam. But his appeal and maneuvering also had little effect. Hanoi was not interested in bargaining; it wanted unconditional surrender. General Dung's artillery intensified its shelling of Saigon while his fifteen-division main force, which had encircled the city, tightened its iron grip. On April 29, President Ford ordered the crash evacuation of the Americans from Saigon. He chose to do so following the bombardment of the Tan So Nhut airport near Saigon and in the face of the imminent entry into the South Vietnamese capital of North Vietnamese army units. Clearly the overriding consideration of the American president must have been his concern for the physical safety of the Americans there. Washington received word from Hanoi—via Moscow—that the North Vietnamese troops would not interfere militarily with the American evacuation.[24] The promise was kept. The last Americans, including Ambassador Martin, left the embassy unharmed. Over 100,000 Vietnamese fled by air and sea to safety. On April 30, 1975, Dung's tanks rolled onto the streets of Saigon and "Big" Minh capitulated.

It was time to say a requiem.

* * *

The sudden collapse of South Vietnam caught everyone by

surprise, especially the victors, who had made plans for a much longer war and expected a conquest no earlier than 1976. Their "silent partner," the Kremlin, was almost as taken aback as the North Vietnamese Politburo. Once it absorbed the situation, however, the Soviet leadership moved quickly to seize the advantage in the balance-of-power shift they knew would develop.

As a first step, the Kremlin called on the nations of Asia to revitalize the long dormant Russian plan for an "Asian Collective Security System." The Soviet leaders maintained that the ten principles set forth in the final act of the "Helsinki Conference on European Security and Cooperation" could be applied to the Asian continent to effect a multilateral treaty that would bring lasting peace to all of Asia. Hoping the acceptance of the plan would thwart Maoist attempts to extend Chinese influence in the area, the Kremlin leaders further directed the Soviet propaganda machine to "expose" in detail Peking's "subversive activities" in Burma, Thailand, Malaysia, and the Philippines. Their high card in this endeavor was a denunciation of the Chinese for publishing maps showing Mongolia, Korea, Vietnam, Cambodia, Laos, Burma, Malaya, Thailand, part of the territory of India, the Japanese Island of Ryukyu, and the Sulu Archipelago of the Philippines as "Chinese territories wrenched away by the imperialist powers." Finally the Soviets attacked the "cold warrior Mao and his retinue" for trying constantly to provoke a major clash between the USSR and the United States and for spreading the view that a world thermonuclear war was unavoidable.

The Chinese, of course, counterattacked. The Asian Security System, they contended, constituted a telling and dangerous move on the part of the USSR to occupy the place relinquished by the United States in Southeast Asia and to establish hegemony in that area. They proclaimed far and wide that it was Moscow, not Peking, that sought dominance in Asia; it was the Soviets, not the Chinese, who had stepped up espionage activities, cultivated anti-governmental elements, and interfered in internal affairs in the nations of Southeast Asia.

The exchange grew increasingly bitter after the September issue of *Kommunist* (the Soviet Communist party monthly) issued a call "to all comrades in China" to "smash Maoism" and after Brezhnev's stinging attack on Maoist ideology and policy at the Twenty-fifth Congress of the Soviet Communist party. Now the Chinese denounced Brezhnev's policy of détente with the West as a cheap trick to distract attention from Soviet preparations for armed expansion. Chinese diplomats in Washington meanwhile warned their American counterparts of the dangers inherent in arms control negotiations with the Russians.

Sino-Soviet tension continued unabated following Chairman Mao's death in September 1976. The new Chinese leader, Hua Kuo-feng, appeared as hostile as his predecessor to Russian appeals for reconciliation. In the best Maoist tradition, his leadership continued "resolutely" to oppose "modern revisionism" and pronounced "Soviet social imperialism" more dangerous than "decaying U. S. imperialism." Interestingly, some familiar Western themes began to surface in the Chinese charges as well; for example, the "new Tsars" in the Kremlin were assailed for their suppression of human rights at home and in Eastern Europe.[25]

In marked contrast to its belligerency toward the Chinese, toward America the Kremlin extended a hand, velvet-gloved, in a gesture of "détente." In that rosy ambience known to both sides as a "relaxation of tensions," the Soviets managed to equal, if not surpass, American military might in some fields; to assure a transfer of American know-how that would bring the Soviet Union fully into the computer age; and to secure the Kremlin against a threat of a two-front crisis. Most important, they worked steadily to induce the United States to formally abandon its traditional policy of containment of Communist expansion.

As "détente" progressed, however, the Russian security mania reasserted itself: distrust grew, upsetting an otherwise beneficial array of joint technical, scientific, and cultural Russo-American projects. The spectacular agreement on the prevention of nuclear war contained no assurance against an accidental major war or of an involvement by either of the superpowers in lesser wars. The temporary curb on the arms race served to weaken NATO by upsetting the strategic equilibrium based on nuclear parity and exposing Europe to Russia's superior conventional military machine. Meanwhile the development of new weapon systems on both sides made strategic arms limitation agreements outdated even before they were ratified. As the days and months passed, it became obvious that the Soviets viewed "détente" as nothing more than another stage in the historic struggle between communism and capitalism, a struggle which "inevitably would eventuate in the victory of communism." With this realization, American enthusiasm for "détente" abated. Nevertheless the United States policy of containment fell by the wayside. After the Vietnam debacle, American policy-makers concluded the United States was no longer in a position to shelter nations from Communist aggression. Instead, they moved toward recognition of a state of "dynamic equilibrium," whereby it was assumed the major powers would pursue diverse strategic policies aimed at securing influence while at the same time concluding alliances for and against each other in order to create a delicate power balance. This new multi-polar approach, complicated and ill-defined as it was, did little to impress the Kremlin, and there was reason to believe that the existing balance of power rested chiefly on a shaky balance of terror.

Meanwhile, in Southeast Asia, the Soviet efforts effectively to fill the vacuum left by the American military withdrawal met with a few small successes and many large frustrations. In Thailand and the Philippines, Soviet diplomacy gained a mere foothold, nothing more, in establishing diplomatic and commercial relations. Indonesia agreed to only a moderate expansion of economic cooperation. Japan's policy of rapprochement with Mao's China contributed even further to the alienation of Tokyo from Moscow. In addition, unexpected difficulties arose on the Indian peninsula. The pro-Soviet Sheik Mujibur Rahman's regime in Bangladesh was overthrown. Soviet influence failed to block the resumption of normal relations between India and China; and—perhaps most important of all—the Russians suffered an incalculable setback with the downfall of their friend Indira Gandhi.

On the Indochina peninsula, Chinese influence with the Khmer Communists continued to foil Soviet efforts to normalize relations with Cambodia, and Chinese advice often disrupted Russian activities in Laos. But the most galling situation prevailed in Vietnam, where Hanoi adopted a neutral position and appeared determined to stick with it. Brezhnev and his colleagues had to live with the fact that although their Vietnamese allies had endorsed "détente" they would not support the "Asian Collective Security System." Even more irritating, Hanoi launched a policy drive to make all of Southeast Asia "a zone of independence, peace and neutrality." And there were other problems. Le Duan did not offer basing rights to the Soviet Pacific Fleet at Cam Ranh Bay or at other naval bases built by the United States in South Vietnam. The Unified Socialist Republic of Vietnam joined the World Bank and the International Monetary Fund, two international financial institutions considered by Moscow to be "tools of American imperialism." (Russia, of course, is not a member of these U. N. organizations, and moreover had prevented all the East European countries except Yugoslavia and Rumania from gaining admission there.) Hanoi let it be known that in the realm of foreign trade Vietnam was looking forward to constructive economic exchange with all countries; Vietnam was not to be considered for all practical purposes as a member of the "socialist community," much less as a member of the Soviet-led communism, but as an integral part of the rapidly expanding international world trading system.[26] At the same time, the Russians could do nothing but offer large-scale economic aid if they wished to keep their "fraternal ties" with Hanoi. Nor could they dominate or even influence the Lao Dong party, which in the post-victory period had become more and more critical towards the Russians as well as the Chinese, propagating its own correct, independent, and sovereign line of socialist collectivism at home and nationalism abroad.

In short, the extension of Soviet influence to the Indochina peninsula proved to be a much harder task than the Kremlin leaders had originally thought. Moscow somehow, for all its aid and influence, did not emerge from the conflict as the principal champion and mentor of the "national liberation movements." It could not contain Chinese influence. It could not replace the United States as a leading power in the area. And, finally, by its material and moral support for the North through the long years of the war, it created a new Communist power center—a united Vietnam—which, in the long run, will in all certainty weaken Soviet influence in the already polycentric world of communism.

NOTES

CHAPTER I

1. Apparently Ho's revolution was not in line with Stalin's perspective. The Russian dictator wanted first a Communist takeover in France and a solution to the Annamite (Vietnamese) independence later. In this respect it is interesting to remember that on September 25, 1945, the Stalinist French Communists in Saigon issued a document urging the Vietnamese Communists to make sure that their actions met the criteria of what was then the Kremlin's policy. They warned that any "premature adventures" in Annamite (i.e., Vietnamese) independence might "not be in line with Soviet perspective." Bernard B. Fall, "Tribulations of a Party Line," in *Foreign Affairs* 33, no. 3 (April 1955):500.

2. George McTurnan Kahnin and John W. Lewis, *The United States in Vietnam* (New York, 1967), p. 32.

3. The Vietnamese Communist party was reestablished only in 1951 as the Vietnamese Workers' party (Dang Lao Dong Viet Nam), *Yearbook on International Communist Affairs* (Stanford, 1967), p. 371.

4. For details of the Geneva Conference, see *The Pentagon Papers*, Gravel ed., 4 vols. (Boston, 1971), 1:108–78.

5. For comprehensive treatment of the battle of Dien Bien Phu, see: Bernard B. Fall, *Hell in a Very Small Place: The Siege of Dien Bien Phu* (New York, 1966); Jules Roy, *The Battle of Dienbienphu* (New York, 1965); and Vo Nguyen Giap, *Dien Bien Phu* (Hanoi, 1964). See *also* Nikita S. Khrushchev, *Khrushchev Remembers,* trans. and ed. Strobe Talbott (Boston, 1970), p. 482.

CHAPTER II

1. See "Working Paper of U.S. State Department on the North Vietnamese Role in the War in South Vietnam," in Richard A. Falk, ed., *The Vietnam War and International Law* 2 vols. (Princeton, 1969), 2:1192–93.

2. As one of Khrushchev's protegés, Mukhitdinov became a Presidium member in 1957. From 1957 to 1961 he was also secretary to the Central Committee with responsibility for the Moslem republics of the USSR. For further details, see Michel Tatu, *Power in the Kremlin* (New York, 1972), p. 553.

3. For text of the resolution concerning the foundation of the NLF and the statements of the foreign delegates, see *Third National Congress of the Vietnam Worker's Party: Documents* (Hanoi: Foreign Languages Publishing House, n.d.). See also *Népszabadság* (Budapest), September 6, 1960.

4. For further details concerning infiltration statistics, see Falk, "Working Paper of U.S. State Department," 2:1194.

5. Douglas Pike, *Viet Cong* (Cambridge, 1967), pp. 74–84; see also *The Pentagon Papers*, 1:337–46.

6. Hungarian government officials needed special permission from the Protocol Department before they could accept an invitation from the U.S. legation or from other Western missions, but they were free to attend at will parties given by embassies of the Soviet bloc countries. After the break with Mao Tse-tung, Politburo members were seldom seen at the Chinese Embassy, and the Protocol Department had difficulty sending even a cabinet minister or a higher ranking military official to the Chinese national holiday party. Kádár himself hated ceremony but liked to attend receptions, where he could mingle with the crowd and have long face-to-face talks with diplomats. He spoke only Hungarian and on most occasions had only a Russian language translator with him. When he wanted to speak with a Western representative, he would ask me to be his ad hoc interpreter.

7. Assignments abroad for persons below the rank of ambassador or minister were approved or disapproved by the foreign minister. In the case of the second man in an embassy or legation (counsellor), approval had to be given by the Secretariat of the party's Central Committee. Administrative formalities for assignments abroad were handled by the Ministry's Personnel Department. The chief of this department could also register an objection to any assignment below that of chief of mission if he was aware of something derogatory in the nominee's file.

The posting of intelligence officers to serve abroad under diplomatic cover could not be questioned by either the Department of International Relations or the Foreign Ministry. This was handled directly between the Administrative Department of the Central Committee and the agency in question, and approval had to be obtained from the Secretariat.

8. For further details, see János Radványi, *Hungary and the Superpowers* (Stanford, 1972) pp. 139–50.

9. *New York Times,* September 16, 1964.

10. State Department Director Harold C. Vedeler informed me about the Mundt amendment on November 16, 1963. Vedeler indicated to me that the introduction of the amendment did not represent a change in the administration position concerning the sale of agricultural commodities on short-term credits guaranteed by the Export-Import Bank. He added that the State Department hoped Congress would not approve the Mundt amendment. For my part, I made it clear that if the deal fell through I would be in no position to convince the Hungarian government of American sincerity for detente. Details concerning the wheat deal can be found in Lyndon B. Johnson, *The Vantage Point* (New York, 1971), p. 39; and Arthur M. Schlesinger, Jr., *A Thousand Days* (Cambridge, 1965), p. 920.

11. During the 1956 Soviet invasion of Budapest, Cardinal József Mindszenty sought refuge at the American Legation in Budapest. The asylum was granted and Mindszenty spent fifteen years at the U.S. mission in Budapest. In 1971, in the "atmosphere of detente" his presence at the American Embassy disturbed U.S.-Soviet relations and became a serious obstacle to a normal relationship between the Church and the Hungarian state. Thus both Nixon and the Pope, after securing him free passage to Austria from the Hungarian government, forced the Cardinal into exile. He died in Vienna.

For revealing details, see Cardinal József Mindszenty, *Memoirs,* (New York, 1974), pp. 232–39.

12. There was only one so-called protest meeting organized in the Cultural Center of the Trade Union, a week after the Tonkin incident. The indifference of the Hungarian party leadership was reflected by the fact that none of the speakers of the rally were members of the Politburo. *Népszabadság,* August 13, 1965.

13. See Seaborn Missions (Canadian ICC delegate's periodical visits to Hanoi from June 1964 until June 1965) in "The Pentagon Papers" (Diplomatic Volumes), 6, C.I., pp. 1–29.

14. The French government forwarded the information to U.S. Ambassador Charles Bohlen, who in turn forwarded it to Secretary Dean Rusk. See Bohlen's cable, *ibid.,* p. 26.

15. See text of U.S. government message to the DRV made public by Hanoi Radio on December 10, 1965. See also *New York Times,* December 12, 1965.

16. Hanoi Radio in English, May 19, 1965.

17. For further details of the Rusk-Dobrynin, Rusk-Gromyko meetings and the Kohler-Firyubin discussion, see "The Pentagon Papers" (Diplomatic Volumes), 6, C. 1., pp. 115–21).

18. *Ibid.,* pp. 124–25.

19. *The Pentagon Papers* (Gravel ed.), 4:297.

20. *Ibid.,* pp. 4:26–33.

21. *Ibid.,* 4:22.

22. My interview with George W. Ball on April 1, 1971, at the Stanford Faculty Club. See *also* the memorandum of George Ball entitled "How valid are the assumptions underlying our Viet-Nam policies?" October 5, 1964, copy in possession of the author and reprinted in the *Atlantic Monthly,* July 1972, pp. 33–49.

23. *The Pentagon Papers* 4:23.

24. David Halberstam, *The Best and the Brightest* (New York, 1972), p. 599.

25. *New York Times,* July 29, 1965.

CHAPTER III

1. Transcript of János Péter's speech at the U.N. General Assembly in 1965, United Nations, General Assembly, *Official Records,* 20th Session, 1350th Plenary Meeting, October 6, 1965.

2. The biographical sketch of János Péter is here reconstructed on the basis of his official biography published in *International Who's Who, 1972–73* (London, 1973), p. 1039, and personal recollection.

3. *Washington Post,* October 7, 1965.

4. Mr. Ford from the State Department was also present and took notes of the conversation.

5. This was true. Péter was referring to Politburo member Jeno Fock's mission to Hanoi. But the Fock delegation, which included Central Committee

Member Árpád Pullai, deputy director of the Central Committee's International Relations, András Gyenes and Major-General Lászlo Szücs of the army, visited Hanoi to discuss economic and military aid matters and questions relating to the international Communist movement with DRV party and government officials and not the DRV's conditions for a negotiated settlement.

6. *Washington Post,* October 8, 1965.

7. United Nations, General Assembly, *Official Records,* 20th Session, 1335th Plenary Meeting, September 24, 1965, pp. 2–3.

8. A year later Rusk extended the same invitation to the Hungarian foreign minister, János Péter. Péter declined because he was sensitive to the possible North Vietnamese reaction.

9. Two years later the Rumanian government would try earnestly to mediate between Washington and Hanoi, but without success.

10. In the course of the conversation with Secretary Rusk the Polish vice minister also reiterated his country's fears for a resurgent militarist and imperialist Germany. He renewed Poland's proposal for a conference to discuss the issue of European security. Personal recollection.

11. Chester L. Cooper, *The Lost Crusade: America in Vietnam* (New York, 1970), p. 330.

CHAPTER IV

1. For an interpretive analysis of the Ia Drang Valley battle, see Halberstam, *The Best and the Brightest* (New York, 1972), pp. 612–14; for North Vietnamese comments: Radio Hanoi, November 29 and December 1, 1965; for American comments: *New York Times,* November 19, 20, and 26, 1965.

2. See report of Radio Nanking, November 24, 1965.

3. *New York Times,* November 26, 1965.

4. *The Pentagon Papers,* Gravel ed., 4:623.

5. *Ibid.*, 4:28.

6. *Ibid.*, 4:2.

7. *Ibid.*, 4:33.

8. Lyndon B. Johnson, *The Vantage Point* (New York, 1971), p. 233.

9. *Ibid.,* p. 234. See also *The Pentagon Papers* 4:33.

10. Johnson, *The Vantage Point,* p. 235; *The Pentagon Papers,* 4:35.

11. In addition to Eric Sevareid's article, "The Final Troubled Hours of Adlai Stevenson," in *Look,* November 30, 1965, pp. 81–86, a comprehensive presentation is offered by Walter Johnson in his article, "The U Thant-Stevenson Peace Initiatives in Vietnam," published in *Diplomatic History* 1, no. 3 (Summer, 1977):285–95. See *also* U.S. State Department transcript of the June 19, 1967, Foreign Policy Conference, as reported in David Kraslow and Stuart H. Loory, *The Secret Search for Peace in Vietnam* (New York, 1968), pp. 105–6.

12. See *Department of State Bulletin* (Washington), January 3, 1966, pp. 10–13, for the text of the Rusk-Fanfani exchange of letters.

13. Liberation Radio (clandestine) in Vietnamese to South Vietnam, 1400 GMT, December 7, 1965.

14. Mansfield expressed his fear as early as February 7, 1965, at a National Security Council meeting, when the bombing of North Vietnam was decided. For further details, see Johnson, *The Vantage Point,* pp. 124–25.

15. Lin Piao, "Long Live the Victory of People's War," *Peking Foreign Languages Press,* September 3, 1965; also *New York Times,* August 31, 1966.

16. *New York Times*, December 21, 1965.

17. *Look,* April 29, 1969 pp. 76–79.

18. *The Pentagon Papers* 4:35–36.

19. "The Pentagon Papers" (Diplomatic Volumes), 6, C.1 (Chapter Pinta: The Rangoon Contact, 3. Chronology p. 1a).

20. Harold Wilson, *A Personal Record: The Labour Government* (Boston, 1971), p. 187.

21. For details of the debate, see Johnson, *The Vantage Point,* pp. 235–37.

CHAPTER V

1. See President Johnson's Baltimore speech of April 7, 1965, in the *Department of State Bulletin* (Washington), April 26, 1965.

2. Cooper, *The Lost Crusade,* pp. 291–92.

3. Radio Hanoi VNA International Service in English, January 4, 1966.

CHAPTER VI

1. Averell Harriman, *America and Russia in a Changing World* (New York, 1971), pp. 117–18.

2. *Ibid.*, p. 118.

3. In 1968 Rapacki reportedly objected to the Soviet invasion of Czechoslovakia and, consequently, was forced to resign.

4. As leader of the Communist-led partisan movement in Poland, Gomulka had remained in Poland throughout the war and visited Moscow only occasionally. In November 1943, Gomulka had been appointed secretary-general of the party. Then in 1944, the Communist-dominated Committee of National Liberation, formed in Moscow, set up a provisional government in Lublin in which Gomulka was appointed first vice president. For further details, see *Yearbook on International Communist Affairs* (Stanford, 1966), p. 707.

5. I learned the details of Ambassador Averell Harriman's travels partly from the ambassador himself during an interview in the summer of 1975, partly from reports of the Hungarian ambassador to Poland, Ferenc Martin.

6. The role of the Polish diplomacy in seeking to bring about negotiations on

Vietnam and the arrival of Wang Kuo-chuang to China was reported from Peking by the Yugoslav news agency *Tanyug* on January 4, 1966.

7. In early 1969 Michalowski, then Polish ambassador to the U.S., met Harriman at the New York governor's mansion and recapitulated the role Poland had played during the 37-day bombing pause. He reported that he found the DRV leaders extremely skeptical, probably unwilling to enter negotiations because of Peking's influence. Michalowski had felt, however, that his visit may have affected Hanoi's subsequent attitude. Harriman, *America and Russia in a Changing World,* p. 120.

8. Kraslow and Loory, *The Secret Search for Peace in Vietnam,* p. 142.

9. Foreign Minister Shiina was not successful in his urgings. Both Gromyko and Kosygin rejected his appeal for aid in bringing peace to Vietnam. *New York Times,* January 21, 1966.

10. According to the Sino-American Security Pact of 1955, Chiang Kai-shek was required to consult with the American government before launching any major military operation against the Chinese mainland. Stephen Pan and Daniel Lyons, *Vietnamese Crisis* (New York, 1966), pp. 224–25.

11. *New York Times*, January 3, 1966.

12. Unpublished Diplomatic Volumes of the Pentagon Papers, as quoted by the *New York Times*, June 27, 1972.

13. W. LaFeber, *America, Russia and the Cold War, 1945-71* (New York, 1972), p. 238.

14. "The Pentagon Papers" (Diplomatic Volumes), 6, C. 1 (Chapter Pinta: The Rangoon Contact, Chronology), p. lb.

15. It is interesting to note that Vu Huu Binh handed over his answer to Byroade 12 hours after the resumption of the air strikes against North Vietnam. Nevertheless, he expressed willingness to listen to what Byroade "may wish to expound on the U.S. position." Actually Hanoi kept the Rangoon channel open for three more weeks, and American and Vietnamese diplomats met twice—on Febuary 8 and 19. On this later date Vu, referring to the U.S.-South Vietnamese Declaration of Honolulu and the resumption of the bombing, told Byroade that "it [was] inappropriate to continue our talks at your request." See transcript of Byroade-Vu meetings in "The Pentagon Papers" (Diplomatic Volumes), 6, C.1 (Pinta-Rangoon), pp. 25–30.

16. *The Pentagon Papers* 4:39.

17. See Memorandum of the Chiefs of Staff to McNamara on January 18, 1966, in *The Pentagon Papers* 4:41–42.

18. *Ibid.*, 4:68.

19. *Ibid.*, 4:38.

20. For details of George Ball's January 25, 1966, memorandum see *Pentagon Papers* 4:51–53.

21. The intelligence report on infiltration activity was released to the press and reprinted in the *Washington Post*, January 25, 1966.

22. For text of Ho Chi Minh's letter, see *New York Times*, January 29, 1966.

23. *Ibid.*, p. 48. Another vivid description of the Rapacki episode can be found in Kraslow and Loory, *Secret Search for Peace,* pp. 152–53. Also Norman

Cousins, "How the U.S. Spurned Three Chances for Peace in Vietnam," *Saturday Review,* July 29, 1969, pp. 45–48.

24. Following their disagreement over Vietnam, tensions between Puja and János Péter increased. In December 1973, Péter resigned and Kádár appointed Puja to the post of foreign minister. Presently Puja is still foreign minister and Péter is one of the deputy speakers of the Parliament.

CHAPTER VII

1. On September 2, 1965, the twentieth anniversary of the defeat of Japan, Chinese Defense Minister Lin Piao recalled the lesson of the protracted struggle with Japan. Referring to Mao Tse-tung's guerrilla strategy, he pointed out: The true revolutionary leader has "to rely on the peasants, build rural base areas and use the countryside to encircle and finally capture the cities." Lin Piao further contended that the world revolution is nothing but a "people's war" of the countries of Asia, Africa, and Latin America—of the "world village" against the states of North America, Japan, Western Europe, and the Soviet Union—the "world city."

2. *Peking Review* 7, no. 46 (November 13, 1964): 14–17.

3. *Pravda,* January 22, 1965.

4. "Refutation of the New Leaders of the CPSU on 'United Action,'" *Peking Review* 8, no. 46 (November 12, 1965): 10–12.

5. For further details and text of the protest notes, see William E. Griffith, ed., *Sino-Soviet Relations 1964–65* (Cambridge, Mass., 1967), pp. 88–91, 403–7.

6. See, for example, *New York Times,* December 23, 1965, which reports Chinese charges that Soviet equipment was old and damaged. On the protocol, see Peking Radio, December 22, 1965. For Russian responses, *New York Times,* December 24, 1965. On further controversy, see Chinese memorandum on the transport of Soviet military supplies in transit to Vietnam; meeting between Vice Foreign Minister Wang Ping-nan and Ambassador S. G. Lapin, Peking Radio, January 15, 1966.

7. "Letter of the CPSU to other Communist Parties Regarding the Split with the Chinese Communist Party," *New York Times,* March 24, 1966.

8. See "Refutation of the New Leaders," *Peking Review,* pp. 10–21; also *Pravda,* November 28, 1965.

9. *Pravda,* December 10, 1965.

10. *Die Welt* (Hamburg), March 21, 1966. Also Albert Parry, "Soviet Aid to Vietnam," *The Reporter,* January 12, 1967, pp. 28–33.

11. The 23rd Congress of the CPSU—held March 29–April 9, 1966—changed the title of the "first secretary" of the party to "secretary general" and the Presidium of the Central Committee was renamed the Politburo—both changes a return to the titles used under Lenin and Stalin. Only full members were entitled to vote although alternate members participated in the debates

and discussion. In May 1973 Brezhnev returned to the organizational pattern of Stalin by bringing back into the Politburo the Defense Ministry, the head of the KGB (intelligence and counter-intelligence service), and the foreign minister. Until then the officials occupying those positions—Marshal Andrei A. Grechko, Yuri Andropov, and Andrei Gromyko—were merely members of the Central Committee, a relatively subordinate body.

12. Soon after Le Duan and Giap left Moscow, the Hungarian party headquarters was informed about the visit through party communication channels. The Hungarians were told that the Soviet Presidium doubled the Vietnamese military aid program and decided to send a party and government delegation headed by Shelepin to Hanoi in December 1965.

13. *Tass International Service,* December 21, 1965.

14. The biographic sketch of Shelepin is based on material in the *Yearbook on International Communist Affairs* (Stanford, 1967), pp. 704–5; Carl A. Linden, *Khrushchev and the Soviet Leadership 1957–1964* (Baltimore, 1967), p. 243; Robert Conquest, "Stalin's Successors," *Foreign Affairs* 48 (April 1970): 509-24; and personal recollection.

15. Actually "the message" was transmitted to Italy by the Italian-language news service of Radio Moscow—*Oggi in Italia*—on January 6, 1966; technical data cited from *Military Balance,* 1968–69 (London: The Institute for Strategic Studies, 1969), p. 54.

16. See text of the speech delivered by A.N. Shelepin at a rally in the North Vietnamese capital, as reported by Hanoi Radio (International Service), January 10, 1966.

17. Details of Shelepin's behind-the-scenes discussion were reported by our embassy in Hanoi. We received further information from Moscow through party channels. During my stay in Budapest, in the summer of 1966, Deputy Foreign Minister Károly Erdélyi revealed to me some of the aspects of the Soviet military aid to Hanoi. According to his information Soviet artillery men were assigned to the surface-to-air missile sites in North Vietnam only as instructors. The bulk of the North Vietnamese rockets forces personnel received training in the Soviet Union. The same was true for the training of the supersonic MIG jet pilots. They got their instructions at the Soviet Air Force schools.

18. *People's Daily* (Peking), January 10 and January 18, 1966.

19. "The Pentagon Papers" (Diplomatic Volumes), 6, C.1 (Chapter XYZ), p. 25.

20. For further details, see statement of former Hungarian intelligence officer, Lászlo Szabó, in *Hearing before the CIA Subcommittee of the Committee on Armed Services of the House of Representatives,* no. 49, 89th Congress, second session, March 17, 1966 (Washington: U.S. Government Printing Office, 1966).

21. Ponomarev was promoted to alternate membership in the Politburo in May 1972, but retained the responsibility for supervising relations between the CPSU and nonruling Communist parties. Richard F. Staar, ed., *Yearbook on International Communist Affairs* (Stanford, 1973), p. 94. Andropov was appointed to head the powerful KGB in 1967 and was elevated to the Politburo in the spring of 1973. *U.S. News and World Report,* May 7, 1973, p. 64.

22. Mazurov's biographical sketch is based on material in Michel Tatu, *Power in the Kremlin* (New York, 1972), p. 552; and personal recollection.

23. See K.T. Mazurov's report on economic reform at the October 1965 session of the Supreme Soviet. *Pravda,* October 2, 1965.

24. The protocol ceremonies of the Brezhnev visit were reconstructed by closely following the official communiqués and reports of the Soviet, Mongolian and East European news media.

25. *Tass* (Moscow), January 15, 1966.

26. *Ibid.*

27. Owen Lattimore, *Nationalism and Revolution in Mongolia* (New York, 1955), pp. 69–81.

28. It was known in Hungarian party circles that the relationship between Khrushchev and Tsedenbal was never harmonious, mainly because the Mongolian Communist party leadership refused to conduct an all-out de-Stalinization policy. Personal recollection.

29. For details, see Radványi, *Hungary and the Superpowers,* p. 4.

30. *New York Times,* January 28 and February 6, 1966.

31. The Treaty of Friendship and Mutual Assistance with the Mongolian People's Republic, signed on February 27, 1946, was a complete facsimile of the Mutual Assistance Pact that the Soviet Union concluded with Mongolia on March 12, 1936. For text and further interpretation of the treaties, see Jan F. Triska and Robert M. Slusser, *The Theory, Law and Policy of Soviet Treaties* (Stanford, 1962), pp. 234–35. Also A.J.K. Sanders, *The People's Republic of Mongolia* (London, 1968), p. 41.

32. These accusations were made in a Chinese diplomatic note addressed to the government of the Mongolian People's Republic. *Christian Science Monitor,* June 30, 1966.

CHAPTER VIII

1. For details on the decision regarding the bombing of Hanoi and Haiphong, see *The Pentagon Papers* 4:102–6; for the increased troop deployment decision: *Ibid.,* 4:322–24.

2. Le Duc Tho's article appeared in the party organ, *Nhan Dan*, February 3 and 4, 1966, and was reprinted in the February 1966 issue of the party's monthly, *Hoc Tap.* See English translation in the *Yearbook on International Communist Affairs—1966* (Stanford, 1967), pp. 687–91.

3. Report of Indochina Resource Center, reprinted in the *Congressional Record—Senate*, May 14, 1975, p. S-8152.

4. For further details see Albert Parry, "Soviet Aid to Vietnam," *The Reporter,* January 12, 1967, pp. 28–33. Also *The Pentagon Papers* 4:324–25.

5. *The Pentagon Papers,* 4:333–34.

6. It was Béla Biszku, the second-highest ranking man in the Hungarian Communist party, who revealed to me the North Vietnamese operations through the DMZ, during my stay in Budapest in July 1966.

7. For details of General Westmoreland's proposals and the Jason study on air-supported anti-infiltration barriers, see *Pentagon Papers* 4:327–56.

8. Documentary history of the Ronning Missions (March and June 1966) in "The Pentagon Papers" (Diplomatic Volumes), 6, C.1, pt. 5, pp. 1–38. For additional information see Chester Ronning, *A Memoir of China in Revolution* (New York, 1974), pp. 255–69.

9. For further details of the June 27, 1966, Lewandowski-D'Orlandi meeting see "The Pentagon Papers" (Diplomatic Volumes), 6, C.2 (Marigold Chronology), pp. 1–3.

10. *Ibid.*, p. 37.

11. Chester L. Cooper, *The Lost Crusades,* pp. 322–23; *also* Johnson, *The Vantage Point,* pp. 251–52.

12. For transcripts of Gronouski-Rapacki negotiations see "The Pentagon Papers" (Diplomatic Volumes), 6, C.2, pp. 39–68 and 75–78.

13. *Ibid.* (History of Contacts-Marigold), pp. 78–80; for communiqué of the Warsaw Pact Political Consultative Committee in Bucharest, see *Pravda,* July 8, 1966.

14. "The Pentagon Papers" (Diplomatic Volumes), 6, C.3 (Chronology), pp. 5–10.

15. See text of Foreign Minister Nguyen Duy Trinh's interview granted to Australian journalist Wilfred G. Burchett, in Radio Hanoi International Service in English, January 28, 1967.

16. "The Pentagon Papers" (Diplomatic Volumes), 6, C.3 (Chronology), pp. 23–24 (Cooper's cable to Secretary of State Dean Rusk and Ambassador Harriman, February 5, 1967).

17. For the full account, see Prime Minister Harold Wilson's memoir entitled: *A Personal Record: The Labour Government, 1964-1970* (Boston, 1971), pp. 345–66; see also George Brown, *In My Way: The Political Memoirs of Lord George Brown* (London, 1971), pp. 141–47; and Johnson, *The Vantage Point,* pp. 253–55.

18. For the entire Presidential message see "The Pentagon Papers" (Diplomatic Volumes), 6, C.3. (Chronology), pp. 29–31 (State Department Cable 132481 to American Embassy, London).

19. *Ibid.*, p. 46 (Cable of Ambassador Bruce to secretary of state 6456, February 10).

20. Wilson, *A Personal Record*, p. 356.

21. *Ibid.*, pp. 364–65.

22. "The Pentagon Papers" (Diplomatic Volumes), 6, C.3 (Chronology), pp. 61–62.

23. *Ibid.*, pp. 69–70.

24. Brown, *In My Way,* p. 146.

25. Summary of Ambassador L. Thompson's report from Moscow on February 18, 1967, in "The Pentagon Papers" (Diplomatic Volumes), 6, C.3, p. 19.

26. Chalmers Roberts also writes about this episode in his book, *First Rough Draft* (New York, 1973), p. 328. He cross-checked my information. It proved that I was correct. But then Roberts spent too much time gathering additional information. In the meantime Hanoi Radio unexpectedly broadcast the Ho-Johnson exchange. Had he broken the story, I think it might have given me a grueling time with the Soviets.

CHAPTER IX

1. Couve de Murville toured Eastern Europe during the summer of 1966 and tried to sell the Gaullist idea of European Europe to the East European Communist regimes with no success.

2. See U Thant-Goldberg discussion in "The Pentagon Papers" (Diplomatic Volumes), 6, C.2 (Marigold), p. 87.

3. See article by Philippe Ben in *Le Monde,* October 22, 1965.

4. After being purged from the Secretariat, Shelepin was permitted to retain his membership in the Politburo only because Trade Union chairmen are traditionally members of that body. Certainly, like the other members, he had the right to vote, but, like his predecessors, he was limited to representing Trade Union matters at the Politburo sessions. It is not without interest to note that Brezhnev waited almost eight years to eliminate Shelepin completely from public life. On April 16, 1975, Radio Moscow announced that "the Plenum [of the Central Committee] has relieved Comrade Shelepin of his duties as a member of the Politburo at his own request." While Shelepin was ousted, Ustinov retained his position in the Secretariat as well as his membership in the Politburo. In the ensuing nine years he remained in charge of party supervision of the Soviet armanent production. In addition, he was closely involved with the Soviet space effort. When, in May 1967, Andrei Grechko died of a heart attack, Ustinov was selected to replace him.

EPILOGUE

1. In December 1967 Ambassador Harriman discussed (at a luncheon) the San Antonio Formula at length with Ambassador Dobrynin. Emphasizing the seriousness of U.S. intentions, Harriman asked if the Soviet government had an alternative plan. Dobrynin had none. "The Pentagon Papers" (Diplomatic Volumes), 6, C.4 (Chronology Mem., Dec. 27, 1967), pp. 17–18.

2. Some of the details of the American peace effort and the talks in Paris were given to me during my meeting with Ambassador Harriman at his Yorktown Heights home in the summer of 1975.

3. During the 1967 General Assembly session in New York, the Rumanians constantly pressured the Americans for a bombing pause. Also, in an attempt to assure international recognition for the political arm of Hanoi, the NLFSV, the Rumanian U.N. delegation circulated the newly adopted text of the program of the Front among the U.N. members. However, this did not contradict the fact that the Rumanians did everything they could to bring about negotiations. For further details, see Harriman, *America and Russia in a Changing World,* pp. 124–25. Also William C. Westmoreland, *A Soldier Reports* (Garden City, New York, 1976), p. 312.

4. For further details, see *The Pentagon Papers* 4:539–49; also Westmoreland, *A Soldier Reports,* pp. 332–33.

5. CIA estimates of Soviet and Chinese economic and military expenditures were revealed in a report of the Washington-based Indochina Resource Center and reprinted in the *Congressional Record,* May 14, 1975, p. 2. The break-

down of military hardware furnished by Moscow and Peking was published by the Institute for Strategic Studies (London) in September 1968 under the title: *The Military Balance, 1968–69* (London, 1968), pp. 13–14.

6. Radio Hanoi in English, April 3, 1968.

7. Radio Moscow, April 2, 1968, and *New York Times,* July 4, 1968.

8. For comprehensive treatment of the 1968 Paris talks see Johnson, *The Vantage Point,* pp. 401–24; and Cooper, *The Lost Crusade,* pp. 381–407. For a balanced account, see also Harriman, *America and Russia,* pp. 126–39.

9. Radio Peking, December 19, 1968.

10. President Johnson acknowledged that Richard Nixon's political friends explicitly told Thieu to stay away from the Paris talks until the election victory of the Republican candidate. For details see Johnson, *The Vantage Point*, pp. 517–21.

11. According to U.S. Intelligence estimates Russian and Chinese economic and military aid totaled $1,215,000,000. For further details, see the *Congressional Records,* May 14, 1975, p. S-8452.

12. See *Background Information Relating to Southeast Asia and Vietnam* (rev. ed.), Senate Committee on Foreign Relations, 93rd Congress, second session, 1974, p. 150.

13. Information concerning Kissinger's Moscow trip was received by the author from Ambassador Jacob D. Beam during an interview on October 25, 1976. For further details see George W. Ball, *Diplomacy for a Crowded World* (Boston, 1976), pp. 75–76.

14. Summary of the Nine Point U.S.-DRV Draft Agreement was revealed by Radio Hanoi on October 26, 1972. Kissinger's confirmation of the Radio Hanoi broadcast can be found in *Department of State Bulletin*, November 13, 1972, pp. 549–58.

15. See text of Nixon's letter to Thieu as published in the *New York Times,* April 30, 1975.

16. In a speech before the U.S. Chamber of Commerce on May 3, 1977, Henry Kissinger revealed that there was discussion of a $3.25 billion Vietnam reconstruction aid program. He added that it would be absolutely absurd to say that the North Vietnamese have the right to economic aid, "having broken every provision of the agreement they signed in Paris." UPI, May 4, 1977. For details see also *Newsweek*, May 16, 1977, p. 49.

17. For text of Pham Van Dong's Four Point proposal, see *Background Information Relating to Southeast Asia and Vietnam* (7th rev. ed.), Senate Committee on Foreign Relations, 93rd Congress, second session, 1974, p. 579. For text of "The Vietnam Agreement and Protocols, Signed January 27, 1973," see *ibid.,* pp. 516–53.

18. General Van Tien Dung and General Van Nguyen Giap, "Great Victory of the Spring 1975 General Offensive and Uprising," *Foreign Broadcast Information Services*—Asian and Pacific, April 7, 1976–May 17, 1976.

19. This vital piece of information was known in the U.S. Embassy as early as the fall of 1974. It was revealed by Ambassador Graham A. Martin during a hearing before the Committee on International Relations, House of Representatives, on January 27, 1976.

20. A detailed account of the collapse of the South Vietnamese Army (ARVN) can be found in Robert Shaplen, "Letter from Saigon," *The New Yorker,* April 21, 1975, pp. 124–38; also, Westmoreland, *A Soldier Reports,* p. 398.

21. The text of the U.S. diplomatic note is reprinted in U.S. House Committee on International Relations, *The Vietnam-Cambodia Emergency.* Hearings, 94th Cong. 1st. sess. (Washington: G.P.O., 1975), p. 453.

22. Keyes Beech, "U.S. Falsely Advised in Vietnam," *Chicago Daily News Service,* May 10, 1975.

23. Testimony of Ambassador Graham A. Martin in U.S. House Committee on International Relations. Hearings, 94th Cong. 2nd. sess. (Washington: G.P.O., 1976), p. 546.

24. *Ibid.,* p. 585.

25. See Chairman Hua Kuo-feng's political report at the Eleventh National Congress of the Communist party of China held August 12–18, 1977, as broadcast by Radio Peking, August 22, 1977.

26. The Board of Executive Directors of the World Bank in September 1976 recognized the membership of Unified Vietnam as a continuation of the membership which South Vietnam had held since 1956. This paralleled action taken by the Board of Executive Directors of the International Monetary Fund, which made one loan of $31 million to Vietnam in January 1977. A five-member World Bank economic mission spent four weeks in 1977 in Vietnam and had wide-ranging discussions on the economic situation with Vietnamese governmental officials in Hanoi. See press release No. 77/3 of the I.M.F., January 11, 1977, and press release of the World Bank dated March 2, 1977.

SELECTED BIBLIOGRAPHY

Aptheker, Herbert. *Mission to Hanoi*. New York, 1966.

Bain, Chester A. *Vietnam: The Roots of Conflict.* Englewood Cliffs, New Jersey, 1967.

Ball, George W. *Diplomacy for a Crowded World.* Boston, 1976.

Ball, George W. *The Discipline of Power*. Boston, 1968.

Beloff, Max, ed. *Soviet Policy in the Far East: 1944–1951*. London, 1953.

Blumenfeld, Ralph, and the staff and editors of the *New York Post. Henry Kissinger: The Private and Public Story*. New York, 1974.

Bohlen, Charles E. *Witness to History: 1929–1969.* New York, 1973.

Brzezinski, Zbigniew. *Soviet Politics from the Future to the Past.* New York, 1975.

Brzezinski, Zbigniew. *U.S.–Soviet Relations.* New York, 1973.

Brown, George. *In My Way*. London, 1971.

Burchett, Wilfred B. *Vietnam: Inside Story of the Guerilla War.* New York, 1965.

Buttinger, Joseph. *A Dragon Defiant.* Washington, 1972.

Cameron, Allan W. *Indochina: Prospects After "The End."* Washington, D.C., 1976.

Chang, Parris H. *Radicals and Radical Ideology in China's Cultural Revolution.* New York, 1973.

Clubb, O. Edmund. *China and Russia: The "Great Game."* New York, 1971.

Cooper, Chester L. *The Lost Crusade: America in Vietnam*. New York, 1970.

Crozier, Brian. *The Masters of Power*. London, 1969.

Dornberg, J. *Brezhnev: The Masks of Power*. New York, 1974.

Draper, Theodore. *Abuse of Power*. New York, 1967.

Dulles, John Foster. *War or Peace*. New York, 1950.

Eisenhower, Dwight D. *The White House Years: Mandate for Change, 1953–56.* Garden City, New York, 1963.

Falk, Richard A., ed. *The Vietnam War and International Law*. Princeton, New Jersey, 1969.
Fall, Bernard F. *Ho Chi Minh on Revolution*. New York, 1967.
Fall, Bernard F. *The Two Vietnams: A Political and Military Analysis*. 2nd ed. Washington, 1967.
Fishel, Wesley R. *Vietnam: Anatomy of a Conflict*. Itasca, Illinois, 1968.
Fitzgerald, Frances. *Fire in the Lake*. New York, 1972.
Galbraith, John Kenneth. *Ambassador's Journal*. Boston, 1969.
Garthoff, Ray L., ed. *Sino-Soviet Military Relations*. New York, 1966.
George, Alexander L.; Hall, David K.; and Simons, William R. *The Limits of Coercive Diplomacy: Laos-Cuba-Vietnam*. Boston, 1971.
Giap, Vo Nguyen. *Dien Bien Phu*. Hanoi, 1964.
Giap, Vo Nguyen. *People's War, People's Army: The Viet Cong Instruction Manual for Underdeveloped Countries*. New York, 1961.
Griffith, William E., ed. *Sino-Soviet Relations, 1964–1965*. Cambridge, Massachusetts, 1967.
Halberstam, David. *The Best and the Brightest*. New York, 1969.
Hammer, Ellen J. *The Struggle for Indochina*. Stanford, 1954.
Harriman, W. Averell. *America and Russia in a Changing World*. New York, 1971.
Hilsman, Roger. *To Move a Nation: The Politics of Foreign Policy in the Administration of John F. Kennedy*. New York, 1974.
Hoopes, Townsend. *The Limits of Intervention*. New York, 1969.
Johnson, Lyndon B. *The Vantage Point*. New York, 1971.
Kahin, George M., and Lewis, John W. *The United States in Vietnam*. New York, 1967.
Kalb, Bernard; and Kalb, Marvin. *Kissinger*. Boston, 1974.
Kalb, Marvin; and Abel, Elie. *Roots of Involvement: The U.S. in Asia, 1784–1971*. New York, 1971.
Kaplan, Morton A.; Chayes, Abram; Netter, G. Warren; Warnke, Paul C.; Roche, John P.; and Fritchey, Clayton. *Vietnam Settlement: Why 1973, Not 1969?* Washington, 1973.
Kearney, Robert, ed. *Politics and Modernization in South and Southeast Asia*. New York, 1975.
Khrushchev, Nikita. *Khrushchev Remembers*. Edited and translated from Russian by Strobe Talbott. Boston, 1970.

Kissinger, Henry. *American Foreign Policy: Three Essays*. New York, 1969.

Kraslow, David; and Loory, Stuart H. *The Secret Search for Peace in Vietnam.* New York, 1968.

Ky, Nguyen Cao. *Twenty Years and Twenty Days.* New York, 1977.

LaCouture, Jean. *Ho Chi Minh*. Le Seuil, France, 1967.

LeFeber, Walter. *America, Russia and the Cold War: 1945–1971*, 2nd ed. New York, 1972.

Lake, Anthony, ed. *The Legacy of Vietnam, The War, American Society and the Future of American Foreign Policy*. New York, 1976.

Lattimore, Owen. *Nationalism and Revolution in Mongolia*. New York, 1955.

Linden, Carl A. *Khrushchev and Soviet Leadership: 1957–1964.* Baltimore, 1966.

Lodge, Henry Cabot. *The Storm Has Many Eyes.* New York, 1973.

Lowenthall, Richard. *World Communism: The Disintegration of Secular Faith*. New York, 1966.

Maneli, Mieczyslaw. *War of the Vanquished*, Translated from the Polish by Maria de Gorgey. Evanston, Illinois, 1971.

Mindszenty, József Cardinal. *Memoirs*. New York, 1974.

Ho Chi Minh. *Prison Diary.* Hanoi, 1967.

Moore, John Norton. *Law and the Indo-China War*. Princeton, 1972.

Morgenthau, Hans J. *A New Foreign Policy for the United States*. New York, 1969.

North, Robert. *Moscow and the Chinese Communists*. Stanford, 1961.

Pentagon Papers, Vols. 1–4 (The Defense Department History of United States Decision-Making). Gravel ed. Boston, 1971.

Pentagon Papers. Unpublished Diplomatic Volumes: United States-Vietnam Relations 1945–1967. Photocopies deposited in the Special Collections of Mitchell Memorial Library, Mississippi State University.

Petrov, Victor P. *Mongolia: A Profile*. New York, 1970.

Pike, Douglas. *Viet Cong: The Organization and Techniques of the National Liberation Front of South Vietnam*. Cambridge, 1966.

Radványi, János. *Hungary and the Superpowers.* Stanford, 1972.

Reinhold, Neuman-Hoditz. *Ho Chi Minh in Selbstzeugnissen und Bilddokumenten.* Hamburg, 1971.

Reshetar, John S., Jr. *The Soviet Policy, Government and Politics in the U.S.S.R.* New York, 1972.

Roberts, Chalmers M. *First Rough Draft*. New York, 1973.

Ronning, Chester. *A Memoir of China in Revolution*. New York, 1974.

Rostow, W. W. *The Diffusion of Power*. New York, 1972.

Roy, Jules. *The Battle of Dien Bien Phu*, Translated from the French by Robert Baldick. New York, 1965.

Sainteny, Jean. *Histoire d'une Paix Manquée*. Paris, 1967.

Salisbury, Harrison E. *War Between Russia and China*. New York, 1969.

Sanders, A. J. K. *The People's Republic of Mongolia*. London, 1968.

Schleisinger, Arthur M., Jr. *The Bitter Heritage: Vietnam and American Democracy,* 1941–1966. Boston, 1966.

Schleisinger, Arthur M., Jr. *A Thousand Days.* Cambridge, 1965.

Shulman, Marshall. *Stalin's Foreign Policy Reappraised*. Cambridge, 1963.

Sorensen, Theodore C. *Kennedy*. New York, 1965.

Sorensen, Theodore C. *The Kennedy Legacy*. New York, 1969.

Strong, John W., ed. *The Soviet Union Under Brezhnev and Kosygin, The Transition Years.* Cincinnati, 1971.

Tatu, Michel. *Power in the Kremlin: From Khrushchev to Kosygin.* New York, 1969.

Taylor, Maxwell. *Responsibility and Response*. New York, 1967.

Taylor, Maxwell. *The Uncertain Trumpet*. New York, 1960.

Thompson, Sir Robert. *Defeating Communist Insurgency: The Lessons of Malaya and Vietnam*. New York, 1966.

Thompson, Sir Robert. *No Exit from Vietnam*. New York, 1969.

Triska, Jan F.; and Slusser, Robert M. *The Theory, Law and Policy of Soviet Treaties*. Stanford, 1962.

Truman, Harry S. *Memoirs*. Garden City, New York, 1956.

Chi, Hoang Van. *From Colonialism to Communism: A Case History of North Vietnam*. New York, 1964.

Villmow, J. *The Soviet Union and Eastern Europe*. Englewood Cliffs, New Jersey, 1965.

Westmoreland, William C. *A Soldier Reports*. Garden City, New York, 1976.

Wilson, Harold. *A Personal Record: The Labour Government: 1964–1970*. Boston, 1971.

Woodside, Alexander B. *Community and Revolution in Modern Vietnam*. Boston, 1976.

Zagoria, Donald S. *The Sino-Soviet Conflict, 1955–1961*. Princeton, 1962.

Zagoria, Donald S. *Vietnam Triangle*. New York, 1967.

INDEX

"An Agreement on Ending the War and Restoring the Peace in Vietnam," 256
and Four Points, 256
signatories, 256
Aldrich, George H., 255
An Loc, battle of, 251
Andropov, Yurii V., 172-173, 177
Asian Collective Security System, 263
Austrian State Treaty, 6

Bălănceanu, Petre, 97-98
Ball, George, 47
and bombing pause, 79, 139
memorandum on McNamara plan, 47
reaction to Lin Piao's article, 86-87
Vietnam, experience in, 47-48
Ban Me Thout, fall of, 259
Bartlett, Charles, 99
Beam, Jacob D., 252-253
Big Four, 1954 foreign ministers' meeting, 6
Bo, Mai Van, 41-42, 168-169
Boncourt, Jean-Paul, 45-46
Brezhnev, Leonid I.
attacks Maoist ideology, 264
and Communist unity, 38
in Mongolia, 176, 179-180
1964 October Revolution speech, 149
and Nixon, 249-250
and Paris deadlock, 244-245
"peace program," 249
powers, 158
Brown, George, 206, 210
Bucharest meeting (Communist bloc), 30-31
Buddhists
in DRV, 22
in South Vietnam, 23-24
Bundy, McGeorge, 107
Bundy, William
memorandum on bombing pause, 79-80, 92-93
memorandum of January 15, 1966, 138-139
and Radványi, 108-109
and Zinchuk, 199-200
Byroade, Henry A., 133-134, 135

Cambodia, 247
Cao Anh Kiet, 13
Catholics
in DRV, 22
in Hungary, 22, 33
in South Vietnam, 23
Ch'en Yi, 25
Chiang Kai-shek, 130-131
China, People's Republic of
anti-Soviet propaganda, 151
attacks Soviet proposal, 263
Communist party (CCP), 153
counter-demonstration in Moscow, 151-152
Cultural Revolution, 90, 147-148, 217-218
ends diplomatic isolation, 249
Great proletarian revolution (cultural revolution), 90
Jen-min Jih-pao (newspaper), 149, 154
prepares for war, 88
propaganda campaign, 89
Sino-Soviet conflicts, 153-154
and Soviet-Mongolian pact, 185
Chistyakov, Anatoliy, 163
Choibalsang, 182-183
Chou En-lai
1964 visit to Moscow, 149-150
speech on war expansion, 89
Chuprong Massif, bombing of, 77
Church, Frank, 93
Churches, National Council of, 99
CIA, 242
Clifford, Clark, and bombing pause, 80, 95
COMECON, 184
Communist movement, international meeting planned by Soviets, 38
Confederation General du Travail, 4
Cooper, Chester, 204-205
Council of National Reconciliation and Concord, 253

Courtade, Pierre, 20
Csapo, Colonel, 233-236
Csatordai, Károly,
 Polish version of Marigold Affair, 200-201
 predicts American defeat, 75
 at U.N., 61-62
 and Wilson-Kosygin visit, 211

Damba, 183
Da Nang, fall of, 259
Declaration of 17 neutral nations, 101
Denisov, G.A., 54
DIA, 242
DMZ, 189-190, 251
Dobrynin, Anatoliy, 34, 45
 and bombing pause, 43, 82, 99-100
 and Four Points, 100
 and Johnson-Ho correspondence, 212-213
 and Marigold Affair, 200
 and McGeorge Bundy, 167
 and Paris deadlock, 245
 recall from U.S., 232-234, 236
 and Rusk, 43
 and Rusk's 12 points, 104, 110
 and San Antonio Formula, 240
 and U.S. strategy, 110
Dong, Pham Van, 16, 24
 and Canadian overtures, 41, 192
 Four Points, 42
 and Michalowski, 126-127
 Molotov's opinion of, 20
 New York Times interview, 201
 and Péter, 218-220
D'Orlandi, Giovanni, 193-194
Duan, Le, 41
 account of DRV's internal situation, 22-24
 and Geneva Agreements, 24
 in Moscow (1965), 159
Duclos, Jacques, 26
Duda, Karel, 99
 and Twelve Points, 110
Dung, General Van Thien, 258-259, 262
Duy, Xuam, 244
Dynamic equilibrium, policy of, 265

Export-Import Bank, 34

Fanfani, Amitori, 83-84
Firyubin, 43
Five Points, 64, 65
Fock, Jenö, 40
Ford, Gerald R., 86
 and Saigon, 259-260, 262
Ford Foundation, 35
Fortas, Abe, 95
Four Points of DRV, 42, 45, 64, 65, 72, 94, 97, 102, 134, 256
Fourteen (earlier Twelve) Points, U.S., 110, 115
French Communist party, 4

Geneva Agreements, 101
Geneva conference, 1954, provisions, 6-7
Geneva Conference, 1962, 66, 101
Giap, Vo Nguyen, 28, 41
 account of Dien Bien Phu, 7-10
 and collectivization, 18
 and Kulikov, 258
 in Moscow (1965), 159
 1965 offensive, 76-77
 and Polish proposal, 127
 strategy, 190
 and Tet Offensive, 243
Glassboro summit meeting, 240
Gogolyák, Gusztáv, 50-51
Gomulka, Wladyslaw, 122-123
Gordon-Walker, Patrick, 42
Gromyko, Andrei,
 and American intervention, 54
 and Marigold Affair, 195
 in Mongolia, 178-179
 and Rapacki, 124-125
 and Rusk, 43
 U.N. speech, 70
Gronouski, John A., 119, 121-122, 197-198
Guerassimov, Luben, 98
Guthrie, John C., 201-203

Ha, Nguyen Thanh, 13
Habib, Philip C., 260
Hallstein doctrine, 230
Harriman, Averell, 117-118, 256
 and Gomulka, 122-123
 and Paris conference, 244, 245
 peace mission, 128-129
 in Poland, 119-123
 and Rapacki, 121
 and Rumanians, 240-241
Hua Kuo-feng, 264
Huang Luong, 65
Humphrey, Hubert H., 131-132
Hungarian People's Republic
 Academy of Sciences, 35
 Agitprop, 39
 Communist party (Hungarian Socialist Workers' party), 37, 39, 50, 227

Communist Youth Organization (KISZ), 39
Department of International Relations, 58
DRV, delegation to, 67
foreign ministry, 10-12
Hanoi embassy, 14-15
Institute of Cultural Relations, 57
Peking embassy, 217-218
Politburo, 38, 58
Politburo, resolution to aid DRV, 40
relations with other countries, 11
U.N. mission, 61
and U.S., 34-36, 39
and Vatican, 33
Washington legation, 31
and West Germany, 230-232

Ia Drang engagements, 77
Indochinese Communist party, 7
International Commission of Control and Supervision (ICCS), 254, 255, 256, 257
International Control Commission for Indochina (1954), 7, 117
International Monetary Fund (IMF), 266

Jason Project, 191
Johnson, Lyndon B.
bombing halt (1968), 243
and bombing pause, 80-81, 91-96, 107-108
bombing pause extended, 107-108
bombing resumed, 142
and Bundy, 111
at Glassboro, 240
and Ho Chi Minh, 243
and Ho Chi Minh, correspondence, 205, 206-207, 209-210, 212
increases troop level, 187-188
letters on bombing pause, 109-110
and McNamara plan, 49
peace effort, 116-117
and Péter's cable, 107-108
Phase A-Phase B message, 208
pressure on, 85
and Rusk-Péter talk, 96
San Antonio Formula, 240
speech at Johns Hopkins University, 44, 101
White House meeting, January 25, 139
and Harold Wilson, 95, 208
Joint Chiefs of Staff, 138

Kádár, János
and Ho Chi Minh, 20
and Péter, 220
and self-sufficiency, 34
speech, 227
and U.S. presidential campaign, 37
KANZUS, 191
Kashmir, 174-175, 176
Kennedy, Robert F., 93
Kennedy administration
concern with Laos, 30
sells wheat to Eastern Europe, 34
Kertész, József, 14-15
KGB, 171, 172
Khan, Ayub, attempt to end war, 41
Khe Sanh, battle of, 243
Khiem, Ung Van, 17
Khrushchev, Nikita S.
and Chinese, 30-31
and Dien Bien Phu, 9
exposes Stalin, 6
and Vietnam, 26
King, Dr. Martin Luther, Jr., 99
Kiss, Károly, 22
Kissinger, Henry
and Jacob Beam, 252-253
and Brezhnev, 252
and China, 248-250
and Chou En-lai, 250
rigid stance, 256
statement before American Society of Newspaper Editors, 260
and Le Doc Tho, 248, 253
and USSR, 248-250
Kohler, Foy, 42-43
and Gromyko, 168
Kommunist, 263
Komocsin, Zoltán, 59
Kontum, fall of, 259
Kosygin, Aleksei N.
and Fourteen Points, 132
at Glassboro, 240
at Hanoi, 150
and Ho Chi Minh, 39
and Humphrey, 131-132
and Johnson's offer, 209
mission to Hanoi, 38
New York Times interview, 155
and Paris deadlock, 245
Presidium responsibilities, 158-159
in Pyongyang, 150
and Thompson, 211
and Trinh's formula, 206
Vietnam, report on, 39-40
and Wilson, 204-209
Kulikov, Victor G., 258
Ky, Nguyen Cao, 46

La Calle Saint Cloud meetings, 257
Lao Dong party, 7
  calls for war against Diem, 26, 28
  Fifteenth Plenum of Central Committee, 26, 28
  Resolution 13, 239
  Reunification Department, 28
  Russians, criticism of, 266
  3rd Congress, 28-29
Lau, Ha Van, 127
Lessiovsky, Victor, 83
Lewandowski, Janus, 193-194
  and Ho Chi Minh, 193
  and Ten Points, 196-197
Lewis, John, 87
Li Fu-ch'un, 29
Liberation Army of South Vietnam, 29
Li Hsien-nien, 166-167
Lin Piao, 86
  article by, 86
  criticism of Soviets, 148
Lisle, Raymond, 44
Liu Shao-ch'i, 90, 148
Lodge, Henry Cabot
  and Marigold Affair, 194, 196-197
  memo against bombing pause, 81
  and Westmoreland, 138
Luong, Huang, 143

Manila Conference, 196
McNamara, Robert
  and bombing pause, 80, 93, 107
  intelligence report, 139
  memorandum of January 1966, 138
  memorandum of July 1965, 46-47, 79
  report to President, 78
  in South Vietnam, 46
  and troop buildup, 49
  and Westmoreland, in Vietnam, 78
Macovescu, George, 241
Malinovski, 178
Manescu, Corneliu, 70-72
Mansfield, Mike, 85, 93
Mao Tse-tung
  aids Viet Minh, 4
  anniversary message for NLFSV, 246
  and Cultural Revolution, 90
  and diplomatic isolation, 249
  and Ho Chi Minh, 26
  and internal affairs, 88
  recognizes DRV, 4
  Soviet charges against, 148
Marigold Affair, 192-201
Martin, Graham A., 262
Mazurov, Kirill, 177-178
Meshcheryakov, Valentin L., 234-235
Michalowski, Jerzy
  Chinese response to trip, 125-126
  in Hanoi, 126-128
  and Ho Chi Minh, 127-128
  interpretation of U.S. position, 121
Mindszenty, József (Cardinal), 35
Minh, Duong Van "Big", 262
Minh, Ho Chi
  and bombing pause, 42
  and Byroade mission, 135-136
  and Chinese aid offer, 190
  and DRV internal situation, 22
  and Indochinese Communist party, 5
  and Italians, 84
  and Johnson, 243-244
  at Lao Dong's third congress, 29
  letter to Johnson, 209-210
  letter denouncing U.S. peace effort, 140-141
  and Michalowski, 127-128
  1945 call to arms, 1
  Prison Diary, 20-21
  proclaims Democratic Republic of Vietnam, 2
  and Radványi, 20-22
  and Shelepin, 165
  and Stalin's disgrace, 18-19
  and Tet Offensive, 242-243
  "translation error," 141-142
Mód, Péter, 100
Molotov, Vyacheslav
  and Georges Biault, 6
  and Ho Chi Minh, 20
Mongolian People's Republic, 176, 178-180, 181-186
  China, border with, 124
  Choibalsang, 182-183
  Mongolian-Soviet mutual aid pact, 176, 180-181, 184-186
  Stalinist rule, 181-182
Montreux Convention, 3
Morse, Wayne, 99
Mukhitdinov, N.A., 29
Münnich, Ferenc, 16, 20, 31

National Front for the Liberation of South Vietnam (NLF; NLFSV), 29, 41, 85, 112, 125, 140, 164, 165, 167, 192, 193, 225, 246
  forms provisional revolutionary government (PRG), 247
  participation in Paris conference, 244

National Security Council, 139
Nehru, B.K., 44
Nemes, Dezsó, 31, 58
Nghi, Le Thanh, 159-160
Nixon, Richard M., 86
  all-out war, 99
  and bombing strike in DRV, 251
  and Brezhnev, 249-250
  and Hanoi-Haiphong bombing, 256
  and Paris conference, 247
  trip to China, 250
Nixon-Brezhnev summit, 249-250, 252
Novikov, Vladimir, 159-160

Oberenko, Valentine, 245
Ochir, Tumur, 183
Operation Hastings, 190-191
O'Shaughnessy, Elim, 39
Outer Space Treaty, 156

Pak Song Chol, 55-56
Paris conference, 247
  breakdown, 256
Pehr, Imre, 215
Péter, János, 31-32, 56-58, 214
  lack of authority, 142-144
  cable of December 28, 108
  cable to Radványi, 105-106
  direct negotiation between U.S. and Hanoi, 113
  and Dong, 218-220
  in Hanoi, 1966, 215-216, 218-220
  Korean trip, 56
  Moscow trip, 1965, 54
  motivations, 228
  news conference, 224-227
  1966 visit to USSR, 214-215
  and Pak Song Chol, 55
  in Peking, 217-218
  and Polish peace mission, 123-125
  and Rusk, on October 6, 221-223
  with Rusk at U.N., 60-62, 65-69
  Russians, useful to, 59
  and Trinh, 218-221
  U.N. speeches, 64-65, 224
  and U Thant, 220, 223-224, 227-228
Phase A-Phase B Plan, 196, 205, 207
Plei Me, attack on, 76
Pleiku, 38, 259
Poland
  DRV, ally of, 121
  Five Points (of U.S. proposal), 121, 126
  ICCI member, 117
  peace efforts end, 198
Polgár, Thomas, 261
Ponomarev, Boris N., 172-173
Provisional Revolutionary Government of the Republic of Vietnam (PRG) 247, 257
Puja, Frigyes, 10, 144-146

Radhakrishnan, 42
Radio Hanoi
  broadcasts Ho's letter, 140-141
  broadcasts Ho's message, 244
  denounces bombing pause in advance, 94
  publishes Johnson-Ho correspondence, 212
  Trinh-Burchett interview, 203
Radio Moscow, 244
Radio Peking, 152
Radványi, János, 2-4
  in Africa, 31
  and William Bundy, 108-109
  cable from Peter, 105-106
  decision to seek asylum, 237-238
  foreign ministry, duties in, 11-12
  and Ho, 21
  and "Hungarian Question," 32-33
  personal consequences of Péter's actions, 228-229
  as protocol chief, 31
  and Rusk, 101-103, 104-105, 106-107, 112, 229
  statement of defection, 238
  and von Stackelberg, 230-231
  at Washington legation, 31-32
  West Coast tour, 233
  and West German relations, 230-232
Rapacki, Adam
  and Gromyko, 123-125
  and Harriman, 121
  and Ho's letter, 141
  and Marigold Affair, 192-195, 197-199
  mediation plan, 123-124
  and "translation error," 141
Rolling Thunder campaign, 198
Ronning, Chester A., 191-192
Rostow, Walt, 210
Rusakov, Konstantin, 163
Rusk, Dean
  and bombing pause, 81, 82, 93, 108
  and Byroade, 134-135
  and Dobrynin, 43
  Four Points, 84
  and Gromyko, 70
  Le Trang, message to, 201-202

and Marigold Affair, 193-194
McNamara, support of, 48-49
NET interview, 84-85
and Péter, 102, 221-223, 228
and Péter at U.N., 36, 65-69
and Péter's cable, 106
and Radványi, 101-103, 104-105, 106-107, 112, 229
and Radványi decision, 238
and Rumanians, 70, 72
Twelve Points, 102
and Winievicz, 72-73

Salisbury, Harrison E., and Pham Van Dong, 201
Sambu, J., 179
San Antonio Formula, 240
Seaborn, J. Blair, 41
Seventeen nonaligned nations, declaration of, (1965), 118
17th parallel, 42, 86, 221, 222-223, 224, 225
Sharp, U.S.G., 47, 138
Shelepin, Alexander N., 160-162
fall from power, 236
in Hanoi, 124, 127-128, 163-166
and Ho Chi Minh, 165
and Li Hsien-nien, 166-167
military aid for DRV, 128, 146
in Peking, 166-167
Politburo, supposed attempt to control, 234-236
and Soviet-DRV communiqué, 164
U.S. peace effort, rejects, 164
Sik, Endre, 10
Soviet-Hungarian Friendship and Assistance Treaty, 3
Soviet-Mongol mutual defense pact, 124
Stackelberg, Herbert A. von., 230-231
Stalin, Josef
and DRV, 2
and Ho Chi Minh, 5
and Mongolia, 181-182
Stevenson, Adlai, 82-83
Sullivan, William H., 85, 253-254, 255-256
Szánto, Zoltán, 4-5
Szilágyi, Béla, 39

Tashkent Declaration, 174-176
Tass, 198
Taylor, Maxwell, 47
Tempo, Svetozar V., 20
Tet Offensive, 241-242
Thach, Nguyen Co, 253-254
Thant, U
bilateral talks, proposal for, 83
1964 proposal, 83
three-month truce, 42
three-stage plan, 191
Thieng, Nguyen Duc, 13-14
Thieu, Nguyen Van, 247-248, 254
Tho, Le Duc
article, 188-189
and Kissinger, 248, 253
and Péter, 227-228
Tho, Nguyen Huu, 25
Thompson, Llewellyn E., 35
bombing pause, urges, 79
and Dobrynin, 109
and Kosygin, 211
and Péter's news conference, 226-227
and Podgorny, 200
Thorez, Maurice, 4-5, 26
Tito, Marshal, 42
Tölgyes, Antal, 260-261
Tolubko, Vladimir, 163
Tonkin Gulf incident, 37
Tonkin Gulf Resolution, 93
Tóth, Janós, 261
Trang, Le, 201-203
Tri-Continental Conference (Havana), 167
Trinh, Nguyen Duy
Burchett interview, 203
and Macovescu, 241
and Polish proposal, 126
Tsedenbal, Yumzhagin, 179-183
Twelve (later Fourteen) Points, 102
Tyler, William R., 39

Union of Soviet Socialist Republics (USSR)
anti-American protests, 155-156
anti-Chinese propoganda, 152-153
Central Committee proposes 36-party meeting, 150
Chinese claims, denounces, 263
Communist party, Soviet Union (CPSU), 153, 163, 165
CPSU 20th Congress, 18
CPSU 24th Congress, 248-249
DRV, aid to, 40, 157, 160
foreign ministry, 12
Kashmir mediation, 174-175
meeting of international Communist parties, 38
NLF, aid to, 157
Peking embassy, 217
Presidium, 158, 170-172
protest note on U.S. intentions, 169
Secretariat, 173

Sino-Soviet conflicts, 151-154
and U.S., détente, 264-265
Vietnamese naval bases denied, 266
United Kingdom peace proposal, 41
United States of America
bombing pause, 42
Budapest legation, attack on, 39
dynamic equilibrium, policy of, 265
"Hungarian Question," State Department memo on, 32-33
and Hungary, 34-36
1968 bombing halt, 246
Radványi asylum, 238
Saigon embassy, 109
secret diplomacy, Pentagon study, 133
State Department warning, 140
U.N. mission, 72
and USSR détente, 265
Vietnam, aid program for, 256
Vietnam, presence in (1963), 30
Ustinov, Dmitri F.
and Brezhnev, 236
Presidium powers, 159

Vance, Cyrus, R., 244
Varga, István, 44
Varga, Lajos, 46
Vatican, the, 33
Viet Cong, 85, 92, 112, 241-242, 243
Five Points, 64, 65
1965 truce proposal, 96
Viet Minh, 1, 10
Vietnam, Democratic Republic of, (DRV), 2
aid for, increased, 189
Budapest embassy, 13
DMZ, violation of, 189-190
foreign ministry, 114, 136, 142
Hungarian delegation to, 67
Moscow embassy, 136
NLF, 38
Politburo, 23, 27, 28, 257-258
Rangoon consulate, 136
Reunification Department, Central Committee, 28
San Antonio Formula, rejection of, 240
Thein Phon cooperative, 17
Vietnam Lap Dong Minh Hoi, 1
Vietnam, South, and PRG, 257
Vietnam (Unified Socialist Republic of Vietnam)
neutrality, 266
joins World Bank and IMF, 266
Vietnamese Independence League, 1
Vietnamese Workers' party, 14
Vinh, Nguyen Van, 28

Wang Yu-t'ien, 25
Warsaw Pact
Bucharest Declaration, 200
consultative meetings, 59
declaration, 194
1965 meeting, 150
Watergate, and DRV strategy, 258
West Germany, and Hungary, 230-232
Westmoreland, William C., 47, 77-78
cable to Pentagon, 138
and KANZUS, 191
Wheeler, Earle G., 46-47
Whiting, Allen, 89
Wilson, Harold
and Johnson, 95, 208
and Kosygin, 204-209
revives Phase A-Phase B, 205, 207
Rostow, criticism of, 210
Winievicz, Jozef, 72-73
World Council of Peace, 4
World Federation of Democratic Youth, 161

Your Side/Our Side Formula, 244

Zinchuk, Alexander I., 94
and Bundy, William, 199-200
and Marigold Affair, 199-200